Sustainability and Wellbeing

The idea that we can meet human needs and simultaneously conserve and even enhance the natural environment is an attractive one. Since the Brundtland report popularised a definition of sustainable development based on the concept of needs, there has been a widespread belief that it should be possible to achieve a good quality of life without compromising natural ecosystems.

Sustainability and Wellbeing fills a gap in sustainable development studies by drawing on a range of case-studies to discuss the challenges and opportunities of using Max-Neef's Human Scale Development (HSD) framework in practice. The first section presents the theory and the methodology of HSD in the context of related literature on sustainable development and wellbeing. The second section discusses applications of the HSD methodology with three different purposes: the design of sustainable development interventions; the engagement of researchers with communities or groups of people in sustainability processes and the consolidation of sustainable community initiatives. Finally, the third section reflects on challenges and limitations of using the HSD approach to define strategies for sustainable development and concludes.

This is an invaluable resource for researchers and postgraduate students in wellbeing, sustainability, sustainable development, and human development.

Mònica Guillén-Royo is a Research Fellow at the Centre for Development and the Environment (SUM), University of Oslo, Norway.

Routledge Studies in Sustainable Development

This series uniquely brings together original and cutting-edge research on sustainable development. The books in this series tackle difficult and important issues in sustainable development including: values and ethics; sustainability in higher education; climate compatible development; resilience; capitalism and degrowth; sustainable urban development; gender and participation; and well-being.

Drawing on a wide range of disciplines, the series promotes interdisciplinary research for an international readership. The series was recommended in the Guardian's suggested reads on development and the environment.

Institutional and Social Innovation for Sustainable Urban Development
Edited by Harald A. Mieg and Klaus Töpfer

The Sustainable University
Progress and prospects
Edited by Stephen Sterling, Larch Maxey and Heather Luna

Sustainable Development in Amazonia
Paradise in the making
Kei Otsuki

Measuring and Evaluating Sustainability
Ethics in sustainability indexes
Sarah E. Fredericks

Values in Sustainable Development
Edited by Jack Appleton

Climate-Resilient Development
Participatory solutions from developing countries
Edited by Astrid Carrapatoso and Edith Kürzinger

Theatre for Women's Participation in Sustainable Development
Beth Osnes

Urban Waste and Sanitation Services for Sustainable Development
Harnessing social and technical diversity in East Africa
Bas van Vliet, Joost van Buuren and Shaaban Mgana

Sustainable Capitalism and the Pursuit of Well-Being
Neil E. Harrison

Sustainability and Wellbeing

Human Scale Development
in Practice

Mònica Guillén-Royo

Routledge
Taylor & Francis Group

LONDON AND NEW YORK

First published 2016
by Routledge
2 Park Square, Milton Park, Abingdon, Oxon OX14 4RN

and by Routledge
711 Third Avenue, New York, NY 10017

First issued in paperback 2018

Routledge is an imprint of the Taylor & Francis Group, an informa business

© 2016 Mònica Guillén-Royo

British Library Cataloguing-in-Publication Data
A catalogue record for this book is available from the British Library

Library of Congress Cataloging-in-Publication Data
A catalog record for this book has been requested

ISBN 13: 978-1-138-59755-6 (pbk)
ISBN 13: 978-1-138-79239-5 (hbk)

Typeset in Goudy
by Florence Production Ltd, Stoodleigh, Devon, UK

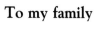
To my family

Contents

Illustrations

Acknowledgments

Several colleagues read early drafts of the manuscript and provided very helpful advice. I would especially like to thank Laura Camfield for being a constant support in the writing process and always available to provide feedback. Thanks also to Harold Wilhite, Ian Gough, Sidsel Roalkvam, Desmond McNeil, Felix Rauschmayer and Tim Kasser for their insightful comments to draft chapters. Inez Aponte with her contribution to Chapter 7 has made the book relevant for those involved in sustainable communities. Maria del Valle from the Universidad Austral de Chile provided me with masters theses and reports from studies using the Human Scale Development (HSD) approach in different contexts and parts of the world for which I am grateful. My time was jointly funded by a grant (208847/H30) from The Research Council of Norway and by the Centre for Development and the Environment (SUM) at the University of Oslo (Norway). I would especially like to thank Kristi Anne Stølen, the director of SUM, for her unconditional support and her belief in the value of this project.

The book would have not been possible without the collaboration of research assistants and colleagues who have supported the facilitation of HSD workshops, recorded and transcribed discussions and organised coffee breaks and recruitment processes. I would like to thank Jorge Guardiola and Fernando García-Quero for the engaging discussions and the enthusiasm with which they approached HSD workshops in Granada (Spain) in 2014. Thanks to Nina Zelenkova and Martin Lee Mueller for their collaboration in the study carried out at the University of Oslo (Norway) in 2013. Martin has also been of great help editing two key chapters in this manuscript. Veronica Laos, Gabriela Stöckli and Ignacio Pezo made a great team assisting my research in Lima. I am also grateful to Percy Reina and Pamela Flores for their commitment and personal involvement in the organisation and facilitation of workshops in Acostambo and Huancayo (Peru) in 2011 and 2012. I am particularly indebted to the people from the neighbourhoods of Vistas and Costas (Acostambo) for their engagement in the participatory action research project we did in their district in 2012–2013 and their generosity sharing their time and knowledge with us. Gemma Farré and Teresa Farré were a great help during the first set of workshops I facilitated in Lleida in 2009; without that first experience, I would most likely not have engaged in the study of the theory and methodology of HSD.

Finally, I would like to thank my family for their interest and direct involvement in my research. My mother Maria Dolors Royo provided practical and logistic support during workshops in Lleida (Catalonia) and Lima (Peru). My aunt Paquita Arturo collaborated finding a venue for workshops in Lleida and contacting potential participants. My sister Cristina, my cousins Laura and Mat, my uncle Paco and his wife Stefania, my friends Araceli and Laura and my family-in-law (Liv Berit, Halvor, Odd, Martin and Kristin) have always shown a genuine interest in my research for which I am deeply grateful. Finally, without the advice, the editing efforts and the patient reference checking of my husband Jakob, I would have never finished the manuscript. I thank him for his love and encouragement.

Introduction

Purpose

The purpose of this book is to contribute to a reflection around the relevance of Human Scale Development (HSD) as a framework for the analysis and encouragement of sustainable development processes. The HSD proposal was developed by Chilean economist Manfred Max-Neef and his collaborators in the 1980s with the goal of supporting grassroots movements and communities in the design and implementation of their own development processes. It was articulated around three interdependent pillars concerning the promotion of self-reliance, balanced relationships among people, institutions and governance dimensions, and the satisfaction of fundamental human needs. The latter was based on a theory of needs that stressed the difference between universal needs and culturally relative satisfiers (among them values, attitudes, laws, institutions, actions, spaces and environments) and provided a practical tool to support communities and local movements to identify their own strategies to meet needs.

The methodology suggested in the HSD proposal, as described in Max-Neef's book *Human-Scale Development – Conception, Applications and Further Reflections* (1991), revolved around a series of participatory workshops aiming to stimulate collective reflection around the satisfiers that hampered or promoted needs fulfilment in a specific society. Since its publication, the HSD methodology has been adapted to address different socio-economic and environmental challenges by local communities, development practitioners and researchers alike. The fact that HSD focusses on meeting needs establishes a direct parallel between the proposal and the main goal of sustainable development (SD) understood following the definition of the World Commission on Environment and Development (WCED) as 'development that meets the needs of the present without compromising the ability of future generations to meet their own needs' (WCED 1987: 43). Meeting fundamental human needs requires, following the tenets of HSD, arriving at satisfiers that are both efficient at meeting one or more needs and environmentally sustainable, so that their generation does not reduce the possibilities of other needs being met now and in the future.

This book has been inspired by the learnings from my own studies using the HSD methodology, and by the increasing reference to HSD by proponents of alternative approaches to sustainable development that highlight the impossibility of achieving sustainability with the current understanding of SD based on economic growth. I have aimed to provide a text which:

1   offers a reflection on the insertion of the HSD proposal within current debates on the green economy-interpretation of SD, and within alternative discourses around SD that are not centred on economic growth;
2   discusses some of the possible uses of the methodology to support needs-based sustainable development, namely those concerning: a) the identification of sustainable development measures or policies through exploratory workshops, b) the understanding of human-nature interdependencies through the involvement with local communities, and c) the strengthening of ongoing local sustainability projects by encouraging a deep reflection on human needs; and
3   draws on the practical applications of the HSD methodology with communities or groups of people to propose a conceptual link between the system of satisfiers that contribute to needs fulfilment at the local level and the interdependent personal, social, economic and environmental features that constitute a sustainable society.

Thus, the book touches on contextual, conceptual and empirical aspects of the HSD proposal with regards to its relevance for sustainable development practice.

Background

The idea that we can meet human needs and simultaneously conserve and even enhance the natural environment is an attractive one. Since the Brundtland report (WCED 1987) popularised a definition of sustainable development based on the concept of needs, there has been a widespread belief that it should be possible to achieve a good quality of life without compromising natural ecosystems. Despite an equal weight given to economic efficiency, social equity and environmental protection in the outcome documents of the influential United Nations conferences on sustainable development in Rio in 1992 and 2012 (UN 1992, 2012), the main mechanisms put in place at the national and international levels to progress towards sustainable development have been based on economic efficiency. This has been materialised through stressing sustainability policies on investments in technological innovations that enable the production of increasing amounts of goods and services while reducing the environmental impact of production. Despite the WCED emphasis on the quality of economic growth, what has guided SD policy has been the 'quantity' of economic growth, as policy-makers around the world have continued to buy into the tenets of neoclassical economics, associating human wellbeing with the expansion of material production and consumption (Guillén-Royo and Wilhite 2015).

Investments in resource efficiency, renewable energy and recycling facilities have not challenged trade liberalisation and the geographical expansion of industrialised consumption and production patterns that have characterised the neoliberal approach to international development since the 1970s (Jackson 2006, 2009; McNeill and Wilhite 2015). Sustainable development interventions that could threaten the expansion of the global economy – such as binding agreements on CO$_2$ emission reductions, or policies for low-carbon lifestyles – have not been given a top priority. As a result, we are witnessing increasing damages to ecosystems and biodiversity, a progressive warming up of earth climate systems and rising inequalities within and across countries (Martínez-Alier *et al.* 2010; Wilkinson and Pickett 2010). The limited contribution to environmental conservation and enhancement of the current sustainability policies suggests that in order to place societies in a sustainable development path, a more radical transformation of our socio-economic and political structures is needed.

Alternatives to the efficiency-based approach to sustainable development are manifold and are often linked to post-growth or post-development paradigms (Daly 1974; Martínez-Alier 2009; Muraca 2012). These are characterised by rejecting a direct positive association between economic growth and human wellbeing, and by allocating a subsidiary role to the economic system in relation to the biophysical and social systems. Thus, economic growth becomes a by-product of measures to reduce environmental degradation and social injustice (van der Bergh 2010). Or, as the proponents of sustainable degrowth maintain, economic growth becomes something that should be reversed in order to achieve a 'socially sustainable and equitable reduction (and eventually stabilisation) of society's throughput'[1] (Kallis 2011: 874). In line with these alternative perspectives, Max-Neef emphasises the need to give the economy an instrumental role, as its ultimate goal is to serve the people, not the opposite. Serving people, in Max-Neef's view, is about providing the economic, socio-technical, cultural and environmental resources that will help humans meet their fundamental needs. This, he argues, should be the goal of any development policy. Any such policy should also be guided by the twin-premises that no economy is possible in the absence of ecosystem services, and that the economy is a sub-system of a larger and finite system, the biosphere. In Max-Neef's view, these premises fully negate the possibility of permanent growth (Smith and Max-Neef 2011: 154).

In addition to theoretical approaches arguing for removing economic growth from the conceptualisation and practice of sustainable development, research and grassroots initiatives demonstrate through empirical research and real-life practice that environmental sustainability and human needs fulfilment can be reconciled through a set of interdependent satisfiers, addressing technological, organisational, cultural, political and personal factors that do not depend on a more voluminous global economy. Recent research shows that economic growth and wellbeing are not necessarily linked. Examples include research on measures of welfare that account for environmental and social costs not included in the calculation of GDP (Costanza *et al.* 2014), the research on wellbeing determinants (Easterlin 2015; Frey and Stutzer 2002), and the experience of people in sustainable communities already experiencing a low-impact lifestyle (Hopkins 2013; Phillips *et al.* 2013). Though they do acknowledge the importance of technological efficiency, these approaches have a stronger focus on strategies such as lower consumption levels, shorter working hours, progressive taxation and carbon quotas that are 'disruptive' to business-as-usual, as they question accumulation and growth, the main goals in capitalist societies.

Linking to the abovementioned evidence, and drawing on his own research which indicated a lack of association between quality of life and economic growth (Max-Neef 1995), Manfred Max-Neef and his collaborators developed a proposal for Human Scale Development (HSD) in the late 1980s. Their proposal was based on popular participation, and it was articulated around three interdependent pillars. The first of these pillars increasing levels of self-reliance, placing the local community at the core of the development process. The second pillar focussed on the balanced interdependence of people with nature and technologies, of global and local processes, of personal and social goals, of planning and autonomy, and of civil society and the state (Max-Neef 1991: 8). Finally, the third pillar concerned the achievement of high levels of quality of life through actualising fundamental human needs.

The HSD proposal considers fundamental human needs to be universal and changing at the slow pace of human evolution. These needs concern the following nine axiological categories: Subsistence, Protection, Affection, Understanding, Participation, Idleness, Creation, Identity and Freedom. Each of those nine categories can be expressed according to four existential categories: Being, Having, Doing and Interacting. Crossing fundamental human needs and existential categories produces a matrix with 36 empty cells that represent *satisfiers* (values, attitudes, institutions, regulations, actions, customs, forms of organisation, spaces, etc.). Satisfiers characterise the ways needs are pursued in a society and could be categorised depending on their positive or negative impact on needs. Thus, the goal becomes for local communities and societies to identify those *synergic satisfiers* which promote more than one human need and are not detrimental to any need, and to engage in endogenous and/or exogenous strategies to make them available in their society. Satisfiers that are harmful to the natural environment will reduce the capacity to meet needs in the short, mid or long run and will not be appraised as synergic.

Max-Neef and his collaborators suggested drawing on the approach to needs and satisfiers in participatory workshops that engage local communities or grassroots groups in finding solutions to their socio-economic and environmental challenges. The methodology proposed has been applied since the 1980s in different countries around the world and with different purposes. Topics that have been addressed using the HSD framework and tools include: racial discrimination, HIV prevention, sustainable housing, health promotion, rural development, end-of-life care and sustainable consumption (Buscaglia 2013; Cuthill 2003; García Norato 2006; Guillén-Royo 2010; Jorge 2010; Mitchell 2001; Peroni 2009). Some of this work has been research-oriented and some practice-oriented. Some has followed the methodology as suggested by Max-Neef and collaborators, and some has adapted the methodology or parts of it to suit the goals of a project or to meet the requirements of a funding body. There are also some researchers who have used the HSD perspective on needs and satisfiers for the development of indicators and the assessment of economic or social trends in society (Cruz *et al.* 2009; Jackson and Marks 1999).

In addition to influencing academic and development practice, the HSD proposal has been used by communities since its publication in Spanish in 1986. Its resonance among grassroots organisations in South America at the time was illustrated by the fact that it became 'the most photocopied document on the continent' (Smith and Max-Neef 2011: 176). Max-Neef reflected on the success of the proposal in the following terms:

> The first lesson we learned from those experiences was that the language of Human Scale Development and its Needs Theory can be easily understood by simple people who lack any formal education beyond a few years of primary school. The second lesson was that no true development can succeed without the understanding, participation and creativity of the people themselves. The third lesson was that what mobilises common people does not necessarily mobilise academics. In fact, what took the peasants almost no time to understand took about 15 years to generate interest at academic levels. Now Human Scale Development is finally in the academic system and its Human needs Theory is recognised as one of the most important contributions in the field.
>
> (Smith and Max-Neef 2011: 176)

Scope and limitations

This book is not intended to be a comprehensive survey of the past or current applications of the HSD proposal. Efforts are being made in this regard by Max-Neef's team at the Universidad Austral de Chile. HSD has been applied in very diverse contexts and interpreted in many different ways by practitioners, communities and researchers since the publication of the HSD book in English in 1991. Most of these applications have never been codified or made accessible to the general public. This reduces the capacity of a researcher with limited financial resources to even attempt mapping the historical applications of the proposal. It is also important to clarify that I do not intend to present an impartial or objective analysis of the relevance of the HSD proposal for SD. I believe that the HSD proposal offers both a sound theoretical and methodological framework from which to support societies towards SD. This belief is the main reason why I wrote this book.

Thus, this volume takes a relatively narrow look at the practice of HSD and discusses current or potential ways the methodology can be used with groups of people or communities to advance towards societies with high quality of life and low ecological impact. In order to do this, I draw on my own experience applying the HSD methodology in Spain, Norway and Peru. I also refer to the work of other researchers and practitioners that have used the HSD framework to identify pathways towards environmental sustainability and human wellbeing in different parts of the world. However, since the focus of the book is eminently practical, I do not explore in depth other conceptual, theoretical and desk-based contributions that are not based on participatory workshops. Finally, most of the chapters reflect on different aspects of the methodology: the challenges of participatory methods, the role of the facilitator or researchers, the importance of following a specific sequence of workshops, the greater awareness derived from participating, and the evidence suggesting that the system of synergic satisfiers emerging from needs-based workshops unveils a supportive structure on which to base sustainable development policies. The latter is the main conceptual aspect of the HSD approach that I will address in depth in this book.

Chapter outlines

The book is divided into three parts that can be read in sequence or in any other order. Nevertheless, Chapters 3 and 4 are of particular relevance, as they introduce the most important characteristics of the HSD proposal and of the methodology suggested to engage people and local communities, which will be frequently referred to throughout the book.

The first part includes three chapters that contextualise the HSD proposal within the sustainable development debate and introduce its main tenets and methodological underpinnings. Chapter 2 discusses the interpretations of SD from the original concept in the Brundtland Report to the current notion of the 'green economy' promoted by international organisations. The chapter also discusses alternative perspectives which associate sustainability with a reduction in the volume of the global economy and the satisfaction of human needs. The relevance of the alternative paradigms is supported by a discussion on the evidence against: (1) the possibility that technological innovations reduce the environmental impact of increasing levels of production, and; (2) against the belief that economic growth brings higher quality of life (Easterlin 2015; Jackson 2009; Smith and Max-Neef 2011).

Chapter 3 provides an overview of the historical context in which the HSD proposal was devised and discusses the three interdependent pillars of self-reliance, balanced relationships and human needs actualisation. It also analyses the strong commitment to democracy and popular participation inherent in the proposal. The chapter finishes by comparing the HSD understanding of human needs and satisfiers with Doyal and Gough's theory of human need and Sen's and Nussbaum's capabilities approach. The latter are two alternative accounts of human development that separate material prosperity from quality of life and are increasingly used as theoretical frameworks in the academic debate on sustainability (Gough 2014; Lessmann and Rauschmayer 2013; Sen 2013).

The last chapter in this part, Chapter 4, analyses in detail the HSD methodology. This is based on a sequence of participatory workshops aiming at unveiling what opportunities a community has to satisfy the needs of its members. The chapter discusses how the HSD methodology has been adapted to address environmental sustainability and looks at issues regarding the role of facilitators, the recruitment of participants and the claim that the experience of participation contributes to empowering people and communities. To illustrate the arguments presented, the chapter introduces examples of the application of the methodology in different contexts and with different purposes.

The second part of the book presents different applications of the HSD framework illustrated with examples of my research in Lleida (Catalonia) and Acostambo (Peru), the experiences of researchers studying sustainability in Belgium (Jolibert et al. 2014), and those of a practitioner engaged in the Transition movement[2]. In this part, the HSD proposal is first addressed as a tool to identify sustainable interventions at the local and regional levels; second, as the guiding framework in participatory action research (PAR) processes; and third, as a tool to consolidate ongoing bottom-up community initiatives such as transition towns, ecovillages and eco-municipalities. Most of the examples detailed in this part concern local communities in line with the emphasis on empowering civil society inherent in HSD.

Chapter 5 discusses the usefulness of HSD workshops as a methodology to explore avenues for sustainable development at the local level. It looks at the sequence of needs-based workshops described in Chapter 4 with regards to The Natural Step framework commonly used to plan sustainability interventions and Theory U that addresses the phases of deep learning processes for sustainability innovations (Holmberg 1998; Scharmer 2009). The goal of this exercise is to highlight both the relevance of the HSD process in the search for sustainable solutions and the quality of the outcomes achieved through deep reflection and deliberative discussions. This is illustrated by the adaptation of the HSD methodology by Jolibert and colleagues (Jolibert et al. 2014) to study needs-based scenarios at the regional level and by the research I carried out in Lleida to explore the linkages between synergic satisfiers and environmental sustainability.

Chapter 6 concentrates on the study of processes of HSD through long-term engagement with participants and communities. It discusses the challenges associated with PAR designs and participatory development approaches; particularly the fact that they might reproduce, exacerbate and generate power imbalances (Cooke and Kothari 2004; Cornwall 2011). It illustrates the importance of paying attention to processes through a PAR study in Acostambo, a rural municipality in the Peruvian Andes. The analysis of the implementation of the synergic satisfier 'parents' school' in parallel with the cultivation of organic vegetable gardens (another synergic satisfier identified by participants) suggests that both projects were positively contributing to human needs in the community through increased knowledge and social cohesion. It also indicates that environmental sustainability in the local area was improved by the new organic agricultural practices, as participants reported to have a greater respect for the natural environment after the PAR project.

Chapter 7 is the last in the second part of the book. It analyses the goals and characteristics of sustainable communities belonging to the eco-municipality, ecovillage, and transition movements with regards to the pillars of the HSD proposal. It presents the experience of Inez Aponte,[3] using the concept of human needs and satisfiers with members of the transition movement. She highlights the relevance of a reflection in terms of needs and satisfiers to strengthen transformative action at the local and national levels. The chapter explores the idea that sustainable communities represent a 'real-life' example of HSD, analysing the needs-enhancing properties of the system of satisfiers characterising their everyday activities.

The third part in this volume revolves around the challenges, limitations, and opportunities of using HSD as a framework of reference for the study and practice of sustainable development. Chapter 8 concentrates on three particular challenges. The first concerns the capacity of the HSD methodology to access people's 'inner' dimension, which has direct consequences for the depth of changes that can be expected from engaging in HSD processes. The second is related to the capacity of needs-based workshops to empower participants. Both topics are illustrated by drawing on the specific applications of the methodology discussed in Part II and also on the findings of exploratory workshops carried out in Oslo (Norway) to explore the relationship between participating in HSD workshops and people's goals and values. The last part considers the difficulties of integrating the holistic approach of the HSD proposal in SD policy.

In the concluding chapter, Chapter 9, I describe the journey followed in HSD processes from an understanding of the personal, socio-economic and environmental problems associated with a low level of needs actualisation, to the design and implementation of needs-enhancing solutions that contribute to environmental sustainability. The journey takes us to the discussion of associating synergic satisfiers with sustainable satisfiers, and to the opportunities of drawing on the HSD framework to advance towards sustainable societies. The chapter finishes by encouraging researchers to continue analysing the theory and practice of HSD: both to increase the visibility of real-life experiences that draw on the approach, and to contribute to a deeper understanding of the linkages between human needs fulfilment and the protection of the natural environment.

Notes

1 Throughput is defined as the natural resources and energy used during the life cycle of a product that finishes when it returns to nature as waste (Daly 1996).
2 Information about the transition movement is available at www.transitionnetwork.org/, accessed 4 May 2015.
3 Inez Aponte is an educator and community activist and founder of Growing Good Lives where she uses the HSD approach to design and deliver seminars, training and consultancy to 'unleash human potential for the common good'. She has been developing participatory learning processes since 1998 and has designed and delivered programmes for, among others, WWF, The Soil Association, Danish Institute for Studies Abroad, Lille Institute of Political Studies and Schumacher College, as well as for activists working in the New Economy movement. She is an accredited Trainer for the Transition Network and works for Totnes-based Futurebound on their Leadership for Resiliency programme (www.growinggoodlives.com).

References

Buscaglia, A. (2013). Propuesta participativa de desarrollo local para la comunidad de Coya, Region de O'Higgins, desde la perspectiva del desarrollo a escala humana. In Moreno, A. (ed), *Tesis 2013. Piensa un país sin pobreza*. Fundación superación de la pobreza, pp. 102–23, (www.superacionpobreza.cl/wp-content/uploads/2014/06/TESIS-2013-final-web.pdf, accessed 21 April 2015).

Cooke, B. and Kothari, U. (eds) (2004). *Participation. The New Tyranny?* 3rd edn. London: Zed books.

Cornwall, A. (ed.) (2011). *The Participation Reader*. London: Zed books.

Costanza, R., Kubiszewski, I., Giovannini, E., Lovins, H., McGlade, J., Pickett, K. E., Ragnarsdottir, K. V., Roberts, D., de Vogli, R. and Wilkinson, R. (2014). Time to leave GDP behind. *Nature*, 505: 283–5.

Cruz, I., Stahel, A. and Max-Neef, M. (2009). Towards a systemic development approach: Building on the Human Scale Development paradigm. *Ecological Economics*, 68, 2021–30.

Cuthill, M. (2003). From here to utopia: Running a human-scale Development workshop on the Gold Coast, Australia. *Local Environment*, 8(4): 471–85.

Daly, H. E. (1974). The economics of the Steady State. *The American Economic Review* 64(2): 15–21.

Daly, H. E. (1996). *Beyond Growth*. Boston: Beacon Press.

Easterlin, R. (2015). Happiness and economic growth: The evidence. In Glatzer, W., Camfield, L., Møller, V. and Rojas, M. (eds), *Global Handbook of Quality of Life: Exploration of Well-being of Nations and Continents*, New York and London: Springer, pp. 283–99.

Frey, B. S. and Stutzer, A. (2002). *Happiness and Economics*. Princeton: Princeton University Press.

García Norato, O. M. (2006). Matriz de necesidades y satisfactores con mujeres rurales de Siachoque, Boyacá, Colombia. Apuntes del CENES. 16(41), Centro de Estudios Económicos, Universidad Pedagógica y Tecnológica de Colombia, (http://virtual.uptc.edu.co/drupal/files/rac_52.pdf, accessed 15 August 2014).

Gough, I. (2014). Climate change and sustainable welfare: The centrality of human needs. New Economics Foundation Working Paper, (http://b.3cdn.net/nefoundation/e256633779f47ec4e6_o5m6bexrh.pdf, accessed 1 April 2015).

Guillén-Royo, M. (2010). Realising the 'wellbeing dividend': An exploratory study using the human scale development approach. *Ecological Economics*, 70: 384–93.

Holmberg, J. (1998). Backcasting: A natural step in operationalising sustainable development. *Greener Management International*, 23: 30–51.

Hopkins, R. (2013). *The Power of Just Doing Stuff*. Cambridge: Green Books.

Jackson, T. (2006). *Earthscan Reader in Sustainable Consumption*. London: Earthscan.

Jackson, T. (2009). *Prosperity Without Growth*. London: Sustainable Development Commission.

Jackson, T. and Marks, N. (1999). Consumption, sustainable welfare and human needs – with reference to UK expenditure patterns between 1954 and 1994. *Ecological Economics*, 28: 421–41.

Jolibert, C., Paavola, J. and Rauschmayer, F. (2014). Addressing needs in the search for sustainable development: A proposal for needs-based scenario building. *Environmental Values*, 23: 29–50.

Jorge, M. (2010). Patients' needs and satisfiers: Applying human scale development theory on end-of-life care. *Current Opinion in Supportive and Palliative Care*, 4: 163–9.

Kallis, G. (2011). In defence of degrowth. *Ecological Economics*, 70: 873–80.

Lessmann, O. and Rauschmayer, F. (2013). Re-conceptualizing sustainable development on the basis of the capability approach: A model and its difficulties. *Journal of Human Development and Capabilities*, 14(1): 95–114.

Martínez-Alier, J. (2009). Socially sustainable economic degrowth. *Development and Change*, 40(6): 1099–119.

Martínez-Alier, J., Pascual, U., Vivien, F.-D. and Zaccai, E. (2010). Sustainable de-growth: Mapping the context, criticisms and future prospects of an emergent paradigm. *Ecological Economics*, 69: 1741–7.

Max-Neef, M. (1991). *Human Scale Development: Conception, Application and Further Reflection*. London: Apex Press.

Max-Neef, M. (1995). Economic growth and quality of life: A threshold hypothesis. *Ecological Economics*, 15: 115–8.

Max-Neef, M. (2011). The death and rebirth of economics. In Rauschmayer, F., Omann, I. and Frühmann, J. (eds), *Sustainable Development: Capabilities, Needs and Well-being*, London: Routledge, pp. 104–20.

McNeill, D. and Wilhite, H. (2015). Making sense of sustainable development in a changing world. In Hansen, A. and Wethal, U. (eds), *Emerging Economies and Challenges to Sustainability*, London: Routledge, pp. 32–56.

Mitchell, J. A. (2001). Propuesta metodológica en el diseño de un asentamiento humano en una zona rural del centro- oeste de la República Argentina. *La casa de América*, pp. 209–39 (ISBN-970-694-063-4).

Muraca, B. (2012). Towards a fair degrowth-society: Justice and the right to a 'good life' beyond growth. *Futures*, 44(6): 535–45.

Peroni, A. (2009). El desarrollo local a escala humana: experiencias de desarrollo comunitario en el sector salud. *Polis*, 8(22): 99–120.

Phillips, R., Seifer, B. F. and Antczak, E. (2013). *Sustainable Communities. Creating a Durable Local Economy*. Abingdon: Routledge.

Scharmer, C. O. (2009). *Theory U: Leading From the Future as it Emerges. The Social Technology of Presencing*. San Francisco, CA: Berrett-Koehler.

Sen, A. (2013). The ends and means of sustainability. *Journal of Human Development and Capabilities*, 14(1), 6–20.

Smith, P. B. and Max-Neef, M. (2011). *Economics Unmasked*. Cambridge: Green Books.

UN (1992). Report of the United Nations Conference on Environment and Development, Rio de Janeiro, Brazil, 3–14 June, (www.un.org/documents/ga/conf151/aconf15126–1annex1.htm, accessed 4 May 2015).

UN (2012). Report of the United Nations Conference on Sustainable Development, Rio de Janeiro, Brazil, 20–22 June, (www.uncsd2012.org/content/documents/814UNCSD per cent20REPORT per cent20final per cent20revs.pdf, accessed 4 May 2015).

van den Bergh, J. C. J. M. (2010). Relax about GDP growth: Implications for climate and crisis policies. *Journal of Cleaner Production*, 18: 540–3.

WCED (1987). *Our Common Future*. Oxford: Oxford University Press.

Wilhite, H. L. and Guillén-Royo, M. (2015). Wellbeing and sustainable consumption. In Glatzer, W., Camfield, L., Møller, V. and Rojas, M. (eds), *Global Handbook of Wellbeing and Quality of Life*. Frankfurt: Springer, pp. 301–17.

Wilkinson, R. and Pickett, K. (2010). *The Spirit Level: Why Equality is Better for Everyone*. London: Penguin.

Part I

2 Sustainable development, economic growth and human wellbeing

Introduction

The concept of sustainable development (SD) as popularised by the report of the World Commission on Environment and Development (WCED 1987), brought together concerns for equity, economic progress and environmental conservation and enhancement (Adams 2009). The commission's report was the response to long-expressed concerns at the national and international levels about the negative impacts of human activities on the natural environment and on the precarious material conditions that most people in poor and middle-income countries were experiencing. SD suggested a process of social and economic transformation that respected the right to natural resources of current and future generations, enabled people to satisfy their needs and used technologies and forms of organisation in a way that limited the impact of the socio-economic systems on the natural environment. This new concept of development was expected to transform the general understanding of progress from a mere materialistic focus to one that took account of social as well as environmental factors.

SD demands action on its three dimensions – the economy, their society and the environment – and as long as these are activated through policies fostering economic growth, greater social equality and the reduction of negative environmental impacts, the needs of current and future generations are expected to be enhanced. A perspective of SD that relies on economic growth is widely supported in international circles as it does not challenge the tenets of global capitalism. While there are a variety of ways that these tenets are manifested at the national level, they represent the most widespread way of organising economy and society. The capitalistic framework is also the one supported by most international institutions and summarised in the ecological modernisation or green economy approach[1] stressing efficiency, technology and an increasing availability of goods and services for the world's poor. Alternative approaches also account for the need to improve the lives of the global poor but do not rely on economic growth as the main mechanism for achieving it. Steady-state, degrowth and other perspectives like the Human Scale Development proposal, argue for the reduction or stabilisation of the volume of the global economy through the efficient use of resources, income redistribution, increased community participation and the relocalisation of production practices.

This chapter discusses the concept of SD from its conception to its current identification with the green economy paradigm. It analyses two of the pillars of the green economy approach to SD, namely, (1) the possibility of arriving at technical innovations that allow continued growth with a minimal environmental impact (decoupling), and (2) the need to promote economic growth to achieve equitable societies and quality of life. The chapter finishes by outlining sustainable development approaches that do not revolve around the necessity of economic growth; among them the Human Scale Development proposal based on self-reliance, a balanced articulation of technology, nature and society and human needs fulfilment.

Sustainable development

The World Commission on Environment and Development (WCED) was established by the UN General Assembly in December 1983 with the goal of finding solutions to global ecological challenges through the promotion of multilateral agreements (Adams 2009). It produced a report 'Our common future', presented to the General Assembly in 1987, that became the reference document for the definition of sustainable development in the decades to come. Sustainable Development was defined as 'development that meets the needs of the present without compromising the ability of future generations to meet their own needs' (WCED 1987: 43). It associated human wellbeing with the satisfaction of basic needs for food, clothing and shelter and jobs, particularly in developing countries, but it also discussed fulfilling aspirations, the legitimate ambition of achieving a better life, as one of the objectives of development. Thus, within the sustainable development discourse, human wellbeing was interpreted both from an *objective wellbeing* perspective where the appropriate material, social and political conditions are available for the population to experience a good life, and from a *subjective wellbeing* perspective as people's experiences of their lives and of the opportunities available to them were also taken into consideration (Gasper 2005).

SD as understood in the WCED report has three interdependent dimensions; economic, social and environmental. Economic growth is seen as a necessary instrument for developing countries so they can catch up with more advanced economies in terms of total product, technology and basic social services. As the report was written during a long decade of stagnation in developing countries, a rise in per capita income in those countries over a rate of 5 per cent was considered a priority. Poverty and environmental degradation were seen as interlinked, so growth was the way forward in those countries (Dasgupta 2011). At the time there was still a shared belief, promoted by the institution of the Washington consensus[2] that poor people would benefit from economic growth through the 'trickle-down' effect, which implied an improvement in the conditions of the poor through the higher employment rates and wages expected in growing economies. In addition, the application of the Kuznets curve to environmental conditions claimed that as income levels in a country increased, the initial negative impact on the environment would subside and environmental conditions improve (Common and Stagl 2007).

SD had to account for the limitations that the environment poses in terms of natural resources and sink capacity.[3] By limiting economic expansion through ecological considerations, SD was incorporating the concerns of the environmentalist and ecological traditions of the mid-twentieth century, alarmed by the predatory effects of industrialisation and the expansion of modern lifestyles into former European colonies (Adams 2009). These traditions associated economic expansion, both within and across countries, with human wellbeing, but saw the latter threatened by pollution, resource depletion and the extinction of plant and animal species. This perspective was also supported by the results of the modelling exercise by the Club of Rome described in the 1992 report *Limits to Growth* (Meadows *et al.* 1972) which maintained that due to the environmental limits associated with resources scarcity, pollution and waste, economic growth could not continue indefinitely. However, the criticism to economic growth was not incorporated in the report, as economic growth continued to be seen as a 'critical objective for environment and development policies' (WCED 1987). Instead, environmental limits were expected to be respected through technological innovations. As the WCED (1987: chapter 2, 10) report stated 'ultimate limits there are, and sustainability requires that long before these are reached, the world must ensure equitable access to the constrained resource and reorient technological efforts to relieve the pressure.'

The WCED understanding of sustainable development provided the guiding principles for the United Nations Conference on Sustainable Development in Rio in 1992, where a framework to address the negative impacts of economic development on the environment was established. As expected, the policy recommendations were mainly of a techno-centric character organised around incentives for better scientific research and information dissemination together with the diffusion of efficient technologies, which resulted in some analysts considering it a 'reformist' approach as it did not challenge the way capitalist economies were organised (Adams 2009). However, Agenda 21 – the document detailing the policies needed to implement the measures suggested in the Rio declaration – went beyond technical efficiency and institutional reform to point to the need to change consumerist lifestyles, which expanded the reformist approach of the SD definition to contemplate more radical transformations of society (Jackson 2006). Lifestyle changes are not usually addressed with specific policy recommendations in international agreements or reports. As they demand cultural, institutional and personal changes that are less straightforward to implement than efficiency measures and could actually slow down or halt economic growth. The potentially threatening character of the policies included in Agenda 21, together with a lack of agreement on a framework to fund its implementation, resulted in a consolidation of the reformist character of SD, where 'consumption means (more) consumption of more sustainable products' (Jackson 2006: 4).

After the Rio Conference in 1992 the SD agenda was consolidated in the World Summit on Sustainable Development in Johannesburg in 2002 and the United Nations Conference on Sustainable Development (Rio+20) in 2012. The World Summit in Johannesburg in 2002 did not change the approach worked out at Rio but focussed more on implementation, particularly of measures directed to reducing poverty and poverty-related environmental questions (safe drinking water and basic sanitation for example). This made explicit the synergies between anti-poverty measures, such as the ones discussed at the Millennium Summit in 2000, and the sustainable development policies debated later in the Rio+20 conference. These synergies have also been a core topic in the debates at the sessions of the Conferences of the Parties to the United Nations Framework Convention on Climate Change (UNFCCC); where a stress on the vulnerability of developing countries to the effects of climate change has been coupled with demands to launch a Green Climate Fund[4] to transfer financial resources from rich to poor countries to assist in their adaptation and mitigation efforts.

Sustainable development and the green economy

The international agreements signed between the Rio Earth summit in 1992 and the most recent UN Conference on Sustainable Development in Rio in 2012 (RIO+20) have not succeeded in halting environmental degradation and have achieved mixed results with regards to human wellbeing. Although rates of ozone depletion have been reversed since the Montreal protocol was signed in 1987, the gases used to replace ozone-depleting substances are now actively contributing to global warming. There are no international official commitments to stop biodiversity loss[5]; agreements on GHG emissions are still on hold, and urban waste is growing uncontrolled (Martínez-Alier *et al.* 2010; World Meteorological Organization 2014). In addition, a recent study by world-leading economists has provided new evidence about the planetary limits that are being dangerously crossed as a consequence of human activity with irreversible consequences on the earth's ecosystems (Rockström *et al.* 2009). Concerning society, although the proportion of people living in absolute poverty has declined, thanks mainly to progress made in this area by China and India, there are still 1 billion people, mostly in sub-Saharan Africa and South Asia, living under life-threatening conditions and 6 million children under the age of 5 dying every year of avoidable causes (Adams 2009; Sachs 2014a).

This context of accelerating environmental destruction and social distress was aggravated in 2008 by the global financial crisis affecting the economies of the US, Europe and their global business partners. In order to address these interdependent economic, social and environmental challenges the UNEP launched in March 2009 a proposal for a Global New Green Deal with the aim of advancing towards a green economy characterised by being low carbon, resource efficient and socially inclusive (UNEP 2011), thus addressing the three fundamental dimensions of the SD framework. A full definition of the green economy is provided in the UNEP webpage:[6]

a green economy is one whose growth in income and employment is driven by public and private investments that reduce carbon emissions and pollution, enhance energy and resource efficiency, and prevent the loss of biodiversity and ecosystems services. These investments need to be catalysed and supported by targeted public expenditure, policy reforms and regulation changes. This development path should maintain, enhance and, where necessary, rebuild natural capital as a critical economic asset and source of public benefits, especially for poor people whose livelihoods and security depend strongly on nature.

UNEP's Green Economy framework relies more heavily than previous approaches to SD on government regulation and intervention in terms of fiscal stimulus and on a set of policy options revolving around institutional, economic and information-based measures. Regarding institutional reforms, stress is placed on laws and norms to encourage long-term and efficient management and use of resources, together with the transfer of technologies and improved government administrative and technical capacities and transparency. Economic measures revolve around increased funding and investment incentives in green sectors (agriculture, energy and waste), environmental taxation, the removal of harmful subsidies and stable and predictable policy frameworks for the support of green sectors. Finally, information-based measures address the use of accurate indicators of progress and a stress on education for a green economy and of improving access of civil society to information and communications technology (Cosbey 2011).

The unwillingness to question the necessity of economic growth is reflected in the Rio+20 outcome document 'The future we want' emphasising the voluntary basis of any measure addressing sustainable consumption patterns or lifestyles. The ten-year framework of programs on sustainable consumption and production adopted by the UN General Assembly had the potential to be transformative as it encompassed measures to integrate sustainable consumption in national education programs and promoted changes in values using scientific information about the root causes of current harmful consumption patterns. But again, as was the case with Agenda 21, this potential will most likely not be realised, as in addition to the voluntary character of measures, funding will not be allocated to sustainable consumption practices if it detracts from other 'high priority' SD activities, as the ones outlined in the UNEP's Green Economy Framework.

Although the green economy perspective was designed to revamp economic growth among rich stagnating economies, environmental issues were considered of equal importance. This resulted in the openness of rich countries to discuss indicators of progress beyond the Gross Domestic Product (GDP). The UN had already been promoting the Human Development Index as a better indicator than GDP for quality of life, but with the green growth proposal and the subsequent Rio+20 resolution, the need to account for environmental and social conditions was given explicit support. Discussions on broadening the indicators of welfare or wellbeing have been convened several times, beginning in the early twenty-first century with the report of the Commission on the Measurement of Economic

Performance and Social Progress in France (Stiglitz *et al.* 2009). Other recent proposals are the European Commission initiative 'Beyond GDP'[7] and the Organisation of Economic Cooperation and Development (OECD) global forums on measuring societal progress (OECD 2011a). A wealth of indexes that go beyond purely economic indicators and include measures of social and environmental welfare or wellbeing have been suggested by academics and organisations since the early seventies. Examples range from the Index of Sustainable Economic Welfare and Genuine Progress Indicator that include social and environmental costs in the accounting (see last section of this chapter) to those that consider, in addition to environmental measures, the subjective wellbeing of the population such as the New Economics Foundation Happy Planet Index, the Kingdom of Bhutan's Gross National Happiness Index and the OECD's Better Life Index (Costanza *et al.* 2014).

Replacing GDP as a measure of welfare is also debated in relation to the new United Nations Sustainable Development Goals (SDG). The Sustainable Development Goals (SDG) will replace the Millennium Development Goals[8] (MDG), eight development targets agreed in 2000 to be achieved by UN members by 2015, in the period from 2015 to 2030. They will apply to all countries, not only to poor or developing ones as was the case for the MDG, and will extend the three pillars of SD to make explicit the goal of eradicating extreme poverty by 2030. Thus, former MDGs emphasising the fight against poverty, empowering women, and improving health and education will be combined with goals addressing social inclusion, environmental sustainability and good governance (United Nations 2013). The SDGs will provide a clear focal point for sustainable development policies around the world. As Sachs put it: 'the SDGs must be the compass, the lodestar, for the future development of the planet during the period from 2015 to mid-century' (Sachs 2014a: 108).

The negotiations to define the new goals and alternative schemes for their implementation started right after the Rio+20 summit, involving consultations at the international, national and regional levels. Early in the process, the Sustainable Development Solutions Network (SDSN) established by the UN Secretary General and including academics, civil society and the private sector, issued a recommendation of ten SDGs. These were structured around ten key areas: ending extreme poverty, promoting sustainable growth and jobs, guaranteeing education, social inclusion and health for all, promoting sustainable agriculture, sustainable cities, sustainable energy and climate change, sustainable biodiversity, good governance and global partnership (Sachs 2014a). Building on the latter and the many inputs from national and international consultations, the UN Open Working Group developed a set of 17 sustainable development goals for consideration by the UN General Assembly in 2013[9]. Most recommendations regarding environmental goals reflect the UNEP's Green Economy perspective based on the belief that technological innovation and regulation would solve the environmental problem, and include specific targets on global food waste, energy efficiency, R&D and conservation of marine areas and forests.

From the very beginning of the process of defining the SDGs, fostering economic growth has been an undisputed component of the package. As I will discuss in the next section, the belief in the 'trickle-down' effect (the idea that economic growth itself will result in wealth reaching the poor and lifting them out of poverty) and the possibility of decoupling economic growth from environmental degradation has resulted in economic growth becoming the core concept of the economic dimension of sustainable development, replacing the broader concept of economic sustainability included in the WCED report. The proposed SDGs even include a specific target of at least 7 per cent per annum GDP growth for least-developed countries, sending a clear signal that GDP still holds a strong position as a measure of welfare.[8] Alternative measures are relegated to the post-SDG period, when it is expected that measurements of progress on sustainable development might be ready to complement GDP in developing countries. There is no mention of a proposal or a decision process regarding the use of alternative welfare indicators in developed countries yet. As Costanza and colleagues (2014: 285) put it: 'GDP remains entrenched. Vested interests are partly responsible. Former US President Bill Clinton's small move towards a "green GDP", which factored in some of the environmental consequences of growth, was killed by the coal industry.'

Discussing the green economy

UNEP's Green Economy Framework is at odds with empirical evidence suggesting 1) the impossibility of decoupling energy and resource use from economic growth and 2) the lack of causal relationship between economic growth and human wellbeing. If decoupling is not feasible and economic growth will not resolve either social or environmental dilemmas, arguments to support the 'green economy' as a viable proposal towards sustainable development crumble. The 'green economy' paradigm becomes yet another intricate architecture to shelter the capitalist system and its 'vested interests' as referred to by Costanza and colleagues.

Decoupling and the rebound effect

The belief that technological innovations can solve the environmental crisis is linked to the concept of *decoupling*, adopted by the OECD in 2001 to describe the possibility of experiencing economic growth without increasing resource depletion or negative externalities such as pollution or CO_2 emissions (UNEP 2011). When resource use or environmental impacts are reduced in absolute terms while the economy continues to grow, we talk about *absolute decoupling*. If the negative impacts are not halted but increase at a slower rate than the economy, we talk about *relative decoupling* (Jackson 2009). The argument expressed by the supporters of the 'green economy' proposal is that investing in technological and organisational innovation will foster absolute decoupling and people, mainly the poor, will be able to increase their levels of consumption at the same time that the environment will experience less negative effects from production and consumption activities. Absolute decoupling is necessary to fight climate change, as a sharp reduction in the net emissions of greenhouse gases is required if we are to stay below the 2 degrees Celsius limit suggested by the IPCC to avert disastrous impacts (Sachs 2014b).

The available evidence so far questions the possibility of achieving absolute decoupling in the near future. That environmental impacts are not decreasing in absolute terms is reflected in the fact that global carbon emissions from energy use have increased by 40 per cent since 1990 (Oliver *et al.* 2013), fossil fuel extraction has kept on rising (although progressively shifting from oil and coal to natural gas) as has the extraction of industrial ores and minerals (OECD 2011b). Furthermore, there is no evidence to suggest that material consumption has dropped. Although some national statistics might show a stabilisation in material consumption caused by the failure to account for the resources and emissions from imported goods (Jackson 2009) the continuous increase in municipal solid waste, expected to reach 1.42 kg per person per day (or 2.2 billion tonnes per year) by 2015, challenges this claim (Hoornweg and Bhada-Tata 2012). Finally, the impact of economic activity on other animal species is not far from predatory. A recent report by the WWF indicates that the total number of wild animals (population sizes of vertebrates) declined by 52 per cent from 1970 until 2010 (WWF 2014).

Despite the grim landscape depicted by a lack of evidence for absolute decoupling, efficiency improvements have been very important in recent decades. Globally there has been a 23 per cent reduction in energy intensity (amount of energy needed to produce one unit of economic output) between 1990 and 2011 (IEA 2013). There has also been a reduction in the global carbon intensity, which declined by 25 per cent from 1980 to 2006, despite the growing emissions from India and China; the latter responsible for 28 per cent of the world's CO_2 emissions (Sachs 2014b). Other evidence of relative decoupling comes from the use of biomass. Harvests have increased while the amount of cultivated land has remained stable. However, the greater use of fertilisers and water for irrigation makes relative decoupling difficult to assess in this particular sector (UNEP 2011).

In general, as production, transport and heating technologies become more efficient, overall production and consumption increases, offsetting the energy and resource savings of the new technologies and processes. As Jackson puts it 'there is little doubt that economic consumption has historically relied heavily on the consumption of material resources; that improvements in resource productivity have generally been offset by increases in scale; and that the goods and services that people actually buy continue to be inherently material in nature' (Jackson 2006: 6). The increases in the total volume consumed as a consequence of efficiency improvements are related to what has been called the 'rebound effect' or the 'efficiency delusion' (Sorrell *et al.* 2009; Wilhite and Nørgaard 2004). Rebound effects are usually classified as *direct* if economic savings from an efficiency increase are used to increase consumption of the same good or service (e.g. savings from energy efficient light-bulbs used to illuminate larger areas) and *indirect* if they increase consumption of other goods and services. Chitnis and colleagues (2014) suggest that the rebound effect applies to all energy efficiency measures implemented to date and that it is important to know their scale and impact across social groups to design better sustainability policies. They also suggest accounting for the interdependence of environmental measures and lifestyle measures, without which no significant energy savings can be expected.

The indications are that relative decoupling will not be a first step towards absolute decoupling in a context of economic expansion, constantly growing global population and the presence of rebound effects. Jackson maintains that to meet the IPCC's target of carbon dioxide emissions below 4 billion tonnes in 2050, annual emissions should be decreasing at an average rate of 4.9 per cent. He writes 'to achieve an average year-on-year reduction in emissions of 4.9 per cent with 0.7 per cent population growth and 1.4 per cent income growth technology has to improve by approximately 7 per cent every year. Almost 10 times faster than it is doing now.' (Jackson 2009: 54) Thus, the positive relationship between economic growth and the environment claimed by the Kuznets curve can no longer be relied on as a justification for more production and consumption. Even if it is true that as societies become rich there is more support for strong environmental policies and there are more funds available to develop technologies to save energy and resources, most environmental impacts are aggravated by economic growth and some, like climate change and biodiversity loss can have a lasting deleterious effect on the earth ecosystems and as a consequence, on human wellbeing.

Human wellbeing and economic growth

The stress on economic growth in the green economy approach to SD does not only make the achievement of environmental conservation difficult but might even impede higher levels of wellbeing. That a greater volume of goods and services at the macro-economic level results in their increased availability for the general population relies on the 'trickle-down' effect, which implies that economic growth, through the benefits that it gives to the rich in terms of profits, will increase the demand for goods and services and provide employment and better wages for the poor. There is little evidence to support the existence of this effect either at the national or global levels. In fact, the industrialised countries that managed to reduce sharply their post-war levels of poverty in the second half of the 20th century were those that succeeded in building sound institutions and creating well-functioning welfare states, not those that experienced higher economic growth (Latouche 2009; Muraca 2012).

The US is often held up as an example of the success of 'trickle down', but the evidence does not support this claim. The US has one of the highest levels of inequality and poverty among advanced economies with a value of the Gini Index[10] similar to that of China, Georgia or Senegal.[11] As the 2014 Human Development Report indicates, when the Human Development Index[12] is adjusted by the level of inequality, the US falls from the fifth position to the 28th position in the ranking (UNDP 2014). At the global level, increasing wealth among the rich has increased global inequalities. As the 2013 Human Development Report illustrates 'the 85 richest people in the world have the same wealth as the 3.5 billion poorest people' and this inequality is also increasing within developing countries. Income inequality within developing countries rose by 11 per cent between 1990 and 2010 (UNDP 2014).

Additional evidence on the relationship between economic growth and human wellbeing is provided by the academic literature in the objective and subjective wellbeing traditions. Objective wellbeing (OWB) is commonly studied through a list of requirements that people should have satisfied in order to live a good or self-actualised life while subjective wellbeing (SWB) depends on people's own accounts of their situation in terms of satisfaction or happiness (Gasper 2005). Objective wellbeing, in addition to wealth and income, can be investigated through indicators on basic needs, capabilities[13] and psychological wellbeing. None of these approaches argue for a strong relationship between economic growth and wellbeing although they vary in the extent to which they believe that quality of life can be improved through the increased production and consumption of economic goods.

For example, Doyal and Gough (1991) in their *Theory of Human Need*, maintain that avoidance of serious harm, which they equate with a situation in which basic needs are satisfied, can only be achieved if the goods and services that are produced have *universal satisfier characteristics*. The latter are defined as: adequate nutritional food and water, adequate protective housing, non-hazardous work and physical environments, appropriate health care, security in childhood, significant primary relationships, economic security, safe birth control and childbearing, and appropriate basic and cross-cultural education (see Chapter 3 for a more extended description of Doyal and Gough's theory). When societies are not concerned with the production of needs satisfiers and rather focus on increasing the availability of luxury goods, economic growth will not necessarily result in increased wellbeing. As Doyal and Gough (1991: 237) put it: 'An economy which prioritises the production of needs satisfiers will, all things being equal, enhance overall opportunities for successful participation to a greater extent than another economy with the same aggregate output but with a higher share of luxury production.'

Amartya Sen proposes a similar approach in his work on human capabilities. If economic growth leads to the expansion of basic capabilities through higher levels of employment, better social services and welfare programmes, then it will make a positive contribution to wellbeing (Clark 2006; Sen 1990). If, on the contrary, it only leads to greater income or increased consumption for a privileged minority, it will not expand the capabilities of the general population and thus it will not have an effect on human wellbeing. Sen defines *capabilities* as the 'combination of *functionings* the person can achieve from which she or he can choose one collection' (Sen 1992: 40) where functionings are defined as 'what people manage to do or to be' (Sen 1985: 10). Capabilities are related to goods and services but only through the skills and freedom that people have to transform them into valuable functionings. Studies analysing the relationship between capability and income/expenditure indicators have confirmed the weak relationship between the two (refer to the work of the Oxford Poverty and Human Development Initiative, www.ophi.org.uk/, Klassen 2000 and Ruggeri-Laderchi 1997 for studies on the topic). A study of minimum income receivers in Finland illustrates how capability expansion does not demand greater consumption (Hirvilammi and colleagues 2013). The authors demonstrated that minimum income receivers achieved the same type of functioning with secondhand household goods than would have been achieved with brand new goods. Collaborative consumption, which does not require increased production, appears here as enhancing both human and ecological wellbeing.

Psychological research adds to the human needs and capability approach by suggesting that a focus on the acquisition of material goods might even be detrimental for wellbeing. Following Self-determination theory, psychological wellbeing is defined in terms of the degree to which the needs for autonomy (people's endorsement of their own actions), competence (being able to function effectively in society) and relatedness (feeling accepted and respected in society) are satisfied (Ryan and Deci 2001; Ryan and Sapp 2007). When people have their competence, autonomy and relatedness needs fulfilled, they are more likely to be intrinsically motivated, to be driven by their curiosity and inner drives. When on the contrary, people are motivated by extrinsic goals such as the pursuit of material or financial success, and those goals become relatively more important than other intrinsic goals such as self-acceptance, family and community, people are more likely to experience lower levels of psychological wellbeing (Kasser and Ryan 1993; Kasser 2002). Kasser and colleagues (2007) maintain that the characteristics of American Corporate Capitalism (self-interest, competition, hierarchical wage labour and a focus on financial profit and economic growth) promote extrinsic goals and thus are detrimental for psychological wellbeing.

Further support comes from the studies investigating the association between economic growth and self-reports on happiness or satisfaction with life. Richard Easterlin's work, using time-series data from a wide array of countries, has provided ample evidence about the lack of relationship between economic growth, measured as GDP growth, and subjective wellbeing or happiness in the long run (Easterlin 1974, 2013). His research indicates that while temporary economic contractions or expansions might influence people's reported wellbeing, long-term economic growth does not have an impact either in rich or in poor or in transition countries. Easterlin (2013) exemplifies these zero-returns to income with the case of China, where the real GDP has multiplied by four in the last two decades but life satisfaction has remained the same.

Easterlin's findings have been often contested by studies suggesting a diminishing marginal utility of income (the smaller the effect on happiness of a given increase in income, the higher the level of income) (for a summary see Frey and Stutzer 2002; Layard 2005; Helliwell *et al.* 2012) or a positive relationship (Stevenson and Wolfers 2008; Sacks, Stevenson and Wolfers 2010). These claims are attractive both for supporters of the green growth approach and of the post-growth movement as they are used to justify economic growth in the Global South and steady-state or de-growth economies in the Global North. However, they have been empirically refuted by Easterlin (2013) who argues that studies addressing the relationship between income and happiness within countries, for example, cannot be used to make any claim about the relationship between these variables over time. He also demonstrates that longitudinal studies that assert a positive relationship over time might be reflecting short and not long-term results.

Beyond sustainable development as green growth

The *green economy* approach to sustainable development accounts neither for the evidence on absolute decoupling nor for the weak or null relationship between income and wellbeing. Alternatives to the green economy that do not revolve around economic growth are manifold, from the Steady-Stage proposal developed in the nineteen seventies to the *Buen Vivir* perspective popularised by the recent Ecuadorian and Bolivian constitutions. The origins of post-growth proposals for development can be traced back to the debate around the *Limits to Growth* report mentioned earlier (Meadows *et al.* 1972). The report raised international awareness about the impossibility of exponential economic and population growth in the context of finite natural resources. Ecological economists such as Herman Daly (1971, 1974), Ernst Friedrich Schumacher (1973) and Nicholas Georgescu-Roegen (1975) developed their alternative conceptualisations of development considering that economic expansion was one of the causes for environmental destruction.

The conceptualisation of alternative development paradigms that do not revolve around economic growth ran parallel to that of indicators that accounted for the social and environmental costs of production and consumption activities. In the seventies, there were few alternative indicators of welfare to the Gross Domestic Product (GDP). The GDP can be calculated in three ways: through the value of the goods and services produced by all economic sectors in a country; by adding up the value of goods and services consumed, the investments undertaken, and the difference between exports and imports; and by calculating the value of the income generated through profits and wages (Mankiw 2011). The three approaches share an accounting based on what has been traded, bought or sold in the market and do not include non-traded goods and services or the social or environmental consequences of the economic activity. Robert Kennedy summarised the problems associated with the use of Gross National Product (a similar measure to GDP that accounts for the production of a country's citizens in and outside the country instead of measuring the production of residents) in a famous speech at the University of Kansas in 1968:

> Too much and for too long, we seemed to have surrendered personal excellence and community values in the mere accumulation of material things. Our Gross National Product,[14] now, is over $800 billion dollars a year, but that Gross National Product – if we judge the United States of America

by that – that Gross National Product counts air pollution and cigarette advertising, and ambulances to clear our highways of carnage. It counts special locks for our doors and the jails for the people who break them. It counts the destruction of the redwood and the loss of our natural wonder in chaotic sprawl. It counts napalm and counts nuclear warheads and armored cars for the police to fight the riots in our cities. It counts Whitman's rifle and Speck's knife, and the television programs which glorify violence in order to sell toys to our children. Yet the gross national product does not allow for the health of our children, the quality of their education or the joy of their play. It does not include the beauty of our poetry or the strength of our marriages, the intelligence of our public debate or the integrity of our public officials. It measures neither our wit nor our courage, neither our wisdom nor our learning, neither our compassion nor our devotion to our country, it measures everything in short, except that which makes life worthwhile.[15]

As discussed earlier, several indicators that account for the environmental and social consequences of economic expansion are now being considered as indicators for the green economy (Kubiszewski *et al.* 2013; Posner and Costanza 2011). Advocates for a post-growth perspective favour the Index of Sustainable Economic Welfare (ISEW) and General Progress Indicator (GPI) as a measure of the total economic welfare derived by the economic activity (Daly and Cobb, 1989; Cobb *et al.* 1995). Both are often used interchangeably and include in a single metric unpaid household labour, social costs, environmental damage, income distribution, the use of natural resources and private consumer expenditure, among other items.[16] Studies in developed and developing countries using these alternative measures indicate that from the late seventies and early eighties onwards GDP has continued to rise while economic welfare measured by the ISEW and GPI has declined (Castañeda 1999; Jackson and McBride 2005; Max-Neef 1995; Stockhammer *et al.* 1997). Max-Neef (2005) drew on these results and his own calculations to propose a 'threshold hypothesis' by which after a certain point, economic growth no longer increased quality of life because of the environmental and social costs associated with it.

The evidence on the 'threshold hypothesis' has been used by ecological economists to propose alternative development pathways not centred on the idea of economic growth but on different notions of welfare or wellbeing. Herman Daly, the proponent of a Steady State economy, defined development in terms of the qualitative improvements that allowed reducing throughput ('the materials and energy a society extracts, processes, transports and distributes to consume and return back to the environment as waste', Daly 1996) through the promotion of values and activities that were more satisfying to people than the ones based on production and consumption (Daly 2008). A lower throughput was presented as opposed to the negative experiences of economic recession, as in Daly's words it 'means high life expectancy for people and high durability for goods', not scarcity of goods or welfare services as is the case in economic downturns. The Steady-State proposal has also different implications for poor and rich countries. Drawing on evidence from happiness and ISEW/GPI-based research, Daly argues that poor countries with strong redistributive policies might still need to experience economic growth and that rich countries 'should reduce their throughput growth to free up resources and ecological space for use by the poor, while focussing their domestic efforts on development, technical and social improvements, that can be freely shared with poor countries', (Daly 2008: 3).

A similar approach to sustainable development assuming economic growth in poor countries and a shrinking economy in terms of throughput in rich countries has been endorsed by advocates of sustainable *degrowth*. The latter is defined as a democratic process of economic reduction with lower levels of consumption and production (Kallis 2011; Martínez-Alier 2009). Both Steady-State and degrowth approaches entail a transformation of society through state intervention based on the generation of suitable technical, organisational and economic conditions for a low impact economy. However, they differ in the stress placed on the need to involve grassroots movements and local organisations in the process of transformation. The degrowth movement underscores the great transformative power of fostering coalitions of experts, policy-makers and grassroots social movements or local and personal initiatives aiming at downshifting and low carbon lifestyles. The interdependences between environmental, social and personal wellbeing are easily observed at the local level and degrowth proponents advocate for the creation of a platform to facilitate the emergence of coalitions and joint initiatives (Martínez-Alier *et al.* 2010). As Kallis summarises it (2011: 874): 'I propose that big social change does not take place by appealing to those in power, but by bottom-up movements that challenge established paradigms; scientists have a role to play as partners in these movements, offering – and problematizing – structuring concepts.'

In the 1980s, Manfred Max-Neef and his collaborators developed the Human Scale Development (HSD) proposal to support grassroots organisations in their quest to improve people's wellbeing without necessarily depending on economic growth (Max-Neef *et al.* 1989; Max-Neef 1991). The HSD takes development as a process geared towards the satisfaction of fundamental human needs and the promotion of increasing levels of self-reliance that break with socio-economic and political dependence. Although the characteristics of the HSD proposal will be thoroughly discussed in Chapter 3, it is useful to highlight here how it provides, in addition to a framework on which to build sustainable development, a specific methodology to support policy-making at the grassroots levels. In the HSD proposal, the role of the state is reversed, from being the designer and implementer of policies to becoming the generator of endogenous sustainable development processes at the grassroots levels. These processes revolve around a participatory exercise to identify *synergic satisfiers*, those values, attitudes, actions, laws, ways of organisation, institutions, infrastructures and natural environments that contribute to the fulfilment of more than one fundamental human need (subsistence, protection, affection, understanding, participation, idleness, creation, identity and freedom).

Although HSD does not exclude the possibility of economic growth, it does not give it a central role. Economic prosperity goes together with competitiveness, urban sprawl, individualism, hectic lifestyles and consumerism which in the HSD proposal are often associated with *harmful satisfiers*; those that reduce people's capacity to fulfil their human needs. In addition, economic growth has a clear negative impact on the environment as captured by studies on planet boundaries, ecological footprints and ECOSONs, a per capita energy budget calculated by Max-Neef. Max-Neef maintains that in order not to exceed the carrying capacity of the biosystem, the energy budget per person calculated at 13,000 kw/pp/yr should not be exceeded (Smith and Max-Neef 2011: 152). His analysis indicates, similar to studies on the ecological footprint, that humanity is already using 33 per cent more primary energy than the one the environment is prepared to assimilate.

The fact that *harmful satisfiers* like consumerism have negative consequences both for people and the environment highlights the interdependence of economic and biophysical systems. This is also represented in the concept of *synergic satisfiers* which are by definition sustainable; as they cannot satisfy more than one need if they destroy or harm the natural environment. This is the most important conceptual contribution of the HSD proposal to the study and practice of sustainability. It draws on a very attractive idea that by targeting human needs fulfilment and not economic growth, societies can actually progress towards reducing CO_2 emissions, halting species extinction and limiting the amount of industrial and household waste. Societies need to provide the population with the means to identify synergic satisfiers and support their production and consumption in a horizontal manner. Thus, the HSD proposal gives the economy a subsidiary role; it should account for the finitude of the biosphere and be at the service of people. As Smith and Max-Neef put it 'no economic interest, under any circumstances, can be above the reverence for [all forms of[17]] life'. (2011: 154).

Finally, it is important to note that an understanding of SD that denies the need for economic growth, challenges the main foundation of the capitalist system. Wilhite and Hansen (2015) explain how three characteristics of capitalism make this system impossible to maintain if we want to progress towards sustainable development. The first is related with the 'growth imperative', the need for capitalist firms to engage in profit generating activities in order to remain in the market. This impels capitalist firms to expand markets, and even if they improve their technical efficiency (relative decoupling), to use more resources and sell more products (Smith 2010). The second is based on evidence from current neoliberal policies where a continuous and dialectical response is established between market expansion and social agents that, after continuous pressures, end up adopting the practices and beliefs characterising the system (Polanyi 2001). The detrimental effect of the beliefs behind neoliberal policies is supported by psychological research indicating that citizens in countries with a more 'liberal market fashion' (US and UK) place a higher value on self-enhancing aims (achievement) and care less about self-transcendent aims (universalism) than people from countries with a more cooperative orientation such as Germany and

Austria, for example (Kasser 2001). Finally, Wilhite and Hansen (2015) discuss the fact that under capitalism increases in efficiency associated with energy or resource-saving technologies are used to reduce prices and expand markets. This results in continuous increases in production and consumption as discussed earlier when addressing the impossibility of decoupling and the existence of rebound effects.

In summary, the fact that alternative approaches such as the Steady-State, Degrowth and HSD proposals challenge the need for economic growth to achieve SD reduces its popularity among international organisations and policy-makers. As Kallis maintains, degrowth 'even if socially sustainable, is likely to shrink the surpluses and profits of private enterprises, redistribute costs between capital and labour and hence meet the resistance of those who have economic and political power (Spangenberg 2010)', (Kallis 2011: 875). He allies with those who suggest that it will not be possible to transform society to include sustainable degrowth without radically changing the way jobs, property and financial resources are allocated and as a consequence creating an alternative system to capitalism (Jackson 2009; Kallis 2011; Latouche 2009).

Conclusion

Sustainable development understood as the process of development that takes into account the possibilities of current and future generations to satisfy their needs does not require that economies experience economic growth. However, since the UN Rio+20 conference, the 'green economy' paradigm has consolidated approaches to SD based on technological and organisational innovations together with a stress on regulation and equitable distribution that protect economic growth from being challenged. Empirical evidence suggests that it is impossible with current technologies to decouple economic growth from environmental degradation and that a direct relationship between increases in material production and consumption and people's experienced wellbeing does not exist. Despite this evidence, it is quite likely that the new Sustainable Development Goals define a specific growth rate for developing countries; which in the last two decades have been experiencing increasing levels of inequality together with above average growth rates.

Alternative approaches to SD that do not revolve around economic growth are manifold. They have not entered the discussions at the level of international organisations because they constitute a direct challenge to capitalism. The capitalist system requires economic growth for its reproduction. Approaches to SD that advocate for the centrality of human needs and highlight the negative effects on people and the environment of the current economic system based on increased levels of production and consumption are thus not generally supported. That, on average, rich countries reduce their throughput, middle-income countries aim for a Steady-State and poor countries consider increases in consumption that meet the material needs of their population does not imply reductions in the wellbeing of the population. It might even enhance it, if human needs are at the centre of policy-making and self-reliance, and balanced articulations between the global, regional and local and between nature, society and technologies are pursued. The next chapter will address how the Human Scale Development approach presents itself as an alternative to the SD perspective characterised by economic growth.

Notes

1 The ecological modernisation discourse stresses the compatibility between economic growth and environmental protection as the mitigation of environmental impacts through technological innovations and increased efficiency are considered beneficial both in economic and environmental terms (Dryzek *et al.* 2013).
2 The Washington consensus refers to the approach to policy reforms endorsed by the US Congress and Treasury, international financial institutions such as IMF and the World Bank and some Washington think tanks with regard to debtor countries in Latin America and elsewhere in the eighties. These reforms were based on ten policy instruments, among them privatisation, deregulation, trade liberalisation, fiscal discipline and the encouragement of foreign direct investments (Peet and Hartwick 2009).
3 The sink function of the natural environment is defined by the OECD as 'the capacity of the environment to absorb the unwanted by-products of production and consumption; exhaust gases from combustion or chemical processing, water used to clean products or people, discarded packaging and goods no longer wanted', (https://stats.oecd.org/glossary/detail.asp?ID=6569; accessed 5 April 2015).
4 The goals of the Green Climate Fund and the characteristics of the projects funded can be found at http://news.gcfund.org/.
5 WWF's Living Planet Report 2014 indicates that biodiversity has declined by 52 per cent since 1970 (http://wwf.panda.org/about_our_earth/all_publications/living_planet _report/; accessed 30 March 2015).
6 Refer to www.unep.org/greeneconomy/, accessed 30 March 2015.
7 http://ec.europa.eu/environment/beyond_gdp/index_en.html
8 The MDGs were a set of development goals agreed by the States Members of the UN in 2000 to be achieved by the end of 2015. Most MDGs were concerned with improving subsistence conditions for the global poor with a special stress on monetary poverty, physical health, gender equality and primary education. One of the MDGs related explicitly to environmental sustainability through calls to reverse natural resources and biodiversity losses, reduce water pollution and improve sewage systems particularly in urban slums and rural areas of the developing world (www.un.org/ millenniumgoals/). Significant progress has been achieved in most MDGs mostly due to the remarkable progress of China and India. However, 1.2 billion people still live in extreme poverty, 25 per cent of children are stunted due to malnutrition, 57 million children are not in primary education, 2.5 million people are infected with AIDS on an annual basis and 2.5 billion people lack access to improved sanitation facilities.
9 The full report of the Open Working Group of the General Assembly on Sustainable Development Goals is issued as document A/68/970, available at http://undocs.org/ A/68/970.
10 'Gini index measures the extent to which the distribution of income or consumption expenditure among individuals or households within an economy deviates from a perfectly equal distribution. A Lorenz curve plots the cumulative percentages of total income received against the cumulative number of recipients, starting with the poorest individual or household. The Gini index measures the area between the Lorenz curve and a hypothetical line of absolute equality, expressed as a percentage of the maximum

area under the line. Thus a Gini index of 0 represents perfect equality, while an index of 100 implies perfect inequality', (http://data.worldbank.org/indicator/SI.POV.GINI, accessed 12 December 2014).

11 Data from the World Bank (http://data.worldbank.org).

12 The UNDP defines the HDI as 'a summary measure of average achievement in key dimensions of human development: a long and healthy life, being knowledgeable and have a decent standard of living. The HDI is the geometric mean of normalized indices for each of the three dimensions', (http://hdr.undp.org/en/content/human-development-index-hdi, accessed 30 March 2015).

13 Refer to Chapter 3 for a description of the characteristics and scope of the basic needs and capabilities approaches.

14 Both GNI (Gross National Income) and GDP (Gross Domestic Product) are economic measures of national income. The GDP measures the country total output while the GNI includes, in addition, the income generated in other countries by residents such as dividends or interests and excludes the income earned in the domestic market by non-residents.

15 The complete speech by R.F. Kennedy at the University of Kansas on 18 March 1968 can be found at the J.F Kennedy Presidential Library and Museum's website, (www.jfklibrary.org/Research/Research-Aids/Ready-Reference/RFK-Speeches/Remarks-of-Robert-F-Kennedy-at-the-University-of-Kansas-March-18–1968.aspx, accessed 30 October, 2014).

16 Following Jackson and McBride (2005: 19) the ISEW can be expressed as 'ISEW = Personal consumer expenditure – adjustment for income inequality + non-defensive public expenditures + value of domestic labour + economic adjustments – defensive private expenditures – costs of environmental degradation – depreciation of natural capital. The GPI adds to the above components adjustments for crime, divorce, changes in leisure, time and unemployment.

17 I included 'all forms of life' between parentheses because this is the expression used by Max-Neef in the same paragraph from where the quote is extracted.

References

Adams, W. M. (2009). *Green Development: Environment and Sustainability in a Developing World*. Abingdon: Routledge.

Castañeda, B. (1999). An index of sustainable economic welfare (ISEW) for Chile. *Ecological Economics*, 28: 231–44.

Chitnis, M., Sorrell, S., Druckman, A., Firth, S., and Jackson, T. (2014). Who rebounds most? Estimating direct and indirect rebound effects for different UK socioeconomic groups. *Ecological Economics*, 106(0): 12–32.

Clark, D. A. (2006). Capability approach. In Clark, D. A. (ed.), *The Elgar Companion to Development Studies*. Cheltenham: Edward Elgar.

Cobb, C., Halstead, E., and Rowe, J. (1995). *The Genuine Progress Indicator: Summary of Data and Methodology*. Washington, DC: Redefining Progress.

Common, M. and Stagl, S. (2007). *Ecological Economics. An Introduction*, (2nd edn). Cambridge (UK): Cambridge University Press.

Cosbey, A. (2011). Are there downsides to a green economy? The trade, investment and competitiveness implications of unilateral green economic pursuit (1 March). United Nations Conference on Trade and Development, (http://r0.unctad.org/trade_env/green economy/road2rioGE2.asp, accessed 23 March 2015).

Costanza, R., Kubiszewski, I., Giovannini, E., Lovins, H., McGlade, J., Pickett, K. E., Ragnarsdottir, K. V., Roberts, D., de Vogli, R. and Wilkinson, R. (2014). Time to leave GDP behind. *Nature*, 505: 283–5.

Daly, H. E. (1971). Toward a steady-state economy. In Harte, J., Socolow, R. H. (eds), *Patient earth*. New York: Rinehart and Winston Inc, pp. 226–44.

Daly, H. E. (1974). The Economics of the Steady State. *The American Economic Review*, 64(2): 15–21.

Daly, H. E. (1996). *Beyond growth*. Boston: Beacon Press.

Daly, H. E. (2008). A Steady-State Economy. Sustainable Development Commission, UK, 24 April, (www.sd-commission.org.uk/data/files/publications/Herman_Daly_thinkpiece.pdf, accessed 23 March 2015).

Daly, H. E. and Cobb, J. (1989). *For the Common Good*. Boston: Beacon Press.

Dasgupta, C. (2011). Reflections on the relationship between the 'green economy' and sustainable development. In UNCTAD. *The Road to Rio+20: for a development-led green economy*. New York; Geneva: United Nations, pp. 33–5.

Doyal, L. and Gough, I. (1991). *A Theory of Human Need*. New York: Palgrave Macmillan.

Dryzek, J. S., Nørgaard, R. B. and Schlosberg, D. (2013). *The Oxford Handbook of Climate Change and Society*. Oxford: Oxford University Press.

Easterlin, R. A. (1974). Does economic growth improve the human lot? In David, P. A. and Reder, M. S. (eds), *Essays in Honour of Moses Abramovitz*. Massachusetts: Academic Press, pp. 89–125.

Easterlin, R. A. (2013). *Happiness and Economic Growth: The Evidence*. IZA DP No. 7187. January 2013.

Frey, B. S. and Stutzer, A. (2002). *Happiness and Economics*. Princeton: Princeton University Press.

Gasper, D. (2005). Subjective and objective well-being in relation to economic inputs: Puzzles and responses. *Review of Social Economy*, 63(2): 177–206.

Georgescu-Roegen, N. (1975). Energy and economic myths. *Southern Economic Journal*, 41(3): 347–81.

Helliwell, J., Layard, R. and Sachs, J. (eds) (2012). *World Happiness Report*. New York: Earth Institute, Columbia University.

Hirvilammi, T., Laakso, S., Lettenmeier, M. and Lähteenoja, S. (2013). Studying well-being and its environmental impacts: A case study of minimum income receivers in Finland. *Journal of Human Development and Capabilities*, 14(1): 134–54.

Hoornweg, D. and Bhada-Tata, P. (2012). What a waste: A global review of solid waste management. Urban development series; Knowledge Papers no. 15. Washington DC: The Worldbank, (http://go.worldbank.org/BCQEP0TMO0, accessed 13 November 2014).

IEA (2013). CO2 emissions from fuel combustion. International Energy Agency, (www.iea.org/publications/freepublications/publication/co2emissionsfromfuelcombustion highlights2013.pdf, accessed 12 November 2014).

Jackson, T. (2006). *Earthscan Reader in Sustainable Consumption*. London: Earthscan.

Jackson, T. (2009). *Prosperity Without Growth*. London: Sustainable Development Commission.

Jackson, T. and McBride, N. (2005). Measuring progress? A review of 'adjusted' measures of economic welfare in Europe (www.surrey.ac.uk/ces/files/pdf/1105-WP-Measuring-Progress-final.pdf, accessed 3 November 2014).

Kallis, G. (2011). In defence of degrowth. *Ecological Economics*, 70: 873–80.

Kasser, T. (2002). *The High Price of Materialism*. Cambridge, MA: MIT Press.

Kasser, T. (2011). Values and human wellbeing. Commissioned paper for *The Bellagio Initiative: The Future of Philanthropy and Development in the Pursuit of Human Wellbeing*.

Kasser, T. and Ryan, R. M. (1993). A dark side of the American dream: Correlates of financial success as a central life aspiration. *Journal of Personality and Social Psychology*, 65: 410–22.

Kasser, T., Cohn, S., Kanner, A. D. and Ryan, R. M. (2007). Some costs of American corporate capitalism: A psychological exploration of value and goal conflicts. *Psychological Inquiry*, 18(1): 1–22.

Klassen, S. (2000). Measuring poverty and deprivation in South Africa. *Review of Income and Wealth*, 46: 33–58.

Kubiszewski, I., Costanza, R., Franco, C., Lawn, P., Talberth, J., Jackson, T. and Aylmer, C. (2013). Beyond GDP: Measuring and achieving global genuine progress. *Ecological Economics*, 93(0): 57–68.

Latouche, S. (2009). *Farewell to Growth*. Cambridge: Polity Press.

Layard, R. (2005). *Happiness. Lessons from a New Science*. London: Penguin Books.

Mankiw, N. G. (2011). *Principles of Economics*, 5th edn. South-western Cengage Learning.

Martínez-Alier, J. (2009). Socially sustainable economic degrowth. *Development and Change*, 40(6): 1099–119.

Martínez-Alier, J., Pascual, U., Vivien, F-D. and Zaccai, E. (2010). Sustainable de-growth: Mapping the context, criticisms and future prospects of an emergent paradigm. *Ecological Economics*, 69: 1741–47.

Max-Neef, M. (1991). *Human Scale Development: Conception, Application and Further Reflection*. London: Apex Press.

Max-Neef, M. (1995). Economic growth and quality of life: a threshold hypothesis. *Ecological Economics*, 15: 115–18.

Max-Neef, M. (2005). Foundations of transdisciplinarity. *Ecological Economics*, 53: 5–16.

Max-Neef, M., Elizalde, A. and Hopenhayn, M. (1989). Human Scale Development: an option for the future. *Development Dialogue*, 1: 17–47.

Meadows, D. H., Meadows, D. L, Randers, J. and Behrens, W. (1972). *The Limits to Growth*. New York: Universe Books.

Muraca, B. (2012). Towards a fair degrowth-society: Justice and the right to a 'good life' beyond growth. *Futures*, 44(6): 535–45.

OECD (2011a). *How's Life?: Measuring Well-being*. Paris: OECD Publishing, (http://dx.doi.org/10.1787/9789264121164-en).

OECD (2011b). *Towards Green Growth: Monitoring Progress: OECD Indicators*. OECD, Paris: Green Growth Studies.

Oliver J. G. J., Janssens-Maenhout, G., Muntean, M. and Peters, J. A. H. W. (2013). *Trends in Global CO2 Emissions, 2013 Report*. The Hague: PBL Netherlands Environmental Assessment Agency; Ispra: Joint Research Centre.

Peet, R. and Hartwick, E. (2009). *Theories of Development*, 2nd edn. New York: The Guilford Press.

Polanyi, K. (2001). *The Great Transformation: The Political and Economic Origins of Our Time*. Boston: Beacon Press.

Posner, S. M. and Costanza, R. (2011). A summary of ISEW and GPI studies at multiple scales and new estimates for Baltimore City, Baltimore County, and the State of Maryland. *Ecological Economics*, 70(11): 1972–80.

Rockström, J., Steffen, W., Noone, K., Persson, Å., Chapin, III, F. S., Lambin, E., Lenton, T. M., Scheffer, M., Folke, C., Schellnhuber, H., Nykvist, B., De Wit, C. A., Hughes, T., van der Leeuw, S., Rodhe, H., Sörlin, S., Snyder, P. K., Costanza, R., Svedin, U., Falkenmark, M., Karlberg, L., Corell, R. W., Fabry, V. J., Hansen, J., Walker, B., Liverman, D., Richardson, K., Crutzen, P. and Foley, J. (2009). Planetary boundaries:

Exploring the safe operating space for humanity. *Ecology and Society*, 14(2): 32, (www.ecologyandsociety.org/vol14/iss2/art32/).

Ruggeri-Laderchi, C. (1997). Poverty and its many dimensions: The role of income as an indicator. *Oxford Development Studies*, 25(3): 345–60.

Ryan, R. M. and Deci, L. E. (2001). On happiness and human potentials: A review of research on hedonic and eudaimonic well-being. *Annual Review of Psychology*, 52(1): 141–66.

Ryan, R. M. and Sapp, A. R. (2007). Basic psychological needs: A self-determination theory perspective on the promotion of wellness across development and cultures. In Gough, I. and Allister McGregor, J. (eds), *Wellbeing in Developing Countries: From Theory to Research*. Cambridge: Cambridge University Press.

Sachs, J. D. (2014a). Sustainable Development Goals for a new era. *Horizons*, Autumn, 1.

Sachs, J. D. (2014b). The climate breakthrough in Beijing gives the world a fighting chance. *The Huffington Post*, (www.huffingtonpost.com/jeffrey-sachs/the-climate-breakthrough_b_6145998.html, accessed 26 January 2015).

Sacks, D. W., Stevenson, B. and Wolfers, J. (2010). Subjective well-being, income, economic development and growth, IZA Discussion Papers 5230, Institute for the Study of Labor (IZA).

Schumacher, E. F. (1973). *Small is Beautiful: A Study of Economics as if People Mattered*. London: Blond and Briggs.

Sen, A. (1985). *Commodities and Capabilities*. Oxford: Elsevier Science Publishers.

Sen, A. (1990). Development as capability expansion. In Griffin, K. and Knight, J. (eds), *Human Development and the International Development Strategy for the 1990s*. London: Macmillan, pp. 41–58.

Sen, A. (1992). *Inequality Reexamined*. Oxford: Oxford University Press.

Smith, P. B. and Max-Neef, M. (2011). *Economics Unmasked: From Power and Greed to Compassion and the Common Good*. Cambridge: Green Books.

Smith, R. (2010). Beyond growth or beyond capitalism? *Real-world Economics Review*, 53: 42.

Sorrell, S., Dimitropoulos, J. and Sommerville, M. (2009). Empirical estimates of the direct rebound effect: a review. *Energy Policy*, 37: 1356–71.

Spangenberg, J. (2010). The growth discourse, growth policy and sustainable development: two thought experiments. *Journal of Cleaner Production*, 18(6): 561–6.

Stevenson, B. and Wolfers, J. (2008). Economic growth and subjective wellbeing: Reassessing the Easterlin paradox. *Brookings Papers on economic activity*, 2998(Spring): 1–87.

Stiglitz, J., Sen, A. and Fitoussi, J.-P. (2009). Report by the Commission on the Measurement of Economic Performance and Social Progress. Paris: Commission on the Measurement of Economic Performance and Social Progress.

Stockhammer, E., Hochreiter, H., Obermayr, B. and Steiner, K. (1997). The index of sustainable economic welfare (ISEW) as an alternative to GDP in measuring economic welfare. The results of the Austrian (revised) ISEW calculation 1955–1992. *Ecological Economics*, 21: 19–34.

United Nations (2013). A life of dignity for all: Accelerating progress towards the Millennium Development Goals and advancing the United Nations development agenda beyond 2015, (www.un.org/ga/search/view_doc.asp?symbol=A per cent2F68 per cent2F202, accessed 26 January 2015).

UNDP (2014). Human development report. Sustaining human progress: Reducing vulnerabilities and building resilience, (http://hdr.undp.org/en/2014-report/download, accessed 26 January 2015).

UNEP (2011). Towards the Green Economy. Pathways to sustainable development and poverty eradication, (www.unep.org/greeneconomy).

WCED (1987). *Our Common Future*. Oxford: Oxford University Press.

Wilhite, H. and Hansen, A. (2015). Reflections on the meta-practice of capitalism and its capacity for sustaining a low energy transformation. In Zelem, M. (ed.), *Sociologie de l'Energie*. Toulouse: Presse de l'Universite de Toulouse.

Wilhite, H. and Nørgaard, J. (2004). Equating efficiency with reduction: A self-deception in energy policy. *Energy & Environment*, 15(6): 991–1009.

World Meteorological Organization (2014). Assessment for decision-makers: Scientific assessment of ozone depletion: 2014. Global Ozone Research and Monitoring Project, Report No. 56, Geneva, Switzerland.

WWF (2014). Living Planet Report 2014: species and spaces, people and places. McLellan, R., Iyengar, L., Jeffries, B. and Oerlemans, N. (eds). Gland, Switzerland: WWF.

3 The Human Scale Development proposal

Introduction

This chapter revolves around the proposal for an alternative development paradigm by economist Manfred Max-Neef, sociologist Antonio Elizalde and philosopher Martin Hopenhayn, detailed in the book *Human Scale Development: Conception, Applications and Further Reflections* published in 1991 by Apex Press.[1] The book was the result of a collaboration between CEPAUR (Centre for Development Alternatives) founded by Manfred Max-Neef in Santiago de Chile and the Dag Hammarskjöld Foundation in Uppsala (Sweden). It collected the transdisciplinary work undertaken by South American, Canadian and Swedish professionals during the eighteen months search for a more human paradigm for development practitioners and theorists.[2] The first part of the book, where the Human Scale Development (HSD) proposal is contextualised and described, had already been published in Spanish (1986) and English (1989) in two different issues of *Development Dialogue*, the academic journal of the Dag Hammerskjöld Foundation. The second part of the book was sole-authored by Max-Neef and included two essays on the language of economics and the differences between knowledge and understanding.

This chapter can by no means replace a careful reading of the original work by Max-Neef and his colleagues[3]. The overview provided here concentrates on the conceptual framework of the HSD proposal in order to facilitate its comparison with other approaches to human development and inform its application. The chapter starts by placing the HSD proposal in the context of the authors' frustrations with decades of failed development policies in Latin America in the nineteen eighties. Then, it continues by describing the authors' vision of a development based on self-reliance, human needs actualisation, participation and balanced relationships. Next, I discuss the HSD approach to human needs and satisfiers through the matrix of human needs; a methodological tool intended to support grassroots organisations and communities in the design of their own development processes. Finally, I address the HSD understanding of human needs and satisfiers and its relevance for sustainable development in relation to Doyal and Gough's theory of human need and Sen's and Nussbaum's capabilities approach. The latter, are two wellbeing theories increasingly drawn on in the sustainability debate to justify alternative accounts of human development to those focussing on material prosperity.

Human Scale Development as an alternative development paradigm

Manfred Max-Neef and his colleagues undertook the task of putting together a proposal for a new development paradigm that could replace the failed attempts of structuralism and neoliberalism to address poverty and marginalisation in Latin America. Structuralism or 'developmentalism' was the approach to development generalised in the region following the work of United Nations' Economic Commission for Latin America and the Caribbean (ECLAC) established in 1948 with the goal of promoting economic development. ECLAC's approach to development influenced many national and regional policies of the time through its stress on structural reforms and protection of exports (Prebisch 2008). Max-Neef and colleagues acknowledged the successes of structuralism in encouraging economic diversification, technological upgrading and creative solutions to the problems of underdevelopment and for having raised the issue of the multiple dependencies experienced by people in peripheral countries from rich countries and local elites. However, they considered that, in addition to the high level of international debt resulting from this development model, the failure of structuralist policies lay in its purely economic focus, with social and political realities often disregarded and resource accumulation by local elites encouraged. The authors concluded that these consequences had rendered the model inadequate to effectively contribute to human development.

Neoliberalism[4] presented additional challenges to human development to those of structuralism. It emerged during the seventies after the previous development model failed to address the huge level of debt in Latin America linked to the international oil shocks. The neoliberal policies as applied in the region during and after the debt crisis of the eighties were characterised by what Max-Neef and colleagues called 'a concoction of prescriptions' also known as the economic policy prescriptions of the 'Washington consensus' favoured by the International Monetary Fund, the World Bank and the US Treasury Department. These were, by and large, based on: encouraging a free market through low levels of tariffs; the privatisation of public companies; deregulation of prices, currencies and the labour market; and redirecting investments towards new and diversified exports (Peet and Hartwick 2009). Following Max-Neef and colleagues, the neoliberal development paradigm was a good recipe for economic growth but it deepened inequality as the poor and marginalised remained excluded from the markets and concentration of economic power was further encouraged by lack of regulation of oligopolistic[5] practices (Max-Neef 1991: 6).

Having analysed the shortcomings of previous and contemporary development approaches to contribute to the satisfaction of human needs in Latin America, Max-Neef and colleagues generated a proposal for a people-centred approach to development. This proposal was contemporary to a diversity of alternative perspectives on human development such as Sen's capability approach (1985, 1992), Streeten *et al.*'s (1981) emphasis on basic needs, Doyal and Gough's (1991) theory of human need and Freire (1970) and Fals Borda's (1987) understanding of development as participation and empowerment. It aligned with alternative approaches to the mainstream by not focussing on transforming economic structures from the top-down but on providing a platform for people and grassroots movements to design their own development strategies. That is why they did not call their approach a theory or a model, but a 'proposal' that could only come to life when applied. As Max-Neef and colleagues state 'there is nothing in the proposal that advocates a final solution, since we are fully aware that human beings and their surroundings are part of a permanent flow which cannot be arrested by rigid and static models' (Max-Neef *et al.* 1991: 12).

One of the main features of the HSD proposal is the central role given to popular participation. The stress on participation resulted from the authors' frustration with top-down development policies that did not account for, and even disregarded, the richness and complexities of people's everyday lives. It was also a consequence of the author's critical stance concerning the traditional lack of interest or ability of the Latin American states to provide spaces for popular participation and to empower civil society (Max-Neef 1991; Max-Neef 1992). The latter brought HSD close to community-led approaches in international development such as those promoted by Chambers (1983, 1992) but with a greater stress on horizontal relationships between the communal/local, regional, national and global levels than the one characterising other participatory development models (refer to Chapter 6 for a discussion on participation in development research and practice). This made the HSD proposal more resistant to the critics of participatory development but it raised the question of the political support such an alternative proposal could raise among different levels of government and across communities with diverse goals and aspirations (Nederveen Pieterse 1998).

The HSD proposal was not openly anti-capitalistic or anti-state regulation (Max-Neef 1992). It did not argue against private property, international trade or salaried work or even economic growth, for example, but was very critical of any economic or social, cultural or political relationship based on dependence or alienation. The objectives of HSD processes were achieving *synergy* and *self-reliance*; with human needs realised through the process of development and people involved from the outset. The economic system that could support HSD was neither defined nor determined by the authors although its principles were developed by Max-Neef through his many writings criticising orthodox economic thinking and advocating for a more humane economics (Max-Neef 1992; Cruz *et al.* 2009; Max-Neef 2014; Smith and Max-Neef 2011). Nevertheless, the original authors gave indications about the type of organisations that would characterise a human scale economy or an economy of everyday life. These organisations would be small and interconnected with the macro-structures in society, would capture the creativity and initiative at the grassroots level and would be financed by local savings institutions managed in a cooperative way by the community (Max-Neef 1991: 68–76).

The role of the state was envisaged as complementary and supportive of local initiatives. The authors gave some suggestions about how this should be brought about, for example through idea banks gathering information on local initiatives; networks of research centres closely linking research and practice under the leadership of the grassroots and through deriving structural policies at the regional and national levels to support needs enhancing transformations occurring at the community level. Max-Neef and colleagues stressed that governments should design policies to strengthen and activate what they call 'non-conventional resources' such as social awareness, dedication, commitment and solidarity. These are plentiful among grassroots movements and organisations and are direct contributors to human needs satisfaction (see Chapter 7 for an exploration of synergic satisfiers in sustainable community initiatives). They make it possible to extend personal development into social development so the personal and the collective are integrated (Max-Neef 1991: 79–80). How this should be done is not made explicit in the HSD book, although the authors warn about the risk of co-option by authorities of local initiatives as this would reduce or erase the beneficial effects of its characteristic features.

The next sections address the pillars of the HSD proposal. Max-Neef (1992) and colleagues saw self-reliance, organic articulations and human needs satisfaction as the three main supporting pillars of the proposal and people's participation and engagement as the solid foundations on which it would be articulated. However, the image of three pillars might detract from comprehending the larger scope of the proposal based on an ontological understanding of human needs as interdependent with the needs of the natural environment in terms of conservation and enhancement. Under this perspective, the three pillars might be better viewed as the normative components of an alternative development path revolving around people's needs but with dynamic trajectories modelled through participatory processes.

Increasing levels of self-reliance

Advancing towards self-reliance, understood as giving people a central role in the development process, could be considered the overarching goal of Human Scale Development. Stressing self-reliance, as Waldo Emerson (1990) did when he advocated for individuals to break with conformism and follow their own ideas and intuitions in the nineteenth century, is done as a reaction to repeated situations of dependence, experienced by people, communities and societies. Particularly, Max-Neef and colleagues understood self-reliance to be in opposition to the dependence resulting from adjustment policies, based on market liberalisation and the shrinking of the State, imposed by the International Monetary Fund and the World Bank on Latin America during the nineteen eighties. Dependence was not only seen in economic, technological or geo-political terms but also regarding lifestyles and consumption patterns.[6] The latter, exported from rich to poor countries and promoted by local elites, were making Latin American countries highly dependent on imported luxury goods and were causing serious imbalances in the region's balance of payments at the time. Max-Neef and colleagues considered that 'a price which should not be tolerated' (Max-Neef 1991: 63).

Self-reliance in international development had already been popularised by Galtung and colleagues (1980) in the early eighties. Galtung defined it as

> producing what you need using your own resources, internalising the challenges it involves, growing with the challenges, neither giving the most challenging task (positive externality) to somebody else on which you become dependent or export negative externalities to somebody else to whom you do damage (who may also become dependent on you).
>
> (Galtung 1986: 103)

He advocated for a more local and community-based economic development that takes into account a broad range of causes and effects but that does not necessarily lead to self-sufficiency. The latter was only recommended when it comes to meeting basic needs for food, shelter, energy or clothing that should by and large be produced locally and only traded when consumption exceeded production. Galtung's approach is not very different to that of Keynes' regarding what should be managed locally and what should be spread internationally. As Keynes (1933) put it, 'Ideas, knowledge, art, hospitality, travel – these are the things which should of their nature be international. But let goods be homespun whenever it is reasonably and conveniently possible; and, above all, let finance be primarily national.' The former connects to the HSD concept of non-conventional resources that should be spread and shared across borders. The latter links to the HSD proposal of supporting the emergence of local saving cooperatives serving the community through investments and the encouragement of residents' creativity.

Self-reliance also means reversing the way development is approached as in Chamber's sustainable livelihoods proposal (Chambers 1992). People and their initiatives become central to the process of development and the role of institutions (also academic institutions) is to support them and encourage their emergence. Thus, public and private institutions should look for these emergent initiatives (youth groups, women's organisations, trade unions, entrepreneurs, ecovillages, indigenous groups and so forth) and provide the financial or technical support for them to flourish (Max-Neef 1991). However, and contrary to some experiences of self-reliant development in Africa that were articulated around existing traditional hierarchical or unidirectional relationships at the local and regional levels (Fonchingong and Fonjong 2003), HSD sought to connect self-reliant development at the local level with larger national and supra-national networks of knowledge and experience sharing.

Finally, implicit in the concept of self-reliance is the belief that people and communities are able to analyse their situation and design the strategies to transform the way human needs are pursued. This has been questioned in the development literature as there are many examples of unsuccessful initiatives decided by grassroots groups in bottom-up participatory processes (da Cunha and

Pena 1997; Cooke and Kothari 2004). However, it is not clear what the reasons for the failure of local development processes aimed at self-reliance are. It often seems that projects originating in the minds of experts, bureaucrats or activists from NGOs, government agencies or civil society organisations are able to involve people but do not manage to commit participants in the project's success (Long 1999). In many cases, what appears as a participatory process ends up consolidating 'hierarchical relationships between central and local governments, between ordinary citizens and the administrative elite and between the poor and the national project of development' (Green 2010: 1241). This is exactly what Max-Neef and colleagues argue against. They maintain that people and communities are meant to collaborate with experts, politicians, planners and even local elites but that collaboration should be based on interdependent relationships and not on dependence.

Balanced interdependence

In the HSD book (pages 57 to 62), Max-Neef and colleagues describe balanced interdependence in terms of organic articulations concerning the personal and the social, the micro and the macro, planning and autonomy and the state and civil society. A common denominator is the requirement to acknowledge interdependence, complementariness and to strive for horizontal relationships in these often unbalanced interactions. Of particular interest to address environmental sustainability is the authors' call for a different articulation to the one we have today of the relationship between people, nature and technologies. They criticise the prevalence of an anthropocentric cosmology that has resulted in the exhaustion of natural resources and the trespassing of many planetary boundaries (MEA 2005; Rockström *et al.* 2009; Smith and Max-Neef 2011). They consider that the reproduction of this destructive cosmology, that does not understand the economy as a sub-system of the larger biophysical system,[7] is supported by welfare indicators such as Gross Domestic Product that, as discussed in Chapter 2, do not account for the negative externalities on people and the environment of harmful production processes and the defensive consumption associated with the arms race, purchase of security services or health care expenses and consequences of pollution of water sources and land.

A balanced articulation between people, nature and resources entails reversing socio-economic priorities, from a focus on increasing production to a focus on human needs satisfaction and environmental conservation. As Max-Neef and collaborators put it:

> Since Human Scale Development is concerned mainly with the fulfilment of fundamental human needs of present as well as future generations, it advocates a concept of development which is essentially ecological. This implies on the one hand, creating indicators capable of discriminating between what is positive and what is negative and, on the other hand, designing and using technologies that can be adapted to a truly eco-humanist

process of development and thus ensure the conservation of natural resources for the future.

(Max-Neef 1991: 59)

The HSD proposal builds on a systemic view of society and of the relationship between society and the natural environment. This means departing from the linear logic that dominated economics, the most influential science behind the modern idea of development, during the last century (Cruz *et al.* 2009). Aligning with perspectives from ecological economics, quantum physics and biology, Max-Neef argues for expanding systemic thinking to the analysis of society and its relationship with nature linking with current complexity approaches in international development (Bevan 2010; Burns 2014) and co-evolutionary approaches in ecological economics (Nørgaard and Kallis 2011). Burns (2014) defines a systemic approach to society as revolving around the interconnections between people, the processes they engage with and their social and natural environment. Systemic approaches do not reduce the analysis to actors or institutions but to their interactions, which are defined as unstable and dynamic. This has an effect in the way that change can be pursued, as a systemic approach opens up for an understanding of environmental protection linked with improved social assistance programmes, for example. As Burns put it:

> it is possible to create change in one part of a system even though the 'problem' appears to be in another part. Seeing change as part of a wider system rather than something that directly impacts on an issue or a problem is an essential part of systems thinking.
>
> (Burns 2014: 5)

Thus, challenges to human needs fulfilment become threats to environmental protection, and vice versa.

Approaching society as a system implies not relying on specific policies but understanding, through direct involvement as researchers or practitioners, the supports that some processes need to be more effective in providing needs satisfaction. It is the opposite of seeing development as a linear process, where policies are applied after experts' analysis of the situation, and outcomes monitored through a set of indicators. The key here is to create what Max-Neef and colleagues identify as a *healthy system* where there is enough flexibility to support grassroots initiatives to initiate processes of innovation and qualitative change. This can only be achieved if the different parts of the system are organically articulated, meaning that there are no significant imbalances between the different constitutive parts.

A systemic view of society is at odds with a monodisciplinary approach to human development. In the 1991 book Max-Neef included an essay criticising the mechanistic and formal approach of the economic, science. He based his criticism on two main points that were later developed in a couple of articles published in the journal *Ecological Economics* (Max-Neef 1995, 2014) and several other publications (Cruz *et al.* 2009; Smith and Max-Neef 2011). These points were: the focus on knowing and not on understanding and the impossibility of any single science to provide answers to the complex questions defining current societies. Although Max-Neef recognises the great level of knowledge achieved by the scientific rational method in the twentieth century he also blames it for the exclusion of intuition as a valid method for research, as it precludes the understanding of complex phenomena. He posited 'you can only understand that of which you become a part, when the *Subject* that searches and observes becomes inseparably integrated with the *Object* searched and observed' (Max-Neef 2005: 15). Thus, the mechanistic worldview adopted in economics based on a linear logic is reductionist and cannot help increase our understanding of the world and of the complex processes behind human wellbeing and ecological sustainability.

Complex problems have to be addressed through a transdisciplinary approach. Max-Neef (2005) advocates for *strong transdisciplinarity*,[8] one based on the acknowledgement of different levels of reality, of different levels of perception that unify single-level contradictions (such as economic growth/environmental destruction; local solutions/global solutions, etc.) and the use of a complexity approach. Following a transdisciplinary perspective the questions of human wellbeing and ecological sustainability should be addressed not as opposites and not by a single science but as elements of a level of reality (for example, based on reason) that can only be accessed from a higher level of reality and perception (for example, a level based on intuition). In this new level both elements are unified and can be integrated in a process of transformation, where people, scholars, planners and/or policy-makers should immerse themselves. The immersion of all participants in the development process is also one of the key characteristics of the HSD approach.

Participation

Drawing on a transdisciplinary logic and the belief that understanding is only possible through immersion, Max-Neef and collaborators gave popular participation a pivotal role in the articulation of HSD. The goal was empowering people and civil society so their endogenous potential could be unleashed and pave the way for a self-reliant development. Using the language of complexity science, participation was seen as a prerequisite to create the conditions that would enable the emergence of socially, economic and environmentally sustainable development paths. Max-Neef suggested increasing participation by reinforcing existing local participatory initiatives, such as indigenous peasant communities, resistance movements, youth-groups or ecovillage movements and by generalising participation at any level of governance through direct democracy institutions (Max-Neef 1992).

A development proposal based on participation was not new in the nineteen eighties. Already in the mid-twentieth century Brazilian educator and philosopher Paulo Freire (1970) saw research as a form of social action. He devised literacy projects in collaboration with people from oppressed groups to identify and develop policies that would bring out social change by empowering participants (Herr and Anderson 2005). He was the initiator of the participatory research movement associated with the adult education movement and with great impact in Latin America and in countries such as Tanzania, India and Bangladesh. The idea of empowering marginalised people through participation was taken beyond educational programs by Colombian sociologist Orlando Fals Borda (1987), among other contemporary development scholars and practitioners (Reason and Bradbury 2013). He developed the term Participatory Action Research (PAR), where research, theory making and activism are combined to challenge internalised patterns of dependence and engage people in their own development processes (refer to Chapter 6 for a more comprehensive discussion on participatory approaches to development practice and research).

Since Freire's initial work, participatory approaches have been used in development and sustainability projects to address a wide array of problems from lack of irrigation to the establishment of micro-credit schemes in rural areas (Lund and Saito-Jensen 2013). Robert Chambers' work on sustainable livelihoods has been one of the most influential approaches to participatory and rural development. Chambers defined sustainable livelihoods as adequate stocks and flows of food and cash to meet basic needs, which should be identified and provided in direct collaboration with rural communities (Chambers 1983). Chambers (1992) maintained that rural development projects should search for what people want and need; support small farmers' and pastoralists' own experiments; and work with communities to enable them to devise and test new approaches for managing their common and private resources. He suggested drawing on Participatory Rural Appraisal (PRA): a set of techniques (transect walks, seasonal calendars, wellbeing and wealth rankings) derived from rapid rural appraisal, applied anthropology and activist participatory research, among others, to empower rural people to change their economic conditions (Chambers 1992).

Chambers' approach extends the concept of participation to encompass the role of development researchers and practitioners. As Chambers (1992: 228) puts it, 'rural people have shown an unexpected ability to present and analyse complex and diverse local systems and relationships' so they do not depend on the researcher/planner to be able to analyse, act and plan on their situation although they would always benefit from collaboration. In a similar vein, adherents to the de-growth paradigm discussed in Chapter 2 have been calling for a continuous dialogue between scientists and practitioners to increase the spaces where sustainable development is discussed and practised. Martínez-Alier and colleagues (2010), for example, emphasise the need for researchers to ally with grassroots social movements and support the formation of local, national and international coalitions, where these movements can converge and push for the low environmental impact measures they are advocating (renewable energy, economic justice, rights of nature, etc.). Furthermore, action-oriented approaches to promote low carbon lifestyles have also drawn on participatory methodologies to facilitate the creation of knowledge and the implementation of changes to increase the uptake of carbon reduction technologies (Reason *et al.* 2009).

As just discussed, the HSD proposal was neither the first nor the only one to integrate people's direct participation as a pillar of an alternative development proposal. Chapter 6 in this book will present in more detail the problems associated with participatory development regarding the reproduction of power structures and the co-option of bottom-up participatory initiatives by the state and local elites, among other challenges to participation discussed in development literature (Cooke and Kothari 2004; Green 2010; Lund and Saito-Jensen 2013). Max-Neef and colleagues were aware of these limitations and they argued that when participation became a tool for authorities to speed up the execution of projects, for example, or when grassroots initiatives were co-opted by the state, development projects lost their local identity and the endogenous objectives for which they were created became diluted. Participation in self-reliant development processes is considered itself a synergic activity (an activity that contributes to the fulfilment of many human needs); managing it under bureaucratic structures is most likely going to reduce its empowering potential.

Human needs and satisfiers: a theory and a tool

Arguably, the most important contribution of the HSD approach to development practice is its understanding of human needs as opportunities for personal and social mobilisation. Until the nineteen eighties human needs in international development had mainly been addressed either as motivations for action or as deprivations (Gasper 1996; Jackson *et al.* 2004). Approaching human needs both as deprivation and potential, aligns with the democratic and empowering vocation of the HSD and its rejection of prescriptive top-down solutions to the problems of development. It also implies that needs might stimulate creative strategies in the pursuit of their satisfaction both at the personal and group levels. Despite not expanding on the psychological evidence behind their proposed list of needs, Max-Neef and colleagues were inspired by Maslow's (1954) classification of needs in terms of physiological needs (hunger, thirst, shelter), safety (security, order, stability), belongingness and love needs (friendship, affection, love, intimacy), esteem needs (mastery, independence, self-respect) and self-actualisation needs (the need to live up to one's unique potential). However, unlike Maslow, they did not take needs as hierarchically related except for the requirement to be alive (subsistence) that they considered had precedence over the rest of the needs. In addition, the authors maintained that there must be a threshold below which the person cannot think but of achieving the means to satisfy the need that is severely undersatisfied (whichever need this is); if a minimum is not achieved, 'all other needs remain blocked and a single and intense drive prevails' (Max-Neef 1991: 49).

The final list of human needs drew on the following premises (Max-Neef 1991: 31):

- The list of needs had to be easy to understand and for people to identify with;

- All the fundamental needs had to be included but the list had to be limited and clearly labelled;
- Needs had to be easily identified as targets of satisfiers;
- The classification had to facilitate the identification of satisfiers that do not contribute to needs actualisation;
- The classification should be useful for the design of alternative satisfiers.

Human needs were not considered as closed categories but part of a system characterised by simultaneities, complementarities and trade-offs. This systemic approach to needs implied that 'deprivation of any of the listed needs will cause shattering within the whole needs system and thereby impacting overall human well-being' (Cruz *et al.* 2009). Representing these interconnections, fundamental human needs were defined as subsistence, protection, affection, understanding, participation, idleness, creation, identity and freedom. In addition the authors maintained that in any cultural or socio-economic context, needs were expressed through four existential categories or existential needs: being, having, doing and interacting. *Being* referred to attributes of the person or groups of people; *having* was associated to institutions, values, tools and forms of organisation; *doing* referred to actions both at the individual and collective levels, and *interacting* to the characteristics of spaces and environments.

The authors considered that the nine fundamental human needs had a socio-universal character; they did not vary with culture and history although they could be felt with different intensities depending on personal/collective attributes or contexts (Cruz *et al.* 2009). However, as the authors acknowledged, needs change with human evolution; they might not all have existed since the origin of mankind. While needs for subsistence, protection, affection and understanding, participation, idleness and creation might be as old as the human species, other needs such as identity and freedom might have arisen at later stages. This could also concern the need for transcendence, a need that the authors did not see as universal and did not include among the list of fundamental needs (Max-Neef 1991: 27).

Max-Neef and colleagues preferred to talk about needs actualisation, realisation or experimentation instead of referring to needs satisfaction as the level at which needs are satisfied might differ across people, social groups and societies or environments. They understood that the way people appraise needs actualisation is subjective but they did not take this as constraining potential analyses on the capacity of different institutional arrangements, environment and attitudes to actualise fundamental human needs, as 'when the object of study is the relation between human beings and society, the universality of the subjective cannot be ignored' (Max-Neef 1991: 26). Thus, the influence of cultural, socio-political and economic arrangements on needs actualisation can be analysed despite its subjective character as subjectivity is common to all human beings and societies.

Since the HSD approach to human needs was eminently practical, the authors proposed a representation of needs and satisfiers through a matrix reflecting the intersection between the four existential needs (top row) and the nine fundamental human needs (first column) to enable its operationalisation (see Table 3.1 below). The resulting empty grids were to be filled in a participatory manner with the *satisfiers* that represent how needs are pursued. *Satisfiers* were defined as social practices, values, attitudes, actions, forms of organisation, political models and environmental characteristics that are used to actualise needs. They were considered to change with history and vary across cultures (Max-Neef *et al.* 1989; Cruz *et al.* 2009). Arguably, the distinction between needs ('inherent to our common human evolutionary heritage') and satisfiers ('the particular means by which different societies and cultures aim to realize their needs') is probably the biggest contribution of the HSD to the international development debate (Cruz *et al.* 2009).

The systemic approach to needs that characterises the HSD proposal implies that there is no two-way correspondence between needs and satisfiers. They are related in a systemic way and people's experience of a particular articulation of satisfiers is what makes them positive or negative contributors to human needs. Satisfiers are related to economic goods but this relationship depends on the type of goods available in their society, which in turn depends on fashion, culture and the socio-economic level of the person, among other factors. For example, the satisfier 'formal education' can give rise to services such as training courses or wi-fi access or goods such as laptops, smart phones or handbooks. As explained in the HSD book 'while a satisfier is in an ultimate sense the way in which a need is expressed, goods are in a strict sense the means by which individuals will empower the satisfiers to meet their needs' (Max-Neef 1991: 25).

Given the many social, economic and environmental pathologies that rich and poor societies suffer from, it is clear that not all satisfiers will be equally successful in their contribution to the actualisation of needs. Max-Neef and colleagues identified five types of satisfiers: *synergic, singular, inhibiting, pseudo-satisfiers* and *violators* or *destroyers* (Table 3.2). The last three are the most

Table 3.1 Matrix of fundamental human needs

	Being	*Having*	*Doing*	*Interacting*
Subsistence				
Protection				
Affection				
Understanding				
Participation				
Idleness				
Creation				
Identity				
Freedom				

Source: Max-Neef (1989)

Table 3.2 Max-Neef's classification of satisfiers

Synergic satisfiers	Satisfy simultaneously different kinds of needs. They usually emerge as a result of endogenous bottom-up processes as do local currencies, farmer's markets and democratic community organisations.
Singular satisfiers	Satisfy the need they are meant to satisfy and are neutral towards other needs. They are common in public or private development programs and interventions.
Inhibiting satisfiers	Over-satisfy a specific need and reduce the prospect of satisfying other needs. They originated in customs, habits and rituals such as paternalistic and overprotecting attitudes and customs.
Pseudo-satisfiers	Mislead people into believing their need is satisfied and puts at risk the satisfaction of the need in the long run. Often induced through propaganda and advertising but, like the overexploitation of natural resources, they might be embedded in socio-economic practices.
Violators or destroyers	Annihilate the satisfaction over time of the need they aim at and they impair the satisfaction of other needs (often related to the need for protection, like censorship, exile . . .).

Source: Adapted from Max-Neef (1991)

potentially destructive because if they are increasingly present in a society they might hinder development and jeopardise wellbeing. In addition, the authors consider that these harmful satisfiers 'are exogenous to civil society as they are usually imposed, induced, ritualized or institutionalized' (Max-Neef 1991: 34). This is not the case for synergic satisfiers that are typically generated by deliberative processes at the local community or grassroots level. Hence, there is an implicit association between satisfiers generated endogenously, from the group or community whose development is at stake, and synergic satisfiers; those that contribute to the actualisation of more than one need. This links needs satisfaction to strong participatory self-reliant local community or civil society insitutions that are capable 'of stimulating the permanent generation of synergistic satisfiers' (Max-Neef 1992: 213).

Needs, capabilities and sustainable development

The HSD emerged in an international context characterised by the search for development alternatives that placed people and not the economy at the centre. These alternatives often revolved around the concepts of human or basic needs understood either as prerequisites for wellbeing or as the avoidance of physical and social impairment (Gasper 1996). Some influential approaches to needs at the time the HSD book was published were the ones by the International Labour Organisation (ILO 1976), the World Bank (Streeten *et al.* 1981) and scholars such as Galtung *et al.* (1980) and Mallmann (1980). These approaches represented an evolution in development theory and policy from an understanding of needs based on physiological and social needs, as in the ILO and World Bank proposals, to more complex perspectives such as Mallmann's, where needs (maintenance, protection, love, understanding, government, recreation, creation, meaning and synergy) were expressed through satisfiers in the personal, social and ecological dimensions. Mallmann's work influenced the HSD approach to human needs as he and Max-Neef had collaborated in the seventies during the latter's engagement at the Bariloche Foundation in Argentina.

Contemporary to the development of the HSD but with a more policy-oriented focus, Doyal and Gough (1991) proposed an approach based on a normative perspective on human need by which basic needs for physical health and autonomy were defined as requirements for full social participation. Their theory of human need was developed parallel to an alternative paradigm based on people's agency and freedom – the capability or capabilities[9] approach by Amartya Sen (1985, 1992) and Martha Nussbaum (1995, 2000). Both the literature on human need and the literature on capabilities inspired the UN Human Development Index, the only index that has been widely accepted to challenge GDP as a measure of human wellbeing (Bagolin and Comim 2008).

Highlighting similarities and differences between the different approaches to human needs and capabilities would require a whole chapter or even a whole book and has been done elsewhere (Alkire 2002a; Doyal and Gough 1991; Gasper 1996; Gough 2003, 2014; Jackson et al. 2004). In what remains of this chapter, I discuss the HSD approach to human needs, satisfiers and sustainable development with regards to its contemporaries Theory of Human Need (THN) and the Capabilities approach, with the goal to explore its singularities further. The latter, together with the HSD proposal, are increasingly being used as alternative paradigms from which to conceptualise sustainable development (Gough 2014; Lessman and Rauschmayer 2013).

Human needs

Max-Neef and colleagues understood human needs as opportunities for personal and societal action. Although this mobilising feature of human needs neither aligns with Doyal and Gough's basic needs theory nor with Sen's and Nussbaum's definition of functionings or capabilities, the three perspectives downplay the role of material accumulation in their definition of wellbeing and argue for human-centred approaches to development. The THN establishes a hierarchy of needs ranked from universal goals through basic needs to intermediate needs. Universal goals are avoidance of serious harm, social participation and critical participation. These are reached through the satisfaction of the basic needs for physical health and autonomy. Physical health concerns more than survival but a level of health that enables participation in one's society. It is supported by goods and services that provide nutritional food and clean water, protective housing, non-hazardous physical and work environments, safe birth control and child-bearing and appropriate health care (universal satisfier characteristics). Autonomy is defined as 'the ability to make informed choices about what should be done and how to go about it' (THN: 53) and is enhanced by the extent to which goods and services with the universal satisfier characteristics of significant primary relationships, security in childhood, physical and economic security, and appropriate education, are available in a society. Doyal and Gough (1991) maintain that people should be able to satisfy their basic needs at a critically optimum level, defined as the highest international standards of need-satisfaction and feasibility. They argue that this level will only be achieved if all social institutions adopt basic needs satisfaction as their operational goal.

Sen's and Nussbaum's approach to human development does not revolve around the concept of needs but that of capability or capabilities. In fact, Sen criticises the language of needs as being paternalistic and addressing people only in terms of what they lack (Sen 1999). *Capabilities* are defined as the choices people have reason to value and *functionings* as the things people have reason to do or be. The stress of the framework is on freedom of choice and on the availability of resources, skills, values and other factors that support the expansion of people's opportunity sets. Despite Sen's initial reticence to support any specific list of capabilities to characterise human wellbeing, Martha Nussbaum proposed ten central human functional capabilities of equal rank that any society should strive to give access to: life, bodily health, bodily integrity, sense, imagination and thought, emotions, practical reason, affiliation, other species, play and control over one's environment (Nussbaum 2000). Beyond the debates on the specific categories included in this or other lists of capabilities, proponents of this approach support selecting them through the use of codified knowledge (existing studies on the topic) and public discussions. How a participatory process to discuss capabilities should work is not elaborated on, but collaboration between experts, organisations and the general public together with openness to different methods and tools is usually favoured (Alkire 2007).

HSD takes needs both as a motivation and a requirement for human development, thus confronting one of the most generalised criticisms to need theory concerning the fact that people are seen as deserving not as agentive individuals. However, this might add a weakness to the proposal in comparison with normative theories of need/capabilities as it could be more affected by *adaptive preferences*, defined as relatively high levels of reported wellbeing associated with objective situations of deprivation (Nussbaum 2000). It could be argued that women, immigrants or other oppressed groups might not be aware of their needs for participation, idleness or creation, for example, and thus not feel mobilised by them. However, the practical orientation of the HSD proposal questions the *adaptive preferences* criticism. First, by stressing the importance to promote the presence of synergic satisfiers in a given society as actualising human needs through this type of satisfiers will not by definition reproduce negative spirals such as the ones associated with gender discrimination, chauvinism or any kind of physical or mental dependence. Second, active participation in HSD processes is likely to lead participants to experience higher levels of autonomy, facilitating more persistent and higher quality motivation, which runs against becoming adapted to demeaning or harmful circumstances.

A common feature of the three approaches is their claim of universality. The HSD considers that human needs change very slowly with human evolution and that, although felt with different intensities, they determine wellbeing across cultures. Similarly, the THN considers that basic needs for physical health and autonomy are universal because, if not satisfied to some degree, people will experience serious impairment in the pursuit of their valued goals. Focussing not on impairment but on opportunities, capability proponents argue that what is universally desirable is the expansion of freedoms as they are intrinsically valuable and important as instruments to attain and mould other desired ends (Gough 2014; Sen 1985, 1992).

The claim for universality brings out the criticism of paternalism that is shared by human needs approaches and Nussbaum's list of fundamental capabilities. Gough (2003) discusses these claims in terms of the THN and Nussbaum's list and concludes that the openness of the two approaches to confront professional knowledge with that of ordinary citizens, exonerates them from the accusation. This argument is even stronger in the HSD framework as the list of human needs is presented as open for modification and satisfiers are seen as culturally, socially, technologically, economically and environmentally determined. Additionally, the HSD was designed to break with the multiple dependencies experienced by people in the developing and developed world thus calling for the organic articulation of knowledge from experts, policy-makers, grassroots organisations and the individuals involved in the development process.

Satisfiers

Max-Neef and colleagues defined satisfiers as the ways needs are expressed in particular cultures and societies. The HSD categorisation of satisfiers as *synergic*, *singular, inhibiting, pseudo-satisfiers* and *destroyers* does not find parallel in the capabilities approach although it resonates with the distinction between needs satisfiers and luxuries in the THN. Some central human functional capabilities such as the ones related to *institutions protecting affiliation* or *being able to hold property*, for example, could be considered singular satisfiers in HSD terms, and intermediate needs or universal satisfiers characteristics in the THN. In addition, intermediate needs such as basic education in the THN could be interpreted as a satisfier for the need of understanding, subsistence, protection and participation in the HSD framework.

Doyal and Gough (1991) agree with Max-Neef and distinguish between needs and need satisfiers. They propose a list of eleven 'universal satisfier characteristics' or 'intermediate needs'[10] that define the goods, services, activities and relationships that contribute to need satisfaction in any given culture. This is akin to an *a priori* identification of synergic or singular satisfiers[11] and it is done by drawing on 'scientific/technical knowledge' on the factors affecting physical health and autonomy, and 'comparative anthropological knowledge' about the ways needs are met in different cultural contexts. However, Doyal and Gough also call for including experiential knowledge, that of the people or groups concerned, in the definition of the characteristics of needs satisfiers. As Gough (2014:17) puts it, defining satisfier characteristics 'requires *a dual strategy* of public policy formation which values compromise, provided that this does not extend to defining the general character of basic human needs (THN: 141). Thus, the HSD and the THN approaches suggest similar processes to identifying synergic or singular satisfiers; which in the former is based on participatory enquiry on the ways of being, having, doing and interacting that best meet human needs and in the latter on expert, academic and grassroots representatives discussing the suitability of the eleven 'universal satisfier characteristics'.

An important aspect of human needs satisfiers in the HSD is that they are systemically related to each other and with human needs. There are rarely one-to-one relationships in the HSD proposal. For instance, singular satisfiers are defined as those whose aim is the actualisation of a single human need but they still depend on the presence of other satisfiers for their positive effect; as singular satisfiers might be more or less effective in actualising the need they aim for through interaction with other satisfiers. This is the reason why the focus of HSD is on the articulation of satisfiers that represent a healthy system, not on specific satisfiers or 'satisfier characteristics' that have a particular negative or positive effect on needs. A systemic understanding of basic needs or capabilities is not explicitly addressed by their proponents. In the THN the relationship between satisfier and basic needs for physical health and autonomy is presented as linear. As long as satisfiers have the eleven universal satisfier characteristics, they will contribute positively to human needs. However, the fact that 'certain packages of need satisfiers are necessary for the avoidance of harm' (Gough 2014: 17) suggests that systemic relationships can be easily integrated in the framework. The capabilities approach does not explicitly contemplate systemic perspectives either, as in order to achieve certain valued functionings certain resources (commodities and services) and conversion factors (e.g. values, skills, social institutions and natural environments) are required. As long as these resources and conversion factors are available, capabilities are expected to be enhanced.

Sustainable development

As discussed in Chapter 2, a common understanding of sustainable development draws on the World Commission on Environment and Development's (WCED) definition in terms of the 'development that meets the needs of the present without compromising the ability of future generations to meet their own needs' (WCED 1987: 43). The THN, the HSD and the capabilities approach are well suited to integrate in their theoretical and conceptual frameworks the obligation to care for future generations and the natural environment. The ways to account for sustainability derived from these approaches rely, to varied extents, on institutional transparency, direct democracy, well-functioning markets, personal and societal freedom and the diversity of systems of provision; among other institutional and personal factors. However, the three approaches differ in the logic behind the incorporation of sustainability concerns in their conceptual frameworks.

Proponents of the capability approach suggest that sustaining the freedom to choose the life one values across generations would be a way of integrating sustainability in the capabilities framework (Sen 2013). Maintaining freedoms across generations would demand, among other factors, suitable economic, political, social and environmental conditions for current and future generations to achieve valued *functionings*. Lessman and Rauschmayer (2013) point out that this requires that people living now adapt their choices to account for the capability set of future generations. But since this generates a heavy burden on people and implicitly assumes an ethical obligation to care for future generations, they suggest 1) concentrating on the impact of achieved *functionings* on the natural environment to have reliable information to guide public and private choices (through indicators of an ecological footprint, for example) and 2) supporting collective institutions to create common understandings and values that reinforce present and future capability sets.

Gough (2014) proposes to operationalise sustainable development, drawing on ethical and justice arguments to justify the obligation of present generations to consider the satisfaction of needs of future generations. He maintains that basic and intermediate needs are the same across generations since the THN is grounded in the biological, physiological and psychological characteristics of human beings. As human needs are universal, both current and future generations have to be able to meet them, because if present generations do not have their basic needs guaranteed they cannot be asked to assume the obligation to guarantee the needs of others in the future. In addition, Gough adds that from a justice perspective the wants[12] of current generations cannot take precedence over the needs of future generations. Quoting Dobson, he writes 'the futurity that is central to all conceptions of sustainability is represented by the way in which future generation human needs take precedence over present generation human wants. It would be odd for those who argue for the sustaining of ecological processes to put the wants of the present generation of human beings (which might threaten those processes) ahead of the needs of future generations of human beings (which depend upon them)' (Dobson 1998: 46 in Gough 2014: 27).

It is important to highlight that any of the three proposals is better suited to address human wellbeing now and in the future than those focussed on economic growth (or even green growth as discussed in Chapter 2). In my view, the crucial difference between them is that the capabilities approach and the THN require current generations to commit to maintaining the choices available to future generations or their capacity to avoid serious harm. This 'commitment' is usually suggested in terms of legislation, public policies and interventions with the degree of involvement by the grassroots remaining largely unspecified (Alkire 2002b). Alternatively, HSD proposes to work in a participatory manner from the outset to find synergic satisfiers that contribute to the actualisation of as many needs as possible. Since human needs change only with evolution, today's synergic satisfiers are likely to have a positive effect on tomorrow's needs. Nevertheless, satisfiers are not static and their effect on needs will evolve and should be rethought in a constant analysis of the feedbacks obtained through their implementation. In summary, the HSD approach does not require a personal pre-commitment with future generations or the natural environment, but honest and coherent institutions that support the co-generation of synergic satisfiers through the engagement of the population.

Conclusion

This chapter has introduced the Human Scale Development proposal by relating it to the contextual influences that surrounded its emergence as an alternative development model. It has discussed the main characteristics of the proposal articulated around the goal of achieving self-reliance, through participatory inquiry on human needs satisfaction and taking into account organic articulations between governance levels, socio-economic and biological systems and people, technologies and the natural environment.

The central role of human needs actualisation has deserved major attention in this chapter. Considering needs as deprivation and potential and as forces that mobilise people into transformative action, differentiates the proposal greatly from the two major alternative contemporary paradigms, namely Doyal and Gough's Theory of Human Need, and Sen's and Nussbaum's Capabilities approach. The three approaches appear as complementary in that they offer an alternative to development where human beings and not economic interests articulate the development process. However, differences exist with regards to their under-standing of the relationship between and across needs or capabilities. The HSD proposal considers satisfiers to be systemically related and interdependent, while proponents of capabilities and basic needs approaches implicitly understand the relationships between socio-economic, technical and environmental factors and human wellbeing as linear. This is a crucial distinction when one wants to address sustainability in its three dimensions (ecologic, economic and social) as whether these dimensions are seen as systemically or linearly related will define the type of policies that will be applied.

Notes

1 In this book I will refer to Max-Neef, M. (1991). *Human Scale Development: Conception, Applications and Further Reflections* as the HSD book.
2 The transdisciplinary team included economists, sociologists, psychiatrists, philosophers, political scientists, geographers, anthropologists, journalists, engineers and lawyers. They gathered in a series of workshops with the goal of proposing a more human development paradigm (Max-Neef 1991).
3 The book in Spanish is available at www.max-neef.cl, accessed 9 February 2015.
4 Harvey defines neoliberalism as 'a theory of political economic practices that proposes that human well-being can best be advanced by liberating individual entrepreneurial freedoms and skills within an institutional framework characterized by strong private property rights, free markets and free trade. The role of the state is to create and preserve an institutional framework appropriate to such practices' (Harvey 2005: 2).
5 Oligopolistic practices refer to the practices of companies operating in markets with few firms and many buyers and with high barriers of entry (implying that it is difficult

for other companies to enter the market). As a result of this market structure, firms will not compete on price so the consumer will usually pay more and companies will have higher profits than in markets with a higher level of competition (Pass *et al.* 1993).

6 This understanding of dependence resonates with the tenets of dependency theory explaining underdevelopment in countries of the periphery through a history of colonisation and exploitation of natural and social resources by the 'center of the capitalist order'; usually associated with Europe and the US (Peet and Hartwick 2009).

7 Following Common and Stagl (2005), systems are understood here as sets of inter-dependent components that have boundaries separating them from their environment. Thus, analyses focussing on systems will be concerned both with the type of interactions between its components and with the nature of the components. Systems are not predefined units, which implies that some studies will treat the planet earth as a system while others will focus on particular systems such as the economy or the biosphere.

8 Max-Neef (2005) distinguishes between *strong transdisciplinarity* and *weak transdisciplinarity*. The latter is characterised by the coordination of disciplines categorised following the levels of 1) what exists (e.g. ecology and economy); 2) what we are capable of doing (e.g. agriculture and commerce); 3) what we want to do (e.g. planning and law) and 4) what we must do (values, ethics and philosophy). Max-Neef argues that weak transdisciplinarity might be easier to operationalise than strong transdisciplinarity but that the latter characterised by different levels of reality, the principle of the 'included middle' and complexity, enables a deeper understanding of reality.

9 The terms capabilities or capability are used indistinctly here. It is common to use 'capability approach' when referring to Sen's theory and 'capabilities approach' when referring to Martha Nussbaum's functional capabilities framework (Alkire 2002a).

10 As presented in the previous section, universal satisfier characteristics or intermediate needs are classified in 11 categories as follows: nutritional foods and clean water, protective housing, non-hazardous living and work environments, safe birth control and child-bearing, appropriate health care, significant primary relationships, security in childhood, physical and economic security, and appropriate education. The first six are considered to contribute to physical health and the rest to autonomy.

11 'Universal satisfier characteristics' or 'intermediate needs' also resonate with the discussion outlined in Chapter 7 about 'necessary synergic satisfiers'; those that belong to a constellation of satisfiers that are beneficial both in terms of human needs actualisation and of environmental conservation and enhancement.

12 The THN distinguishes from needs and wants arguing that wants depend on individuals' preferences and are not associated with serious harm or impairment if they are not fulfilled. However, there are instances in which needs and wants will overlap. As the authors put it: 'there are wants which are satisfiers of generally accepted needs and others which are not. So you can need what you want, and want or not want what you need. What you cannot consistently do is not need what is required in order to avoid serious harm – whatever you might want' (THN: 42).

References

Alkire, S. (2002a). *Valuing Freedoms: Sen's Capability Approach and Poverty Reduction.* Oxford: Oxford University Press.

Alkire, S. (2002b). Dimensions of human development. *World Development,* 30(2): 181–205.

Alkire, S. (2007). Why the capability approach? *Journal of Human Development* 6(1): 115–35.

Bagolin, I. P. and Comim, F. V. (2008). Human Development Index (HDI) and its family of indexes: an evolving critical review. *Revista de Economia*, 34(2): 7–28.

Bevan, P. (2010). Tracing the 'war against poverty' in rural Ethiopia since 2003 using a complexity social science perspective. Lessons for research and policy in the 2010s. Paper prepared for the Chronic Poverty Conference 'Ten years of war against poverty'.

Burns, D. (2014). Systemic action research: Changing system dynamics to support sustainable change. *Action Research*, 12(1), 3–18.

Chambers, R. (1983). *Rural Development: Putting the Last First*. London: Longman.

Chambers, R. (1992). Sustainable livelihoods: The poor's reconciliation of environment and development. In Ekins, P. and Max-Neef, M. (eds), *Real-life Economics*. London: Routledge.

Common, M. and Stagl, S. (2005). *Ecological Economics*. Cambridge: Cambridge University Press.

Cooke, B. and Kothari, U. (2004). The case for participation as tyranny. In Cooke, B. and Kothari, U. (eds), *Participation. The New Tyranny?* (3rd edn). London: Zed Books.

Cruz, I., Stahel, A. and Max-Neef, M. (2009). Towards a systemic development approach: Building on the Human Scale Development paradigm. *Ecological Economics*, 68: 2021–30.

da Cunha, P. and Pena, M. (1997). The limits and merits of participation. World Bank Policy Research Working Paper, 1838.

Dobson, A. (1998). *Justice and the Environment*. Oxford: Oxford University Press.

Doyal, L. and Gough, I. (1991). *A Theory of Human Need*. New York: Palgrave Macmillan.

Emerson, R. W. (1990). Essays, First and Second Series. New York: Vintage Books.

Fals Borda, O. (1987). The application of participatory action-research in Latin America. *International Sociology*, 2: 329–47.

Fonchingong, C. C. and Fonjong, L. N. (2003). The concept of self-reliance in community development initiatives in the Cameroon Grassfields. *Nordic Journal of African Studies*, 12(2): 196–219.

Freire, P. (1970). *Pedagogy of the Oppressed*. New York: Herder and Herder.

Galtung, J., O'Brien, P. and Preiswerk, R. (eds) (1980). *Self-Reliance: A Strategy for Development*. London: Bogle L'Ouverture Publications.

Galtung, J. (1986). Towards a new economics: On the theory and practice of self-reliance. In Ekins, P. (ed.), *The Living Economy: A New Economics in the Making*. London: Routledge, pp. 97–109.

Gasper, D. (1996). Needs and basic needs. A clarification of meanings, levels and different streams of work. Institute of Social Studies, Working Paper series 210.

Gough, I. (2003). Lists and thresholds: Comparing the Doyal-Gough theory of human need with Nussbaum's capabilities approach. WeD Working Paper 01. Bath: University of Bath.

Gough, I. (2014). Climate change and sustainable welfare: the centrality of human needs. New Economics Foundation Working Paper, (http://b.3cdn.net/nefoundation/e256633 779f47ec4e6_o5m6bexrh.pdf, accessed 1 April 2015).

Green, M. (2010). Making development agents: Participation as boundary object in international development. *Journal of Development Studies*, 46(7): 1240–63.

Harvey, D. (2005). *A Brief History of Neoliberalism*. Oxford: Oxford University Press.

International Labour Organisation (1976). Employment, growth and basic needs: A one-world problem (Geneva).

Jackson, T., Wander, J. and Stagl, S. (2004). Beyond insatiability: Needs theory, consumption and sustainability. Working Paper Series, 2004/2, Centre for Environmental Strategy, University of Surrey.

Keynes, J. M. (1933). National self-sufficiency. *The Yale Review*, 22(4): 755–69.

Lessmann, O. and Rauschmayer, F. (2013). Re-conceptualizing sustainable development on the basis of the capability approach: A model and and its difficulties. *Journal of Human Development and Capabilities*, 14(1): 95–114.

Long, N. (1999). The multiple optic of interface analysis. Background Paper on Interface Analysis. Paris: UNESCO.

Lund, J. F. and Saito-Jensen, M. (2013). Revisiting the issue of elite capture of participatory initiatives. *World Development*, 46: 104–12.

Mallmann, C. (1980). Society, needs and rights. In Lederer, K. (ed.), *Human Needs – a contribution to the current debate*, Chapter 2. Cambridge, Mass: Oelgeschlager, Gunn and Hain, pp. 37–54.

Martínez-Alier, J., Pascual, U., Vivien, F.-D. and Zaccai, E. (2010). Sustainable de-growth: Mapping the context, criticisms and future prospects of an emergent paradigm. *Ecological Economics*, 69: 1741–7.

Maslow, A. H. (1954). *Motivation and Personality*. New York: Harper & Row.

Max-Neef, M. (1991). *Human Scale Development: Conception, Application and Further Reflection*. London: Apex Press.

Max-Neef, M. (1992). Development and human needs. In Ekins, P. and Max-Neef, M. (eds), *Real-life Economics*. London: Routledge.

Max-Neef, M. (1995). Economic growth and quality of life: A threshold hypothesis. *Ecological Economics*, 15: 115–18.

Max-Neef, M. (2005). Foundations of transdisciplinarity. *Ecological Economics*, 53(1): 5–16.

Max-Neef, M. (2014). The good is the bad that we don't do: Economic crimes against humanity: A proposal. *Ecological Economics*, 104: 152–4.

Max-Neef, M., Elizalde, A. and Hopenhayn, M. (1989). Human Scale Development: an option for the future. *Development Dialogue*, 1: 17–47.

Nederveen Pieterse, J. (1998). My paradigm or yours? Alternative development, post-development, reflexive development. *Development and Change*, pp. 343–73.

Nørgaard, R. B. and Kallis, G. (2011). Coevolutionary contradictions: prospects for a research programme on social and environmental change. Geografiska Annaler: Series B. *Human Geography*, 93(4): 289–300.

Nussbaum, M. C. (1995). Human capabilities, female human beings. In Nussbaum, M. C. and Glover, J. (eds), *Women, Culture and Development: A Study of Human Capabilities*. Oxford: Clarendon Press, pp. 193–211.

Nussbaum, M. C. (2000). *Women and Human Development: The Capabilities Approach*. Cambridge: Cambridge University Press.

Pass, C., Lowes, B. and Davies, L. (1993). *Dictionary of Economics*, 2nd edn. Glasgow: Harper Collins Publishers.

Peet, R. and Hartwick, E. (2009). *Theories of Development*, 2nd edn. New York: The Guildford Press.

Prebisch, R. (2008). Towards a theory of change. *CEPAL Review*, 96: 27–74.

Reason, P. and Bradbury, H. (2013). *The SAGE Handbook of Action Research. Participative Inquiry and Practice*. London: Sage.

Reason, P., Coleman, G., Ballard, D., Williams, M., Gearty, M. and Bond, C. (2009). *Insider Voices: Human Dimensions of Low Carbon Technology*. Bath: Centre for Action Research in Professional Practice, University of Bath.

Rockström, J., Steffen, W., Noone, K., Persson, Å., Chapin, III, F. S., Lambin, E., Lenton, T. M., Scheffer, M., Folke, C., Schellnhuber, H., Nykvist, B., De Wit, C. A., Hughes, T., van der Leeuw, S., Rodhe, H., Sörlin, S., Snyder, P. K., Costanza, R., Svedin, U.,

Falkenmark, M., Karlberg, L., Corell, R. W., Fabry, V. J., Hansen, J., Walker, B., Liverman, D., Richardson, K., Crutzen, P. and Foley, J. (2009). Planetary boundaries: Exploring the safe operating space for humanity. *Ecology and Society*, 14(2): 32, (www.ecologyandsociety.org/vol14/iss2/art32/).

Sen, A. (1984). *Resources, Values and Development*. Oxford: Blackwell.

Sen, A. (1985). *Commodities and Capabilities*, Oxford: Elsevier Science Publishers.

Sen, A. (1992). *Inequality Reexamined*. Oxford: Oxford University Press.

Sen, A. (1999). *Development as Freedom*. Oxford: Oxford University Press.

Sen, A. (2013). The ends and means of sustainability. *Journal of Human Development and Capabilities*, 14(1): 6–20.

Smith, B. P. and Max-Neef, M. (2011). *Economics Unmasked. From Power and Greed to Compassion and the Common Good*. Cambridge: Green Books.

Streeten, P., Burki, S. J., Ul Haq, M., Hicks, N. and Stewart, F. (1981). *First Things First: Meeting Basic Human Needs in Developing Countries*. London: Oxford University Press.

4 Methodology and practice of Human Scale Development

Introduction

The matrix of human needs and satisfiers[1] proposed by Max-Neef and colleagues (1989, 1991) has been used as a tool for diagnosis, planning, assessment and evaluation since its formulation in the mid-eighties. Academics and practitioners have drawn on the matrix both as a theoretical framework in desk studies (Cruz et al. 2009; Jackson and Marks 1999; Jorge 2010; Jolibert et al. 2011) and as a participatory tool with groups of people or communities (Cuthill 2003; García Norato 2006; Jolibert et al. 2014; Guillén-Royo 2010, 2012, 2015; Mitchell 2001). The latter was the way Max-Neef and his collaborators envisaged the matrix would be used; as a support for participatory processes towards self-reliance and human needs fulfilment. The HSD book[2] (pages 37 to 42) provided methodological guidance on how to use the matrix in deliberative workshops. Drawing on those initial recommendations researchers and practitioners have adapted and modified them to suit their topics, populations, timeframes and budgets. For example, the HSD approach to human needs has been drawn on by the transition town movement in Europe;[3] it has inspired the ecovillage movement in Sweden and peasant associations in Latin America (Smith and Max-Neef 2011) and has been used as a reference framework to discuss social assistance programmes in the Italian region of Abruzzo (Bucciarelli-Alessi 2013).

This chapter discusses the applications of the HSD methodology articulated around participatory workshops and the concepts of fundamental needs and satisfiers. Most of the discussions revolve around the use of the matrix for academic purposes but some illustrations also refer to its use by practitioners. The chapter starts by presenting the levels and phases of HSD-based projects as suggested in the HSD book and some adaptations of the methodology; particularly those aiming at addressing environmental sustainability. Then, I discuss issues surrounding the organisation of HSD workshops; mainly recruitment of participants, the role of facilitators and the expected outcomes of HSD exercises in terms of emergence and empowerment. In the concluding section, I outline the potential of HSD workshops to capture the systemic relationships between human and ecological systems.

Methodological considerations

The matrix of human needs and satisfiers was designed within the context of the HSD proposal which, as described in Chapter 3, is based on the two additional pillars of self-reliance and balanced interdependencies. It was meant as a tool for development practitioners but also as a way to represent the differences between needs and satisfiers, their interdependence and their systemic relationship. Thus, it emerged as a flexible tool that could be used to reach many interlinked goals such as achieving a deeper understanding of specific development challenges; a greater engagement of people in social transformation processes; or an increased awareness of what was important in community development. It is quite likely that the targeted goals and the characteristics of particular projects (led by academics, practitioners or community members, externally funded or based on work by volunteers, with a short or long-term perspective, diagnostic or action oriented, grassroots or institutionally initiated, etc.) will determine how the matrix and its conceptual underpinnings are adapted and used in practice. Thus, the methodological discussions presented hereafter should be taken as general reflections and by no means considered as precepts or recommendations of good practice.

Levels and phases of a HSD-based research project

Originally, the HSD methodology was structured around two-day workshops attended by a total of 50 people (Max-Neef 1991: 39–42). The goal of the workshops was 'to allow participants to reflect on the reality of their society at large in the light of Human Scale Development theory, in order to design ways of overcoming or coping with the most important problems detected' (Max-Neef 1991: 39). Workshops would follow four differentiated phases with the roles of participants and facilitators/volunteers clearly specified (see Table 4.1 below). After going through the four phases, the community or group would have completed a matrix featuring the most harmful satisfiers that impeded needs fulfilment in their society (negative synthesis matrix).[4] The authors suggested repeating the four phases in order to obtain an additional synthesis matrix (the utopian/positive synthesis matrix) with the synergic satisfiers that should be available in their society for people to experience an optimal level of needs actualisation. An important consideration made by the authors was to avoid having the negative matrix available when discussing synergic satisfiers in order to minimise the risk of people only reporting opposites.

Once the two synthesis matrices are obtained (the negative and the positive/utopian), the authors suggest conducting a plenary session where the two matrices are presented, and dividing people into groups to find the most *synergic bridging satisfiers* (those that would enable a society or community to transition from a situation dominated by harmful satisfiers to another characterised by synergic ones) and reflect on their *exogeneity* (coming from outside the community) or *endogeneity* (mobilised from inside the community). This last part of the process is the least

Table 4.1 Structure of human needs workshops

Phase	Goal	Workshop	Matrix
1 (day1)	Divide the group into five sub-groups of ten people		
	Obtain 5 matrices with the satisfiers that impede human needs actualisation	A total of 8 hours to fill a complete matrix with negative satisfiers using 2 hours for each existential category (Being, Having, Doing and Interacting)	Original matrix with 36 cells to fill with satisfiers
2(day 1)	Generation of the *consolidated matrix*	Facilitators/volunteers generate one matrix out of the 5 obtained by eliminating repetitions and synonyms	Original matrix with harmful satisfiers
3(day 2)	Divide the group into nine sub-groups (one for each fundamental human need)		
	Choose the one or two most harmful satisfiers in every cell	Each group discusses one fundamental need. Consensual choice of most harmful satisfiers.	Focus on the four existential categories of Being, Having, Doing and Interacting
4(day 2)	Generation of the *negative synthesis matrix*	The satisfiers chosen are pinned up on a matrix that is discussed and interpreted in a plenary session	Original matrix with the most harmful satisfiers

Source: Adapted from Max-Neef *et al.* (1991)

elaborated upon in the original work, and how sub-groups are formed and discussions are organised is not made explicit. What is clear is that the goal of this last phase is to identify the most synergic satisfiers that can support a society or group in their quest to improve human needs fulfilment. Coherent with the HSD goal of self-reliance, an additional objective of this last phase is for people to become aware of those satisfiers that are endogenous and can be mobilised within the local community and those that require support from external institutions. A discussion on these terms also increases people's awareness of the connections between the personal and the societal. Participants become aware of the changes in attitudes, values, behaviours and actions that they have to put in place at the personal, family and community levels to stimulate broader transformations.

Most recorded applications of the HSD matrix have not followed the phases recommended by the authors in their original work; which Max-Neef sees as a sign of the flexibility of the proposal to adapt to different contexts and circumstances (Max-Neef 2011). Common in the literature is the use of the matrix of human needs as one of many tools in a research project. It is also common to focus academic studies on eliciting either negative, synergic or synergic bridging satisfiers without following all the phases suggested by the HSD book. One of the reasons why two or three-day workshops have not been used is the fact that HSD-based research projects are typically initiated by researchers and not by grassroots organisations or communities. As a consequence, participants have not always felt strongly about the project (at least in the beginning) and they have limited their participation to a few hours and/or specific days. In addition, researchers have often had a limited amount of funding and time to allocate to the exercise, which has frequently limited the possibility of organising workshops lasting several days.

Having experienced some of the constraints just described in organising community-level workshops, I found it useful to simplify the methodology to three phases each corresponding to one or more workshops resulting in two synthesis matrices and a set of strategies or synergic bridging satisfiers (see Guillén-Royo 2010). Table 4.2 summarises the simplified approach. Ideally, we would have ten people available to participate in the first phase where harmful or negative satisfiers are discussed and a synthesis matrix produced. Another ten people are then invited to attend a second workshop where satisfiers, that enable optimal need fulfilment, are identified, resulting in a second synthesis matrix. Both synthesis matrices are then presented to all 20 participants in a plenary session and people break into four groups corresponding to the four existential categories Being (individual or group attributes), Having (laws, values, institutions, norms), Doing (personal or collective actions) and Interacting (characteristics of times and spaces) to generate a new matrix or alternatively a set of satisfiers with synergic characteristics that can bridge the negative and the utopian scenarios. Thus after three phases, endogenous and exogenous synergic bridging satisfiers are available for people, the community and other interested organisations to co-define practical ways of implementing them (see Chapter 6 for an example on implementation).

Table 4.2 Simplified structure of human needs workshops

Phase	Goal	Workshop	Matrix
1	Co-generating a *negative synthesis matrix*	One or several workshops with groups of 5 to 10 people	Original matrix with 36 cells to fill with harmful satisfiers. Participants to reach a consensus on the one or two most harmful in each cell
2	Co-generating a *utopian synthesis matrix*	One or several workshops with groups of 5 to 10 people	Original matrix to fill with synergic and singular satisfiers. Consensus on the one or two most synergic in each cell
3	Identifying *synergic bridging satisfiers*	Previous participants presented with the two synthesis matrices are invited to identify synergic bridging satisfiers or strategies, both exogenous and endogenous. Participants discuss in plenary or are divided in four groups.	Either use the original matrix or discuss the ways of Being, Having, Doing and Interacting that will enable advancing towards the utopian situation summarised in 3 or 4 categories of satisfiers (see Example 4.1)

Source: Adapted from Guillén-Royo (2010; 2012)

Ideally, Phase 1 of the simplified approach would be carried out in four three-hour workshops, each addressing an existential category. This structure would also be replicated in Phase 2 with regards to synergic bridging satisfiers. Using three hours for each existential category enables deep discussions and the emergence of root causes of the problems, challenges and opportunities present in a society. However, as mentioned earlier, it is not always feasible to get people to attend the workshops when these are not initiated by the community. Thus, quite often, the two phases will have to be completed in one three-hour workshop instead of four workshops. This will give a bigger role to the facilitator than the one originally planned, as she will have to moderate discussions so that matrices are filled within the available timeframe (Guillén-Royo 2012).

It is important to repeat here the suggestion by Max-Neef and collaborators that participants discussing utopian synergic satisfiers do not have the *synthesis negative matrix* available so they do not generate a utopian matrix based on satisfiers that are the exact opposites of the negative ones. One way of avoiding the matrix of utopia being influenced by previous discussions on problems and challenges is inviting different people to join each of the two first phases (Guillén-Royo 2010, 2015). Another strategy, only possible if each phase consists of more than one workshop, is assigning to each group existential categories different from the one they had in Phase 1. However, all these precautions cannot prevent the negative and utopian matrices containing some opposites, as prevalent problems in a society are felt strongly and the opposite is usually desired and sought for. As Cuthill puts it 'when listed together [the negative and utopian matrices], these results provide a startling validation of the identification process. The 'Utopian community' descriptions in almost all cells proved a direct contrast to what had been identified in the negative matrix' (Cuthill 2003: 477).

Phase 3 is of special interest to researchers, practitioners and policy-makers as it is the stage at which *synergic bridging satisfiers* are derived, and interventions and policies designed. Participants in the previous phases and other interested people are usually invited to join this phase. Including new people is possible because we take as a starting point the two *synthesis matrices* that have been produced earlier and time is allocated at the beginning of the workshops for people to read the matrices carefully, discuss any unclear points, and challenge the suggested satisfiers.

Depending on the amount of people joining the last workshop the group can break into four groups corresponding to the four existential categories or keep on working in plenary. The former is advisable when Phase 3 uses the original matrix, as participants will have to discuss bridging satisfiers cell by cell, which demands a detailed and thorough analysis. The latter is more suitable when the researcher/practitioner has analysed the *utopian synthesis matrix* and presents participants with three or four categories that summarise the *synergic satisfiers* in the matrix. If the latter is the strategy chosen, it is important to start the workshops with a discussion of the categories, as participants might disagree and suggest new categories of synergic satisfiers that better capture the meaning of the utopian matrix. The discussion is then organised around the ways of Being, Doing, Having and Interacting that will enable participants to advance towards a society characterised by the utopian categories of satisfiers. The example below illustrates the two versions of Phase 3 used in an exploratory project in Peru.

Example 4.1: HSD workshops across socio-economic groups in Peru

In Autumn 2011, I conducted a study with the goal of understanding the challenges and opportunities to improve needs fulfilment experienced by peoples from different socio-economic groups in Peru,[5] a rapidly growing upper-middle-income country in South America with high levels of inequality and poverty.[6] The study included the facilitation, with the support of local assistants, of a total of 15 HSD workshops in five Peruvian districts: three in Lima (an upper-middle-class district – Miraflores, a lower-middle-class district – Breña, and a shanty town – Huaycan) and two in the Central Andean highlands (an urban – Huancayo, and a rural – Acostambo, district). Districts were selected for their diversity regarding socio-economic and geo-political characteristics, following the selection criteria used by previous research on the cultural constructions of wellbeing by the ESRC Wellbeing in Developing (WeD) countries research group at the University of Bath (refer to Copestake 2008 for an overview of the WeD research in Peru).

Most participants were recruited through a survey on wellbeing and personal values that I was conducting in the five districts as part of a larger research project. The survey included a question on people's willingness to participate in HSD workshops and asked for their contact details[7]. In total, 63 people participated in the study; of which 21 joined more than one workshop in their district. The average number of participants in each workshop was six, distributed unevenly across districts with workshops in the upper-class district of Miraflores having an average of three to four participants and those in the rural district of Acostambo an average of nine. All participants were over 18 years of age and groups were diverse regarding age and gender. The exceptions were Miraflores, where there was only one male participant, and Huancayo where all participants were under 40 years of age[8]. Following the structure described in Table 4.2 participants in both phases were invited to join the last workshop.

The two first phases were conducted following the same structure in the five districts. The venues ranged from a private house in Breña to a municipal hall in Huaycan and Acostambo. Workshops usually started with facilitators (I or a local assistant) presenting the nine fundamental human needs (subsistence, protection, affection, understanding, participation, idleness, creation, identity and freedom) and the four existential categories (being, having, doing and interacting) to address any difficulties or discrepancies in people's interpretation of them. Next, discussions would turn to the need for Subsistence and people would be invited to share their views on satisfiers that hampered (negative matrix) or promoted (positive or utopian matrix) that need with regards to the four existential categories. Following the HSD proposal, *Being* would be identified by adjectives (e.g. chauvinist, authoritarian, compassionate, inclusive, open, etc.), *Having* by nouns concerning values, laws, traditions, tools or institutional agreements (e.g. basic income, greed, formal education, repressive police forces, non-independent media), *Doing* by verbs (e.g. cooperating, excluding, sharing, discriminating, etc.) and *Interacting* by the characteristics of spaces or environments (e.g. free public parks, surveillance cameras, information in indigenous language, sports facilities, spaces for creativity, etc.).

After satisfiers for the need for subsistence had emerged, discussions would be directed to the need for Protection and would continue until the nine fundamental needs and the four ways of expressing them had been addressed. The process would be scheduled to last approximately two-and-a-half hours, after which time most cells would be completed and participants would be invited to take some time to read and reflect on the results of the discussion. A poster-size copy of a human needs matrix with empty cells would be hanging on the wall during the workshop and stickers would be used to pin on each cell the agreed satisfiers. The last half hour was usually devoted to going through the 36 cells and agreeing on the one or two most harmful (Phase 1) or synergic (Phase 2) satisfiers in each cell. This would result in two synthesis matrices that would be presented to participants at the beginning of Phase 3.

Generally, Phase 3 started by debriefing participants on the work undertaken in the previous phases and handing out copies of the two synthesis matrices or hanging them on the wall for all to see. Facilitators and participants would go through the different satisfiers and would modify them if consensus arose about any missing or irrelevant satisfier[9]. As we usually had less than 15 participants, we would then proceed to discuss in plenary the *synergic bridging satisfiers* that would allow transitioning from a society characterised by harmful satisfiers to a society based on synergy. This last workshop would again be articulated around an empty matrix that would be progressively filled with the satisfiers proposed. The focus was always on the 'how' so participants would be encouraged to reflect on the mechanisms, supports and practical tools, both endogenous and exogenous, that would need to be in place for *synergic satisfiers* to become available to them.

After using the approach just described in the three districts of Lima, the research team realised that it was cumbersome for both participants and facilitators to use the original matrix with 36 cells to identify *synergic bridging satisfiers*. Quite often people would find it hard to come up with satisfiers that were not already identified as synergic in Phase 2; particularly regarding the existential categories of *Doing* and *Interacting*. Thus, in Huaycayo and Acostambo, the two last districts where the workshops took place, I analysed the synthesis utopian matrix after Phase 2 and identified common categories under which synergic satisfiers could be summarised (Guillén-Royo 2015). This resulted in a much simpler matrix with three categories of synergic satisfiers (e.g. social cohesion, quality education and higher economic level in Acostambo). The latter were discussed at the beginning of the third workshop to give participants the opportunity to change them if they thought they did not accurately represent the utopian matrix. The workshop was then articulated around the ways of Being, Having, Doing and Interacting that would facilitate the emergence of the envisaged synergic category of satisfiers. People were also asked to reflect on the extent to which the ways of Being, Having, Doing and Interacting could be developed endogenously or required the support of external institutions.

Addressing environmental sustainability

As described in Chapter 3, HSD was a proposal for development based on the search for synergic satisfiers, those that contribute positively to more than one human need now and in the future. The latter concerns the fact that fundamental human needs change slowly with the course of history and synergic satisfiers now are quite likely to remain so in the future. If synergic satisfiers like extensive cycle lanes in urban areas are present, human needs of both current and future generations are likely to be met. However, if singular or inhibiting satisfiers prevail, there are no positive spillovers from the targeted needs to other needs and the prospect of satisfying multiple needs might even be reduced in the mid and long run. This could be exemplified by the use of private transportation in cities, which can be seen as satisfying the needs for identity, freedom, subsistence, leisure and protection but at the same time be detrimental for the same needs, through the effects on carbon emissions, the use of urban space, noise and the promotion of individualist values. The question remains on how to explicitly address environmental issues when using the HSD matrix.

The conceptual clarity of the HSD proposal in embedding ecological sustainability into a system of synergic satisfiers does not always translate in the spontaneous emergence of environmentally relevant satisfiers when carrying out HSD workshops. The synergic satisfiers that emerge in participatory discussions might not be explicitly connected to greenhouse gas emissions, pollution, deforestation, land degradation, biodiversity loss or other environmentally relevant issues. This might result in researchers or practitioners forcing a focus on environmental issues when leading HSD workshops to the detriment of a wider understanding of personal, economic, socio-cultural or political issues that might be essential for the realisation of environmental goals. An example of the need to account for interdependence was made clear to me in a participatory research project I conducted in Acostambo (Peru) following the study described in Example 4.1 where a synergic bridging satisfier identified around the organisation of a parents' school ended up being key for the success of an organic gardens project (see Guillén-Royo 2015 and Chapter 6 for a detailed explanation of this research).

Example 4.2: Four approaches to the study of environmental sustainability

In this section I draw on the available literature on the applications of the HSD to outline four strategies used by researchers or practitioners to adapt the HSD methodology to address environmental concerns.

1) INVITING PARTICIPANTS AFTER MATRICES ARE FILLED TO REFLECT ON THE
RELATIONSHIP BETWEEN SATISFIERS AND SUSTAINABILITY

In a study carried out in Lleida, a medium-sized city in Catalonia, in 2009 I drew on the matrix of human needs to discuss sustainable consumption with 47 local residents (Guillén-Royo 2010). The study followed the three phases described in Table 4.2 and focussed discussions on the satisfiers that 1) impeded human needs satisfaction in their society; 2) would facilitate an optimal fulfilment of human needs; and 3) would enable bridging the negative and the utopian matrices. The last half an hour of each workshop was devoted to reflecting on the relationship between the satisfiers that had emerged in the discussions and the current patterns of consumption in their society. It was common for participants to associate negative satisfiers with unsustainable consumption practices and synergic satisfiers with a society where consumption does not have a destructive impact on the environment. As a participant put it when looking at the matrix with negative satisfiers: 'consumerism reinforces all these limitations [referring to the negative satisfiers in the matrix], everything is interrelated'. In addition, synergic bridging satisfiers such as direct democracy and flexible working times, although not intuitively linked to environmental policies, were considered indispensable to support the transition to a low carbon society in Lleida (see Chapter 5 for a detailed analysis of the synergic satisfiers in this study).

2) USING THE MATRIX TO ANSWER SPECIFIC ENVIRONMENTAL QUESTIONS

In a study aimed at improving sustainable regional planning, Jolibert and colleagues (2014) used HSD-based workshops to identify satisfiers at the individual, community and governance levels that could support interventions for sustainable development in Brabant-Wallon, a Belgian region. In order to do that, they invited eight key stakeholders (a manager of natural areas, a representative of the tourism sector, a manager of economic development, a farmer, a policy-maker, a forester, a sustainability promoter and a local resident) to first fill the matrix individually with synergic satisfiers that are necessary to achieve a sustainable living environment (utopian matrix with sustainability as a goal). They were asked to think both in personal terms and to take into account their professional expertise. Next, participants were invited to share two of their satisfiers with the group and reformulate them in order to obtain a list of collective satisfiers that all participants could endorse. Finally, they drew on this information to encourage participants to co-design a needs-based planning scenario for the region with implicit policy recommendations. This ranged from interventions addressing issues of population and lifestyle to regulations targeted at the agricultural and forest sectors (see Chapter 5 for a more detailed discussion of this research). In summary, Jolibert and colleagues' study addressed ecological sustainability by using the utopian matrix as a basis to discuss individual, community and governance dimensions of a future sustainable living environment and by deliberately choosing stakeholders with interests in the topic.

3) USING THE MATRIX AS ONE OF THE MANY PARTICIPATORY METHODS OF A
PROJECT

A third approach to using the matrix to address environmental issues is the one
chosen by architect A. Mitchell in an Argentinian project co-designing a
sustainable rural settlement in the province of Mendoza (Mitchell 2001). The
target group were 27 peasant families from a street association who lived in
precarious housing. Mitchell started by organising a workshop to discuss
participants' motivations to join the project. Then participants engaged in a
discussion on needs and satisfiers using the HSD matrix and giving particular
attention to the physical spaces required to satisfy human needs in the future
settlement. Next, participants discussed the characteristics of the goods and
services under 'interacting' and listed the activities that would take place in those
spaces characterising them, depending on whether they were seasonal or not and
required open or closed spaces. Finally, the last workshop aimed at co-designing
the future homes, taking into account the characteristics of the local climate and
considerations of energy efficiency. In this case, the matrix of human needs was
used as a starting point for the identification of physical spaces with synergic and
singular satisfier characteristics, and ecological sustainability was purposefully
addressed in the last workshop where dwellings were planned and co-designed.

4) INTRODUCING THE ENVIRONMENT AS THE FUNDAMENTAL CONDITION FOR THE
SATISFACTION OF HUMAN NEEDS

A fourth approach to including environmental sustainability in a discussion on
needs satisfiers is exemplified by Inez Aponte's[10] workshops with members of the
general public, transition initiatives and local organisations in the UK and Europe
(see Chapter 7 for a description of her work with the Transition movement).
Workshops would start with the question: 'What do humans need to thrive?'
Participants would be invited to brainstorm their answers in small groups and
write them up on post-it notes. This would provide a collection of satisfiers and
goods and services ranging from 'bikes' and 'computers' to 'democracy' and 'clean
air'. Then, participants would be asked to stick each post-it in only one of the
nine need categories which would have been stuck in a circle on the wall (see
Figure 4.1). Because the words on the post-it notes are satisfiers or goods and
services, there is usually no strict correspondence between them and fundamental
human needs. This usually results in a discussion around the fact that some of
the words do not fit into any particular category. At this point the difference
between needs and satisfiers is clarified and the term *synergic satisfier* is introduced,
as well as *pseudo-satisfier*, *inhibitor* and *violator* as satisfiers that have a negative
impact on the overall model. Next, participants are given time to reflect on
examples of negative satisfiers in their own lives which raises questions around
personal and collective responsibility. The goal of this phase is to engage
participants in an alternative way of looking at the economy, to invite discussions
on the efficiency of the current economic system in providing needs satisfiers and
to ask where the responsibility lies for the choice of satisfiers.

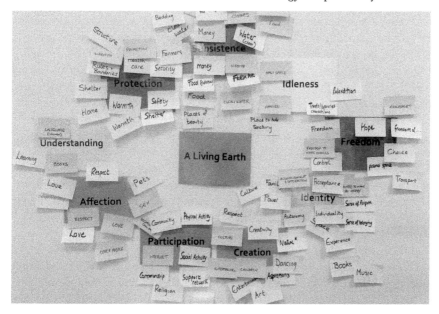

Figure 4.1 The Living Earth as fundamental condition for needs satisfaction
Photo: Inez Aponte

Later, a sticker representing the 'living earth' is placed in the middle of the circle formed by the nine fundamental needs and their current satisfiers. This is the starting point for a deeper discussion on the synergic satisfiers that should be available in any given society for human needs to be better fulfilled and the natural environment preserved and enhanced. The ultimate goal of the entire exercise is to introduce a mode of sustainability-thinking that aligns human needs with the needs of a living earth, and to identify the different alternatives available to provide need satisfiers.

Participants' recruitment and ethical considerations

Ideally, a project based on HSD workshops should be initiated by a local community/grassroots organisation or at least be planned and implemented in collaboration with participants as done in Participatory Action Research (PAR) designs (see Chapter 6 for a discussion on PAR designs). When a community is involved in the planning of a HSD project, it is likely that workshops are well attended and that people are engaged and willing to take the process beyond a mere diagnostic exercise. When the idea of carrying out a HSD project does not come from the local community, as is common in academic or development planning activities, it will be necessary to design a strategy to recruit participants. This will include, among other ethical considerations, an evaluation of the appropriateness of offering incentives, rewards or gifts in exchange for the time spent participating.

Ethical considerations should be taken into account when planning a HSD project for academic purposes in order to avoid any type of harm to people as a consequence of their participation in research activities (Bryman 2008). It is quite likely that academics or practitioners will want to use the HSD proposal to address a problem or a challenge that affects vulnerable groups such as materially poor people, marginalised groups or people exposed to certain health conditions. When this is the case, the goal of the researcher should be to ensure that vulnerable people do not become 'objects' of the research or victims of the research process. The fact that HSD is based on the direct involvement of participants who leave their traditional role as informants to become active agents in the research and development processes reduces the risk of objectifying participants. However, expectations about the personal and structural changes that might derive from participation should be discussed beforehand together with the amount of time involved, the level of engagement of researchers/practitioners and their availability after workshops have taken place.

Three ethical issues might necessitate careful consideration: 1) the information conveyed before initiating the project; 2) the consent required from participants to record or use the data from the workshops; and 3) the incentives or gifts that will be offered to participants. The first issue concerns the verbal or written information that participants have to have access to before engaging in a HSD project. General information about the goal of the project, the institutions participating, the characteristics of the methods used, including their duration, and the future management of the data should be included in the description. The length of workshops and the type of dynamics expected should also be conveyed before people agree to participate and it should be clear that anonymity and confidentiality (the raw data will not be accessible to other institutions or people) are guaranteed.[11] Participants should be asked for their consent after information about the project has been conveyed and made aware that even if they consent to participate they are free to withdraw from the project at any point. This is particularly important for participants in HSD workshops as knowing they have the right to opt out, they might choose not to get involved in discussions or to abstain from joining further workshops and other activities linked to the project if they do not feel comfortable with the groups, the dynamics or the outcomes of the process.

Using video or audio recording during the workshops is very useful as the resulting matrices do not always reflect the richness of the discussions, comments or explanations behind each of the selected satisfiers. Records can be drawn on to validate the meaning of the concepts used to describe satisfiers, and will enable researchers to expand on the interconnections between different sets of satisfiers and human needs. However, it is common that people reject being recorded in contexts of social fragmentation, institutional opacity, violence or mistrust. Then note taking will be the only possible option and will demand that at least two researchers are present, one to facilitate the discussion and the other to take the notes.[12]

Providing incentives or giving gifts is another issue that needs to be addressed when HSD workshops are not initiated by the grassroots. The greatest challenge here is to avoid reaffirming problematic patron–client relationships that would certainly reduce any potential synergic effect from the HSD exercise. However, studies show that small gifts can act as incentives for people to participate in research and that as long as they are kept small, they do not have a significant influence on people's answers or level of engagement[13] (Cobanoglu and Cobanoglu 2003). In addition, it is quite common for researchers to feel grateful to those who generously make time to participate in a research project, that *a priori*, they do not see of direct benefit to them (although this perception of lack of benefit usually changes after people spend three hours discussing satisfiers) and a small gift is usually a socially accepted expression of gratitude.

Example 4.3: Recruiting participants in Lleida and Oslo

The goal of the study in Lleida (Catalonia), outlined in Example 4.2, was to investigate the usefulness of the HSD methodology to support societal transformations towards sustainable consumption (Guillén-Royo 2010). The project was designed in the traditional academic way and the involvement of participants in its design was not initially contemplated. Since there was not an explicit interest in this type of research in Lleida, I needed to devise a strategy to recruit participants for the workshops. I and a local collaborator placed general information about the workshops on a dedicated project website, in posters hung on notice boards at the local University, the public library, non-profit organisations and several neighbourhood associations. An advert was also placed in one of the local newspapers during the three preceding weeks. The poster and advert mentioned that a complimentary coffee break and a small gift would be offered but no detailed information about the type of gift was provided.

Most of the 47 people who joined one or two of the ten three-hour workshops were recruited through *snowball sampling* (Bryman 2008) drawing on people and institutions that were known to us or our local contacts. The posters and ads did not prove very useful to recruit people. Once people agreed to participate they were informed verbally and in writing about the goal of the project and about the anonymity and confidentiality with which the data will be treated. Permission to record discussions was granted by people participating in the ten workshops and notes were taken to facilitate the analysis of data. Regarding the gift, since the topic of the study was human needs and sustainable consumption and the project did not have any external funding, we decided to offer participants the possibility to take home second-hand fiction books. People seemed to welcome the initiative and many chose a book to take with them. However, most participants made it clear that their motivation to attend the workshops had been either their curiosity about the project's methodology or their friendship with the person who had informed them about the workshops.

A more significant incentive or reward was planned for the workshops carried out at the University of Oslo in May 2013. Together with two research assistants and three research partners we designed a pilot study as part of a small project to investigate the relationship between personal values and participation in HSD workshops.[14] The project was articulated around two phases. The first consisted of a self-completion questionnaire on personal values, subjective wellbeing, environmental behaviours and engagement in social or environmental activism. The survey was applied to a convenience sample of 260 students across the natural, social and human sciences. The front cover of the questionnaire included information about the project's ethical considerations and the reward for those respondents who would be invited to attend the workshops organised at a later stage (600 NOK – Norwegian Kroner, approximately 72 Euros, for participation in two workshops). Since one of our goals was to increase our understanding of the relationship between personal values and participation in the HSD process we aimed at gathering two groups of people with different value orientations (extrinsic and intrinsic[15]).

Interestingly enough, and given the fact that most answers to the survey questionnaire were by university students, the possibility to earn a 600 Norwegian Kroner book voucher for participation in two workshops did not act as a powerful incentive. On average, a Norwegian student getting a state student loan, will receive around 10,000 NOK per month, enough to pay for accommodation in a shared flat or university hall and cover food and other living expenses. The 600 NOK made up 6 per cent of their monthly income, which we expected would have worked as an incentive. Nevertheless, most of the 26 people who ended up engaging in the workshops came through a snowballing process started by the team's own colleagues and students. All participants in the workshops accepted the book voucher. However, as it happened in Lleida, most participants indicated that it was not the voucher that had persuaded them to participate but their genuine interest in the project or their acquaintance with our research centre and/or its researchers.

The role of the facilitator

Facilitating HSD workshops is a task well suited to those who are not afraid of losing their status as researchers, NGO workers or community leaders, since it implies that the researchers get personally involved in the research process and somehow influence and get influenced by it. Max-Neef highlights the importance of personal involvement in terms of enabling a deep understanding of the situations that communities go through. As he puts it 'no understanding is possible if we detach ourselves from the object of our intended understanding. Detachment can only generate knowledge not understanding' (Max-Neef 1991: 100). In the academic literature on the HSD proposal, it is common to find that researchers have taken on the role of facilitators (Buscaglia 2013; García Norato 2006; Guillén-Royo 2010, 2015; Mitchell 2001) although there are some examples of workshops carried out by professionals (Cuthill 2003) and by social workers or experts with a long-standing relationship with the participating groups (Bucciarelli and Alessi 2013, 2014). However, if the exercise has to be truly transformative, it seems difficult to justify using people other than the researcher or practitioner in organising and coordinating the workshops.

Openness to engage in a deep understanding of the problems and potentials of a specific community does not always accord with having a predefined purpose or goal. As Max-Neef and colleagues propose, HSD practitioners have to make 'the conscious decision to act synergically' and be aware that at some point in the process different strategies or synergic satisfiers might emerge (HSD1991). Acting synergically implies being reflexive and acting in awareness of one's own needs and expectations and those of the collaborators and participants. It means having gone through a process of personal transformation that goes beyond the mere utilitarian goal of becoming more empathic in order to build rapport with others. It means in summary, changing the focus from wanting to change others to wanting to change oneself. Max-Neef recognised the difficulty of this reversal, as Chambers (1992) called it, but believed it was the only legitimate course of action: 'at this stage of my life, I have reached the conclusion that I lack the power to change the world or any significant part of it. I only have the power to change myself [. . .] Now, the point is that if I change myself, something may happen as a consequence that may lead to a change in the world' (Max-Neef 1991: 113).

Changing oneself in order to be able to lead or support broader transformative projects is obviously not an easy task and there are not many guidelines about how to go about it at the individual level. Rahnema (1990), in a piece criticising participatory action research proponents for their alliance with specific methodologies and ideologies of change, suggests that the way to become an agent of change is to question

> endlessly one's own motives, attitudes, beliefs, ways of life, habits, traditions, and thought processes. And to question is not to be pathologically sceptical about everything; it only means to be critically self-aware and yet passionately compassionate. By fully participating in the world, such a person becomes not only one's own change agent, but one who, by the same token, changes the world.
>
> (Rahnema 1990: 223)

Thus, self-awareness and compassion might be important skills to cultivate when engaging in and coordinating participatory process.

Mackewn (2008) adds to the above requirements, the need to be open to deviating from the initial purpose and the importance of engaging in a continuous reflection on our conceptualisation of group processes, on the wider field in which we operate, and on what he calls 'the choreography of energy'. The first consideration is of a more methodological nature and concerns the impact on the facilitation of our understanding of the development stage at which the community or group is and the need to be aware of the tensions and events that are affecting the community and might not be implicitly discussed in the workshops (see Chapter 6 for a discussion on power and participatory processes).

The second recommendation is a more crucial matter as it depends on the personal capacity to pay attention to the energy flow in the groups and to work with them so that the workshops become a synergic and engaging experience. Mackewn (2008) gives some suggestions about how to increase the energy flow in the group that can be summarised as sensitising ourselves through different exercise and relaxation techniques and integrating creative approaches (such as drawing, theatre playing or miming) into the group dynamics.

As I have learned through carrying out HSD workshops with people with different personal values and goals, synergy and energy flow might not totally depend on the facilitator but on participants sharing common goals or intentions. This is illustrated by the comment from a research assistant from the University of Oslo, asked to keep a reflexive journal of the HSD workshops outlined in Example 4.3.

> At this point I feel my own focus beginning to weaken. I perceive a certain lack in the group, a certain lack of passion. It remains an 'exercise', rather than emerging as a real (small-scale) community effort to make relevant and concrete changes. Why is it that I experience a lack of integration of the participants in the discussion? The discussion appears exerted, without a strong inherent drive. There is also a certain fragmentation, both in terms of contents discussed and participant interplay.

Thus, it might well be that even if we are psychologically, physically and theoretically ready to run HSD workshops, both the processes and the outcomes are beyond our well-intentioned purpose. I will get back to this discussion in Chapter 8 where I will present limitations and challenges of the uses of the HSD methodology.

Emergence and empowerment

Max-Neef and colleagues argued that the participatory discussions people engage with during the workshops enable people to understand the deep roots of the problems affecting a group or organisation. They claim that their 'observations have shown that at some point during the exercise, the urge to unearth truly and honestly (no matter how painful it may be) what is ailing in one's society is highly intensified' (Max-Neef 1991: 43). These sort of participatory discussions are likely to have synergic effects as people feel the urge to do something about the situation they have analysed and might be willing to actively seek solutions to the personally and institutionally rooted satisfiers that block needs actualisation in their societies (Guillén-Royo 2015; García Norato 2006). This deep level of understanding and the increased willingness to mobilise to change a specific situation are related to the concepts of 'emergence' and 'empowerment' associated with participatory processes (Reason and Bradbury 2013).

Using the logic of complexity, one could argue that HSD workshops can provide the enabling environment for new strategies or interventions to emerge and that these strategies have the power to trigger systemic transitions towards a new order. As Mitleton-Kelly (2003: 21) puts it

> the generation of knowledge and of innovative ideas when a team is working together could be described as an emergent property in the sense that it arises from the interaction of individuals and is not just the sum of existing ideas, but could well be something quite new and possibly unexpected.

Through discussions on satisfiers, people deepen their exploration into the structures that define the functioning of their society and they come up with personal, collective and higher level changes that have to be in place for the system to become better suited to satisfy needs. HSD workshops could work as a platform to facilitate the emergence of transformative ideas and, if followed-up through participatory interventions that encourage self-organisation, might have lasting effects on the functioning of the socio-economic system.

Emergence, as a property of the HSD process, links to the concept of social learning as used in sustainability studies. Social learning is defined as a type of learning that goes beyond the mere factual acquisition of knowledge to account for shared understandings and collaborations involving changes in personal values, behaviours and skills (Garmendia and Stagl 2010). This type of learning is central to promote changes towards sustainable societies. As Garmendia and Stagl (2010: 1712) put it: 'deliberative approaches that enhance collective learning processes among a diverse group of social actors, with different types of knowledge and perspectives, are thus central in the creation of new responses to threats for socio-ecological systems'. HSD workshops could be considered a type of deliberative approach that promotes learning and shared understandings that can lead to the generation of new responses through the multidimensional analysis of needs and needs satisfiers (Jolibert *et al.* 2014).

The synergic effects of participation in the HSD workshops might still not be enough to achieve consensus over policies or initiatives. Nørgaard (1994) warns against assuming that syntheses or consensuses are always achievable. He argues that societies are constituted by people with different or even divergent ways of understanding and influencing the socio-ecological systems in which they operate. These divergent perspectives cannot always be reconciled through deliberative or participative approaches but have to be unveiled to understand the plurality operating in social systems. Nevertheless, the fact that HSD is associated with a way of knowing based on systemic relationships and not the linearity and fragmentation characteristic of traditional thinking opens up the possibility for alternative ways of understanding that might facilitate the emergence of consensus over satisfiers, even if these are only relevant in the short run and have to be adapted through a process of constant learning.

Empowerment understood as 'the expansion in people's ability to make strategic life choices in a context where this ability was previously denied to them' (Mikkelsen 2005: 348) is one of the expected consequences of participating in HSD workshops. Max-Neef claims that engaging in a HSD process increases self-awareness and understanding of the underlying causes behind deficient needs satisfaction. This, together with the process of distinguishing between endogenous and exogenous synergic satisfiers might give people the tools to reverse negative situations. The hypothesis that participation increases feelings of empowerment is supported by psychological research on motivation (Ryan and Deci, 2000, 2001). Active participation is likely to make people experience high levels of choice and autonomy when synergic satisfiers are translated into policies or interventions. Experiencing higher levels of autonomy, defined as 'feeling personal value and interest with respect to what one does' (Ryan and Sapp 2007: 76), is associated with higher quality motivation, better internalisation of pro-social and pro-environmental behaviours, and increased wellbeing. As research in self-determination theory (SDT) has shown, the experience of being autonomy-supported by authority figures such as workshop facilitators (as opposed to controlled or coerced via rewards and punishments) leads individuals to feel more motivated to change behaviour, which in turn increases their sense of personal and community wellbeing (Ryan and Deci, 2000).

Whether the higher feeling of empowerment experienced during participation in HSD workshops leads to transformative action is difficult to assess with the evidence available so far. In the three energy and natural resource management European case studies analysed, Garmendia and Stagl (2010) did not find evidence of participatory workshops empowering individuals, with empowerment defined as finding better ways to change institutions. In Chapter 8, I present in more detail the exploratory research undertaken in Oslo where changes in values, environmental attitudes and willingness to participate in socio-environmental activism of people participating in HSD workshops were measured. Answers to the pre- and post-workshop surveys to questions on participants' willingness to engage in social or environmental activism suggest that people in exploratory workshops might not be more willing to engage in activism after their participation.

The fact that most HSD workshops are undertaken with the purpose of a one-off assessment of a situation might limit the benefits of the exercise in terms of empowerment. In most cases, lack of funding and time for researchers to engage with the community in pursuing the synergic bridging satisfiers derived from a HSD exercise makes it impossible to analyse the extent to which participation has led to increased empowerment. However, many reactions from participants after HSD workshops, asking each other 'What now?' or 'What are we going to do with this?' suggest that participants are willing to go beyond understanding to engage in transformative action through the increased sense of trust and fellowship that HSD workshops promote. This willingness manifests in HSD exercises designed as Participatory Action Research, such as the one presented in Chapter 6, as these projects do not stop in the design or identification phases.

Conclusion

This chapter has discussed some methodological issues around the use of the human needs matrix in participatory workshops. It has presented the approach suggested by Max-Neef and collaborators and how researchers have adapted it to suit the requirements of a particular project. The chapter has addressed the ethical challenges associated to the recruitment of participants not initially engaged with the research topic regarding information, consent and gift giving. The role of the facilitator and his/her personal and social skills have also been debated, focussing on the need to engage in personal transformation and to cultivate self-awareness. Attentiveness to the 'choreography of energy' or energy flow in groups appears as a key skill for facilitators without which it will be difficult to assert the trustworthiness of the findings. Allowing for the interplay of intuition and knowledge when facilitating HSD workshops seems the right way forward if we want to experience synergic effects from the research process itself.

Finally, how to address environmental sustainability in the setting of a HSD workshop is an open question. The examples presented in this chapter have given a glimpse on how this has been done so far but there is still more to discuss and debate about the integration of human and environmental wellbeing. The next chapters will deepen in the analysis of practical applications of the HSD framework with the aim to support sustainable development processes. The HSD understanding of the socio-economic system as complex and co-evolving with the ecological system suggests that a use of the matrix that concentrates on environmental issues might fail to unveil the interconnections of the natural environment with the personal, social, economic, cultural, religious and political characteristics of a specific group, community or society. Without accounting for interdependence, sustainable development policies might be insufficient, at the minimum incomplete and at the maximum might risk fatal rebound effects[16] in terms of human and environmental wellbeing. In Max-Neef's own words 'there is nothing wrong in making mistakes; there is something wrong in being dishonest, and it is this which we cannot afford' (Max-Neef 1991: 110).

Notes

1 I use the terms 'matrix of needs and satisfiers' and 'HSD matrix' interchangeably.
2 I refer to the HSD book as the one published in English by Max-Neef, *Human Scale Development: Conception, Applications and Further Reflections*, published in 1991 by Apex Press.
3 Chapter 7 in this book includes an example of the use of the HSD framework with people involved in the transition movement.
4 Refer to Chapter 3 for a detailed description of the human needs matrix and a definition of satisfiers.
5 This study was part of the post-doctoral project 'Sustainable development in Peru – A study of the factors that explain sustainable consumption and wellbeing across socio-economic groups', funded by the *Latin Amerika* programme of the Research Council of Norway between 2011 and 2014. Other outputs of this study can be found in Guillén-Royo, M. (2015). Human needs and the environment reconciled: Participatory action-research for sustainable development in Peru. In Syse, K. and Mueller, M. (eds) (2015). *Sustainability and the Good Life*. Oxford: Routledge; and in Guillén-Royo, M. and Kasser, T. (2015). Personal goals, happiness and socio-economic context: Studying a diverse sample in Peru. *Journal of Happiness Studies*, 16(2): 405–25.

6 Peru is classified as an upper middle-income country by the Development Assistance Committee (DAC) of the OECD following criteria based on GNI per capita, (www.oecd.org/dac/stats/daclist).

7 For more information about the recruitment of participants refer to Guillén-Royo, M. (2015). Human needs and the environment reconciled: Participatory action-research for sustainable development in Peru. In Syse, K. and Mueller, M. (eds), *Sustainability and the Good Life*. Oxford: Routledge.

8 Workshops were conducted during the day at times that participants had suggested would suit them. Some workshops were also scheduled during weekends to facilitate the attendance of people in paid work and students.

9 This part of the workshop should be allocated more time if participants have low levels of literacy as a thorough summary of the matrices should then be made orally. In this project, only some participants from Huaycan and Acostambo had not completed primary education.

10 Personal communication by Inez Aponte (www.growingoodlives.com, accessed 20 April 2015).

11 In a context of violence or mistrust, it might also be advisable to agree with participants not to share what they hear in the workshops with third parties.

12 Participants might support the study by taking notes. It is also good practice that notes are validated by the community.

13 This study refers to survey research and does not address HSD workshops in particular.

14 The findings of this project are discussed in some detail in Chapter 8.

15 Define intrinsic and extrinsic values following Kasser (2002).

16 As discussed in Chapter 2 rebound effects concern the increases in consumption derived from efficiency improvements (Sorrell *et al.* 2009).

References

Bryman, A. (2008). *Social Research Methods*, 3rd. edn. Oxford: Oxford University Press.

Bucciarelli, E. and Alessi, M. (2013). Introduction to the Human Scale Development Methodology Improved by Bucciarelli-Alessi's Innovative Methodological Procedure, (http://dx.doi.org/10.2139/ssrn.2262870).

Bucciarelli, E. and Alessi, M. (2014). *Output delle attività 2.1.3, 2.2 e 3.3. Progetto 'Terzo incluso: il valore aggiunto che fa innovazione'*. Università degli Studi 'Gabriele D'Annunzio di Chieti-Pescara (Italy).

Buscaglia, A. (2013). Propuesta participativa de desarrollo local para la comunidad de Coya, Region de O'Higgins, desde la perspectiva del desarrollo a escala humana. In Moreno, A. (ed.), *Tesis 2013. Piensa un país sin pobreza*. Fundación superación de la pobreza, pp. 102–23, (www.superacionpobreza.cl/wp-content/uploads/2014/06/TESIS-2013-final-web.pdf, accessed 21 April 2015).

Chambers, R. (1992). Sustainable livelihoods: The poor's reconciliation of environment and development. In Ekins, P. and Max-Neef, M. (eds), *Real-life Economics*. London: Routledge.

Cobanoglu, C. and Cobanoblu, N. (2003). The effect of incentives in web surveys: Applications and ethical considerations. *International Journal of Market Research*, 45(4).

Copestake, J. (2008). *Wellbeing and Development in Peru: Local and Universal Views Confronted*. New York: Palgrave MacMillan.

Cruz, I., Stahel, A. and Max-Neef, M. (2009). Towards a systemic development approach: Building on the Human Scale Development paradigm. *Ecological Economics*, 68: 2021–30.

Cuthill, M. (2003). From here to utopia: Running a Human-scale Development workshop on the Gold Coast, Australia. *Local Environment*, 8(4): 471–85.

García Norato, O. M. (2006). Matriz de necesidades y satisfactores con mujeres rurales de Siachoque, Boyacá, Colombia. Apuntes del CENES. 16(41), Centro de Estudios Económicos, Universidad Pedagógica y Tecnológica de Colombia, (http://virtual.uptc. edu.co/drupal/files/rac_52.pdf accessed 15 August 2014).

Garmendia, E. and Stagl, S. (2010). Public participation for sustainability and social learning: Concepts and lessons from three case studies in Europe. *Ecological Economics,* 69(8): 1712–22.

Guillén-Royo, M. (2010). Realising the 'wellbeing dividend': An exploratory study using the human scale development approach. *Ecological Economics,* 70: 384–93.

Guillén-Royo, M. (2012). The challenge of transforming consumption patterns: A proposal using the Human Scale Development Approach. In Bjørkdahl, K. and Nielsen, K. B. (eds), *Development and the Environment. Practices, Theories, Policies.* Oslo: Akademika Publishing, pp. 99–118.

Guillén-Royo, M. (2015). Human needs and the environment reconciled: Participatory action-research for sustainable development in Peru. In Syse, K. and Mueller, M. (eds), *Sustainability and the Good Life.* Oxford: Routledge.

Jackson, T. and Marks, N. (1999). Consumption, sustainable welfare and human needs – with reference to UK expenditure patterns between 1954 and 1994. *Ecological Economics,* 28: 421–41.

Jolibert, C., Max-Neef, M., Rauschmayer, F. and Paavola, J. (2011). Should we care about the needs of non-humans? Needs assessment: A tool for environmental conflict resolution and sustainable organization of living beings. *Environmental Policy and Governance,* 21(4): 259–69.

Jolibert, C., Paavola, J. and Rauschmayer, F. (2014). Addressing needs in the search for sustainable development: A proposal for needs-based scenario building. *Environmental Values,* 23: 29–50.

Jorge, M. (2010). Patients' needs and satisfiers: Applying human scale development theory on end-of-life care. *Current Opinion in Supportive and Palliative Care,* 4: 163–9.

Kasser, T. (2002). *The High Price of Materialism.* Cambridge, MA: MIT Press.

Mackewn, J. (2008). Facilitation as action research in the moment. In Reason, P. and Bradbury, H. (eds), *The SAGE Handbook of Action Research.* London: Sage.

Max-Neef, M. (1991). *Human Scale Development: Conception, Application and Further Reflection.* London: Apex Press.

Max-Neef, M. (2011). The death and rebirth of economics. In Rauschmayer, F., Omann, I. and Frühmann, J. (eds), *Sustainable Development: Capabilities, Needs and Well-being.* London: Routledge, pp. 104–20.

Max-Neef, M., Elizalde, A. and Hopenhayn, M. (1989). Human Scale Development: An option for the future. *Development Dialogue,* 1: 17–47.

Max-Neef, M., Elizalde, A. and Hopenhayn, M. (1991). Development and human needs. In Max-Neef, M. (ed.), *Human Scale Development: Conception, Application and Further Reflection.* London: Apex Press.

Mikkelsen, B. (2005). *Methods for Development Work and Research,* 2nd edn. London: Sage.

Mitchell, J. A. (2001). Propuesta metodológica en el diseño de un asentamiento humano en una zona rural del centro- oeste de la República Argentina. *La casa de América,* pp. 209–39 (ISBN-970-694-063-4).

Mitleton-Kelly, E. (2003). Ten principles of complexity and enabling infrastructures. In Mitleton-Kelly, E. (ed.), *Complex Systems and Evolutionary Perspectives of Organisations: The Application of Complexity Theory to Organisations.* Oxford: Elsevier, pp. 23–50.

Nørgaard, R. B. (1994). Development Betrayed. The End of Progress and a Coevolutionary Revision of the Future. London, New York: Routledge.

Rahnema, R. (1990). Participatory Action Research: The 'Last Temptation of Saint' development. *Alternatives: Global, Local, Political*, 15(2): 199–226.

Reason, P. and Bradbury, H. (2013). *The SAGE Handbook of Action Research. Participative Inquiry and Practice*. London: Sage.

Ryan, R. M. and Deci, E. L. (2000). Self-determination theory and the facilitation of intrinsic motivation, social development and wellbeing. *American Psychologist*, 55 (1): 68–78.

Ryan, R. M. and Deci, E. L. (2001). On happiness and human potentials: A review of research on hedonic and eudaimonic wellbeing. *Annual Review of Psychology*, 52: 141–66.

Ryan, R. M. and Sapp, A. R. (2007). Basic psychological needs: A self-determination theory perspective on the promotion of wellness across development and cultures. In Gough, I. and McGregor, A. (eds), *Wellbeing in Developing Countries: New Approaches and Research Strategies*. Cambridge: Cambridge University Press.

Smith, B. P. and Max-Neef, M. (2011). *Economics Unmasked. From Power and Greed to Compassion and the Common Good*. Cambridge: Green Books.

Sorrell, S., Dimitropoulos, J. and Sommerville, M. (2009). Empirical estimates of the direct rebound effect: A review. *Energy Policy*, 37, 1356–71.

Part II

5 Exploring avenues for sustainable development through needs-based workshops

Introduction

The matrix of human needs and satisfiers was developed as a tool to structure a series of seminars or workshops with communities and groups of people interested in finding strategies to improve the satisfaction of needs. As described in Chapter 4, a process in three phases was proposed first to increase participants' awareness of the deep underlying problems in their society; second to reflect on the characteristics of a society that would enable an optimal satisfaction of human needs; and third to discuss the endogenous (that generated by the community) and exogenous (that which needed external support) satisfiers that would support overcoming the challenges detected and increasing the satisfaction of needs. This process of collective reflection and introspection was meant to contribute to a deep understanding of the root-causes of need deprivation at the same time that it facilitated the identification of a strategy for development directed towards the fulfilment of human needs.

In principle, the process just described would concentrate on finding strategies that would increase the satisfaction of needs of the generations currently present in their society. The processes and outcomes of exploratory or diagnosis-oriented HSD workshops might not seem to imply changes in values, attitudes, organisations, regulations and behaviours that reduce the negative impacts of human activities on the natural environment. However, several studies suggest that through the awareness and understanding that a process of HSD workshops provides, groups of people are able to unveil the articulation of satisfiers that promote both needs fulfilment and a reduced impact on the natural environment (Cuthill 2003; Guillén-Royo 2010, 2012, 2015; Jolibert et al. 2014). This is done either directly, by adapting the HSD methodology to account for sustainable development as a goal (Jolibert et al. 2014) or indirectly, by using the original HSD methodology to identify synergic satisfiers and analysing in a participatory manner their relationship with environmental sustainability (Cuthill 2003; Guillén-Royo 2010).

This chapter discusses the utilisation of HSD workshops to explore avenues for sustainable development at the local level. It reflects on the sequence and dynamics of HSD workshops with regards to The Natural Step framework, a strategy for sustainability planning that takes human needs satisfaction as a guiding principle; and Theory U, a framework used to support sustainable transformations in communities and organisations. It then presents a study of a needs-based planning exercise with stakeholders, that adapts the HSD methodology to support the participatory design of a sustainable scenario for a Belgian region (Jolibert *et al.* 2014). The latter is complemented by the study I carried out in Lleida (Catalonia) in 2009, where HSD workshops with local residents were used following its original design to identify the satisfiers that would contribute to needs fulfilment in the city. The analysis of the set of satisfiers that people considered as contributing to the optimal actualisation of human needs (*singular, synergic* and *synergic bridging satisfiers*) suggests that they are directly or indirectly supporting the emergence of environmentally sustainable societies. I illustrate this point with the example of a *synergic bridging satisfier*, the rationalisation of daily schedules. Both adapting the HSD methodology to target the identification of sustainable policies and using the original approach to identify needs-enhancing satisfiers appear as useful strategies to inform sustainable development policies and processes.

A reflection on the three phases of HSD workshops

In this section, I discuss the HSD methodology with regards to the processes defined in The Natural Step (TNS) framework and Theory U. TNS framework is used to guide strategic planning for sustainability in communities and organisations (Holmberg 1998) and Theory U focusses on the stages of deep learning processes that result in innovations that come from a deep awareness of the future, not of the past. The goal of reflecting on the HSD process with regards to a planning framework and a framework for the generation of sustainable innovations is twofold. First, it highlights the importance of the sequence followed in HSD workshops to arrive at human needs-enhancing solutions. Second, it relates the deliberative process to the quality of the results, which are, arguably, representing a high level of awareness and a deep insight into the interdependent factors influencing the capacity of societies to provide human needs fulfilment.

As described in Chapter 4, the three phases that define exploratory or diagnosis-oriented workshops aim at first identifying negative satisfiers, second suggesting synergic and singular satisfiers and last co-creating strategies to overcome society's challenges, both through endogenous initiatives and with the support of development agents. Table 5.1 below outlines the 4 phases of The Natural Step framework together with the phases of the HSD methodology discussed in Chapter 4, and the ones described in Theory U as necessary to arrive at sustainable solutions (Scharmer 2009).

The Natural Step framework or Framework for Strategic Sustainable Development[1] is a backcasting methodology for strategic planning towards sustainability (Holmberg 1998) popularised by the eco-municipalities movement in Sweden in the nineteen nineties. Backcasting[2], in opposition to the more traditional forecasting, is not based on what is possible or reasonable to achieve in the long term. It is articulated around the generation of images of future scenarios with

Table 5.1 Phases of the Natural Step Framework, Theory U and the HSD methodology

Backasting (from sustainability principles)	Theory U	HSD methodology (as suggested in Chapter 4)
Awareness Baseline mapping	Seeing with fresh eyes and getting rid of old habits	Phase 1: negative synthesis matrix
Awareness and Visioning Creative Solutions	*Presensing*: learning from the emerging future	Phase 2: utopian synthesis matrix
Deciding priorities	Acting in the now: prototyping and exploring new ways of doing things	Phase 3: identifying synergic bridging satisfiers

the help of supporting normative principles or guidelines and the definition of pathways to achieve the desired visions (Carlsson-Kanyama *et al.* 2008: 36). The principles provide the guidelines for a sustainable future and constitute the normative framework for *backcasting* in strategic sustainability planning. They are associated to the requirements of decreasing resource usage, reducing emissions, safeguarding biodiversity and ecosystems, and satisfying fundamental human needs (see Chapter 7 for a more detailed description). In order to articulate *backcasting* exercises drawing on the normative principles of The Natural Step (TNS), Holmberg (1998) suggested following four steps known as the ABCD method that describes a participatory methodology based on Awareness raising, Baseline mapping, facilitating the emergence of Creative solutions and Deciding on priorities and strategies.

Theory U describes the practice and process of generating sustainable strategies from a more conscious and intentional way (Scharmer 2009). It claims that many of the failures to address the current social and environmental challenges stem from the fact that decisions are taken on superficial grounds, without following a process that enables people, communities and organisations to access the 'inner' source or 'blind spot' from which long-term sustainable solutions are created. In order to access the 'inner' source, Scharmer suggests engaging in a learning cycle following a process in three 'movements'. The first consists in opening up and connecting horizontally with people and/or places, the second implies connecting vertically with the deeper sources of 'knowing' and 'self-knowing' and the third is about using the acquired awareness to explore new possibilities (Scharmer 2009, 2010). These processes of deep learning are often experienced by participants in human needs workshops (Cuthill 2003; Guillén-Royo 2010, 2015; Max-Neef 1991; Smith and Max-Neef 2011). Hereafter, I focus in more detail on the parallels between the HSD process, TNS Framework and Theory U process of quality learning using as a starting point the phases of the ABCD method.

In The Natural Step (TNS) framework, A corresponds to *Awareness raising* and it involves the presentation and discussion of the four sustainability principles. In this phase:

participants review the state of the earth's system, including the ecological, social and economic trends that are undermining our ability to create and manage healthy and prosperous ecosystems, businesses and communities, and then place their own organisation, community or project within that context.[3]

Participants appraise their community or their company with regards to the whole socio-economic and natural system in which they operate and through this new awareness, they start to envision new avenues for change. However, as pointed out by the Theory U framework, a greater awareness is not necessarily associated with new or more information but with getting rid or old habits, opening up and connecting with a new way of addressing the challenges at stake. This resonates with the process people engage in in HSD workshops. As participants analyse their society from its capacity to satisfy the nine fundamental needs in their four existential dimensions (being, having, doing and interacting) they discover a 'new way' of looking at problems; they become aware of the interrelated ways of being, having, doing and interacting that are influencing negatively (negative matrix) or positively (utopian matrix) their capacity to meet human needs.

The second step, *Baseline mapping*, is described as an evaluation of the ways current activities of the community or organisation relate to TNS sustainability principles. This involves a thorough analysis of the organisations' activities. Firms would be encouraged to analyse their role as purchasers, resource converters, suppliers and communicators (Holmberg 1998), whereas communities would focus on energy, food, education, health or transportation systems, for example (Phdungsilp 2011). In Table 5.1 Baseline mapping is associated with Phase 1 of the HSD methodology, where negative satisfiers, the ones that hamper needs fulfilment in a given society, are analysed. However, TNS suggests using this phase to also 'look at the social context and organisational culture in order to understand how to positively introduce change'[4] and widens the discussion to include the strengths of the organisation or community that could be used as leverage points to start a potential transformation. This links to what Cruz and colleagues call a *situational human needs matrix*: a matrix that 'represents a given state of affairs or situation, representing the combination of circumstances at a given moment' (Cruz *et al.* 2009: 2025–6). By generating a situational human needs matrix, the problems, obstacles but also the strengths of a group or community would be included in the matrix; giving a more realistic picture of their society than the one represented in the negative matrix. The process of reflecting on the current situation is not necessarily supported by the Theory U framework as it is believed that creative solutions cannot emerge by focussing on the past or the societal, technological or organisational constraints that brought societies or corporations to the current situation.

Designing **Creative solutions** to challenges identified in the previous step through visioning the possibilities of the community or organisation without focussing on current constraints is the third step of TNS backcasting process. As Holmberg (1998: 38) puts it 'the main idea of this step is to free the mind of restrictions set by present circumstances and open the mind for future options'. This is a common step in different backcasting methodologies and it often leads to the construction of scenarios,[5] understood as 'descriptions of possible futures that reflect different perspectives on the past, the present and the future' (Van Notten *et al.* 2003: 424). However, unlike other approaches to backcasting, The Natural Step framework does not aim at the construction of scenarios as

> getting large groups of people to agree on a desired future scenario is often all but impossible – they have too many different perspectives and vested interests. Further, scenarios that are too specific may limit innovation, and distract our minds from the creative solutions needed for sustainable development.[6]

Thus, they recommend backcasting from the four sustainable principles described earlier, among them meeting human needs, and not from a specific scenario detailing the economic, social, technological and environmental characteristics of a future sustainable society as is often the case in sustainability planning (Carlsson-Kanyama *et al.* 2008; Neuvonen *et al.* 2014).

Searching for creative solutions resonates with Phases 2 and 3 of the HSD methodology. When participants discuss and agree on singular and synergic satisfiers for optimal needs actualisation, they are envisioning a specific articulation of satisfiers that is not based on reversing current situations of inequality, poverty, environmental destruction and personal or group marginalisation. Participants are invited to 'dream', to think of singular and synergic satisfiers regardless of their probability to be found in their society in the near future. This collective engagement in the generation of an ideal system of satisfiers is akin to the experience of *presensing* defined by Scharmer (2009) as being present and able to sense or feel the emergence of solutions, which can be achieved through introspection at the personal level and through dialogue and deliberation at the community or group levels. Max-Neef (1991) suggested that participants deliberating on synergic and singular satisfiers in the Utopian matrix, did not have the results of the negative matrix available. This was intended to avoid discussing future possibilities with regards to the problems and challenges of the current socio-economic system. *Presensing* demands looking ahead and creating from the desired future or the future that is emerging when participants explore the personal, economic, technological, cultural and environmental aspects that would enable people to meet human needs.

The last stage in TNS concerns *Deciding on priorities*; on the strategies that will bring the community or the organisation closer to their vision. It is about bridging the current situation defined in step B with the sustainable vision outlined in step C by devising a series of steps or a pathway with a particular timeline where the different drivers and short-term actions that are needed to realise the future are specified. It demands what Theory U calls *acting from the present moment*, where innovation and exploration of new pathways for sustainability are attempted and assessed. This might require being open to make mistakes, to rapidly implement collaborative changes that give immediate feedback and support further learning. In the HSD methodology, this phase is associated with the search for synergic bridging satisfiers, the values, actions, institutions and spaces that will allow people to lift the level of needs fulfilment. However, for a deeper learning process as the one suggested by Scharmer, the identification of synergic bridging satisfiers has to be done in the framework of a development or participatory action research project that implies a long-term commitment with participants and the possibility of learning from the implementation process itself, as Chapter 6 on needs-based Participatory Action Research projects illustrates.

An example of backcasting exercises used to increase environmental sustainability at the local level are the Energy Descent Action Plans (EDAP) carried out by communities in the Transition Town movement. This movement, which will be discussed in more detail in Chapter 7, gathers local communities working to adapt to the challenges of peak oil and climate change at the local level. The 'Energy Descent Action Plans' are generated through participatory backcasting in order to identify the structures and processes that need to be at play for local communities to withstand the effects of environmental degradation (Hopkins 2011). An EDAP provides detailed timelines addressing decarbonisation and localisation of food and education and energy, among other issues, and is commonly created with the involvement of local stakeholders (Hodgson and Hopkins 2010; Hopkins 2013). Both the inclusion of stakeholders and the fact that the visioning and backcasting exercises are initiated by the grassroots have made Energy Descent Action Plans eminently practical (Hopkins 2011). The experience of Totnes (Devon, United Kingdom), the town where the Transition Movement started in 2006, suggests that EDAP are valuable tools to guide both community and council-supported projects towards the sustainable vision envisaged by participants.

To sum up, the sequence of workshops suggested in the HSD methodology reflects the stages of a process to devise sustainable measures such as TNS and engages people in a deep learning journey akin to the one described by Theory U. This suggests that the process of HSD could be easily adapted to frame deliberative exercises aiming at determining specific policies, interventions or personal, social and technological changes in a participatory fashion. Whether the phases and the processes of the HSD methodology ought to be adapted to better suit the goal of achieving a sustainable society, or they can be implemented as represented in Table 5.1 to arrive at *synergic bridging satisfiers* or interventions, is a matter of debate. The next section contributes to this reflection by presenting examples of these two different perspectives.

Devising sustainability measures through needs-based workshops

The goal of HSD workshops is to identify interventions in terms of policies, regulations, collective action or personal transformation that support human needs fulfilment; which is defined as a situation where society is articulated around synergic and singular satisfiers. Max-Neef defined synergic satisfiers as 'those that satisfy a given need, simultaneously stimulating and contributing to the fulfilment of other needs' (Max-Neef 1991: 34). The potential effect on the natural environment of this type of satisfier was not explicitly defined, neither was the fact that it should not have a negative influence on other needs. However, the latter was taken for granted, as harming one need turns a satisfier into a violator, inhibiting or pseudo satisfier.

My experience facilitating HSD workshops in Europe and Peru, together with the results from studies by researchers and students applying the HSD methodology indicates that the process people engage in when participating in needs-based workshops is unlikely to result in a system of satisfiers that is directly harmful to nature (Cuthill 2003; García Norato 2006; Guillén-Royo 2010, 2012, 2014, 2015; Max-Neef 1991; Mitchell 2001). For example, participants in the workshops carried out at the University of Oslo (Norway) with a mix of people with relatively high and relatively low materialist values (see Examples 4.3 and 8.1 in the book for a description of the research) identified 'better transport infrastructures' as a *synergic satisfier* contributing to the needs for subsistence, protection and freedom. 'Better transport infrastructures' included from improving the quality of rural roads to more and better quality cycle lanes and public transport in the city of Oslo. Other interdependent *synergic satisfiers* in the Utopian matrix were 'shortening working times', 'slowing the pace of urbanisation in Oslo' to preserve urban forest and 'generating spaces to devise creative solutions' for the social and environmental challenges affecting society. Thus, although, on its own, 'better transport infrastructures' could be interpreted as a synergic satisfier with potentially negative effects on the environment by encouraging private transportation, the fact that the other singular and synergic satisfiers in the Utopian matrix were associated with the characteristics of low-impact societies suggests that the articulation of satisfiers emerging from the HSD workshop is also environmentally sustainable.

Despite the arguments just outlined and the evidence presented throughout the book on the sustainability of the system of satisfiers emerging from the utopian matrix, researchers and practitioners might still prefer to adapt the HSD methodology to sharpen its focus on sustainability. In the remainder of this section I present two applications that illustrate two of the possible avenues to identify *sustainable satisfiers*. The first adapts the HSD methodology to the specific challenge of creating a needs-based sustainability scenario at the regional level that addresses the conflicts that define the personal, communal and governance dimensions of sustainability. The second uses the three-step HSD methodology described in Table 5.1. It focusses the analysis on the interdependence between human and ecological systems unveiled through the constellation of *synergic* and *singular* satisfiers identified by participants in the Utopian matrix and discusses their sustainability.

Example 5.1 Adapting the HSD methodology to design sustainable scenarios

Jolibert and colleagues (2014) conducted a study with stakeholders involved in an EU-funded project on ecosystem services (EcoChange) aimed at providing 'data, scenarios and associated confidence limits so that policy-makers and land managers can use them for anticipating societal problems and for designing sustainable conservation strategies by accounting the most likely global change effects on biodiversity and ecosystems'[7] in the province of Brabant-Wallon (Belgium).[8] The goal of the study was to investigate the possibility of adapting the HSD approach to apply it in regional planning when constructing a sustainable scenario. The stakeholders invited to participate in the project's workshops were a manager of natural areas, a representative of the tourist sector, a manager of economic development, a farmer, a policy-maker, a forester, a sustainability promoter and a local resident.

The expected output of the study was a sustainable scenario for the region based on the HSD understanding of needs and satisfiers. Researchers were not interested in carrying out a whole backcasting process to identify policies or interventions to advance towards a sustainable society but on presenting a methodology to build sustainable scenarios based on a deep reflection on needs and satisfiers. The authors justified using the HSD approach to human needs in the scenario building process in terms of the centrality of the concept of needs for sustainable development as understood in the Brundtland report[9] (WCED 1987). In addition, they maintained that a needs-based planning process 1) 'helps to foster long-term regional planning by creating more dynamic interactions between stakeholders for social change', and 2) 'highlights not only society's fundamental sameness but also the conflicts that arise between competing values and strategies that can be staged through a scenario' (Jolibert *et al.* 2014: 30–31). Thus, a needs-based scenario methodology was considered to have synergic effects in itself by creating a climate of trust where dynamic interactions between participants were promoted, and by enabling consensus after competing values and perspectives were shared and discussed.

The participatory process organised by the researchers with the eight stakeholders from the Brabant-Wallon region in Belgium was carried out in an afternoon workshop articulated around four phases. As described in Chapter 4, the first was informative and participants were briefed on the EcoChange project and the objectives of building the needs-based scenario. The second revolved around the nine fundamental needs that participants would analyse individually (as citizens but also as representatives of their occupational activity) in order to identify satisfiers that would be required to achieve sustainability in the province by 2050. The third phase involved choosing two of the satisfiers identified individually and sharing them with the other stakeholders in order to, in the fourth phase, jointly generate a list of sustainable satisfiers that would integrate the sustainable scenario. This last phase addressed conflict between satisfiers, as some of the ones suggested by stakeholders were divergent (such as protecting local shops vs attracting new external businesses). But by having the opportunity to discuss the synergic character of individual satisfiers collectively, stakeholders could find common grounds to reach consensus. The resulting collective satisfiers were classified into eight categories (population and lifestyle, economic development, energy tourism, spatial development, environment, transport and mobility, agriculture and forest) and constituted the sustainable scenario for the region in 2050.

Jolibert and colleagues adapted the HSD methodology and conceptualisation of satisfiers to work with stakeholders, commonly understood as 'any group or individual who can affect or is affected by the achievement of the organization's objectives' (Freeman 1984: 48). They used the concepts of *divergent* versus *convergent* and *individual* versus *collective* satisfiers. *Individual satisfiers* were the ones each stakeholder identifies as meeting their personal needs and they may accord or not with those of other group members. *Collective satisfiers* were the ones finally included in the scenario for the region and were arrived at in Phase 4 'after an open discussion in which stakeholders were asked to reformulate their individual satisfiers so that they were *less divergent* with those of other group members' (Jolibert *et al.* 2014: 40). In addition to individual, collective, divergent and convergent satisfiers, the authors also used the concept of *sustainable satisfier* defined as a satisfier that 'meets one or several needs without impeding others needs being satisfied, or other living beings from meeting their own needs'.

This alternative conceptualisation of satisfiers recognises the often conflicting values of stakeholders and their *a priori* reluctance to discuss sustainable futures in a participatory manner with people that they might perceive as adversaries. The fact that participants are given time to reflect on their *individual satisfiers* for a sustainable scenario makes them involved in the deliberative process at their own pace and might make it easy for them to be open about their values and perspectives at later stages. It might also allow stakeholders to approach a vision of a sustainable future in terms of needs and satisfiers and not only in terms of regulation and technical innovations. This first individual phase is common in participative backcasting for sustainability and has been reported to improve the experience of participating in deliberative workshops (Carlsson-Kanyama *et al.* 2008). The next phase makes people aware of the interdependences and potential conflicts between individual satisfiers. The collective task of reform-ulating individual satisfiers to find *convergent satisfiers* is quite likely to unleash the synergic effect of the participatory process tapping into the needs for understanding, participation, creation, and identity among others.

The final scenario contains both *singular* (they satisfy the need they are meant to satisfy) and *synergic* (they satisfy more than one need) satisfiers, which in addition are *convergent* (because they have been identified in a process targeting consensus) and *sustainable* (because both at the individual and collective level satisfiers were identified with the goal of sustainability in mind – not impeding the satisfaction of any need now and in the future). The satisfiers that constituted the sustainable scenario for Brabant-Wallon in 2050 ranged from 'social and environmental consciousness' to 'restoration of extinct fruits and vegetables' (Jolibert et al. 2014: 41). In essence, they comprised satisfiers that, following the HSD methodology described in Table 5.1, would be included in the utopian matrix and/or as *synergic bridging satisfiers*; since many of them were specific enough to become regulations or concrete policies.

The methodology suggested by Jolibert and colleagues brings the HSD proposal close to the logic of planning authorities focussed on resolving conflicts of interest and addressing specific goals such as environmental sustainability. The fact of including an individual phase, giving space for participants to reflect on needs and satisfiers on their own terms, is an interesting addition to the approach. It facilitates a connection with one's values and experiences of needs actualisation before sharing them with the community, which was not explicitly contemplated in the original approach to the HSD methodology.

Example 5.2 Using HSD workshops to unveil the interdependence of need satisfiers and environmental sustainability

In 2009, I undertook an exploratory exercise in Lleida,[10] a medium-sized city in Catalonia, aiming at 1) studying the role of sustainable consumption as a human needs satisfier and 2) identifying policies or interventions towards a low-carbon society (Guillén-Royo 2010). The study was organised in three phases following the HSD methodology captured in Table 5.1 but time was allocated in the last part of each workshop to reflect on current patterns of consumption and their relationship with needs and satisfiers (see Examples 4.2 and 4.3 for a description of the workshop dynamics and the recruitment process). After the first and second phases a negative matrix with violators, pseudo and inhibiting satisfiers and a utopian matrix with singular and synergic satisfiers were obtained. The third phase resulted in the identification of *synergic bridging satisfiers* that were meant to advance their society towards the utopian scenario. The 47 residents engaged in the workshops were between 16 and 64 years of age, mostly women (62 per cent), employed (57 per cent) and with secondary (47 per cent) or higher education (32 per cent). The sample was by no means intended to represent the views of the city's population but geographical and socio-economic diversity was sought with participants coming from nine of the 12 districts in the city.

Figure 5.1 below presents the categories that I used to summarise the satisfiers in the synthesis negative and utopian matrices and the discussion in Phase 3. A detailed description of the satisfiers included under these categories can be found in Guillén-Royo (2010). In general, participants in the first phase agreed on several *violators*, *inhibiting* and *pseudo satisfiers* that were making it difficult for citizens to actualise human needs in Lleida. Complexity and confusion, isolation and individualism and time pressure are the categories that I used to capture the essence of the harmful satisfiers agreed on by participants. Specifically, they discussed the negative effects of the lack of transparency on needs in public

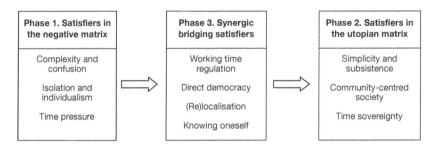

Phase 1. Satisfiers in the negative matrix	Phase 3. Synergic bridging satisfiers	Phase 2. Satisfiers in the utopian matrix
Complexity and confusion	Working time regulation	Simplicity and subsistence
Isolation and individualism	Direct democracy	Community-centred society
Time pressure	(Re)localisation	Time sovereignty
	Knowing oneself	

Figure 5.1 Summary of negative, utopian and synergic bridging satisfiers in Lleida
Source: Adapted from Guillén-Royo (2010)

institutions, lack of trustworthy information from media, excessive bureaucracy, feelings of being trapped or 'locked-in', unsustainable consumption practices, individualism, decline in social interaction, and long and irrational working hours. Those who joined the second phase of the project discussed the synergic effects of satisfiers such as relocalising production activities and decision making, supporting organic and local agricultural production, slowing the pace of everyday activities, achieving work-life balance, experiencing simple living and having universal basic need coverage. I categorised these and other singular and synergic satisfiers included in the utopian matrix as simplicity and subsistence, community-centred society and time sovereignty.

Sustainable consumption (both in terms of consumption of less material or resource intensive products and in terms of lower levels of consumption in general) emerged as a synergic satisfier contributing to the needs for subsistence, protection, understanding and identity. A transformation of consumption patterns was linked to more consumption of local food, energy savings from transporting less food from outside the region and a reduced use of chemicals in agriculture; since organic products were preferred over non-organic. The rationalisation of working times that would reduce the need for commuting at lunchtime would also contribute to sustainability through a lower use of public and private transportation in the middle of the day. The interconnectedness among satisfiers and between them and human needs made explicit during discussions, was also making people aware of the synergies between human wellbeing and the preservation of the natural environment.

The transformations required to advance towards a utopian society, characterised among other things by sustainable consumption patterns were discussed in the workshops organised in the third phase of the study. Regarding *exogenous* and *synergic bridging satisfiers*, participants considered that it was necessary to implement regulations at the state level to increase flexibility in the workplace and to give employees the possibility of deciding their working times together with employers. They also agreed on the need to change democratic participation from representative to direct democracy at the state, autonomous community and municipal levels so people would be consulted more often over issues that directly influence their quality of life. Interlinked with mechanisms to reduce time pressure and increase political participation were demands for a better city planning that maintained the connectedness of the city with its farming and agricultural surroundings through the protection of its agricultural land.

In addition to exogenous synergic bridging satisfiers participants also discussed strategies that had to be initiated from the local community or by people themselves. They considered that 'understanding and accepting who one was, breaking with materialist aspirations and getting rid of personal fears were necessary steps prior to any organised move' (Guillén-Royo 2010). Knowing oneself, is one of the most synergic satisfiers, in Max-Neef's own words, as he thinks of it as the first step towards personal change and consequently towards systemic transformations (Max-Neef 1991: 113). Participants understood that broader changes would occur if people actively engaged in activism. Although getting involved in activism was considered a synergic satisfier by most participants, younger participants perceived that grassroots movements at the time did not have any possibility to fight the current economic and political structures.[11]

It is quite likely that authorities in charge of local sustainability policy would not be interested in the results of a HSD exercise such as the one carried out in Lleida. Most of the *synergic satisfiers* featuring in the utopian matrix and the *synergic bridging satisfiers* co-generated in the last phase of the study concerned political, economic, cultural, infrastructural and technological features of their society that, on their own, might not look to be of direct relevance for the natural environment. However the in-depth reflections that participants engaged in during HSD workshops made it possible to visualise the interdependence of synergic satisfiers and the natural environment. For example, in Lleida, increasing political participation through direct democracy institutions appears to be linked to narrowing the gap between consumers and farmers; which has a great potential to reduce CO_2 emissions from production and distribution activities. Nevertheless, promoting the consumption of local produce is currently done through labelling and information campaigns and does not address larger issues of participation. In Catalonia, the label 'venda de proximitat'[12] (sale of local produce) identifies local agricultural or farming products that have gone through a maximum of one intermediary. The interdependences unveiled by the HSD workshops suggest that this measure is not likely to change the consumption patterns of people who, as it emerged in the workshops, feel trapped in a bureaucratic, non-transparent and individualistic society. Unless their opinions are heard, and this is usually more likely to happen when consultations are held frequently, top-down measures to increase the environmental sustainability of consumption practices in Lleida might not be perceived as part of a process to enhance the quality of life of its residents.

Synergic satisfiers as sustainable satisfiers: discussing time sovereignty in Lleida

Long working hours and irrational timetables described as a two-hour lunch break and late evening meals were appraised as *violators* or *destroyers* by residents in

Lleida. As outlined earlier, they were interlinked with a series of negative satisfiers that represented a situation in which neither human needs nor ecological sustainability were promoted. People discussing synergic and singular satisfiers underlined the importance of increasing one's control over daily schedules, changing to lifestyles characterised by simplicity and guaranteed subsistence and promoting a closer connection between local farmers and consumers. Participants considered that for optimal needs actualisation their relationship with time needed to change in two specific dimensions. The first was related to the pace and tempo at which everyday activities were carried out. The second, interlinked with the above, concerned the rationalisation of working times and the flexibilisation of work schedules. This required generalising flexi-time in the workplace, harmonising school and work schedules and ending with the long lunch break around 2pm. The latter was particularly detrimental for working mothers as the long lunch break often implied a ride home in the middle of the working day to prepare food and eat with the family.

As the consolidated utopian matrix generated by participants in the HSD workshops suggests (see Table 5.2 below), time sovereignty and a slower daily pace are synergic satisfiers with a positive direct effect on the needs for protection, affection idleness and creation. In addition, less time pressure is expected to give space for the emergence of intuition and enable downshifting and simplifying one's life, thus adding to the actualisation of the need for understanding and reducing the environmental impact from consumerism. A 9 to 5 working day was also claimed to free time from the daily midday commute and to enable people to spend more time in their neighbourhoods, volunteer more and get involved in civil society organisations. This would most likely contribute to fulfil the need for participation while reducing emissions from avoiding the midday commute. By promoting participation, the need for identity would also be enhanced and by having time to simplify one's life people will feel freer because they will experience less pressure to consume.

Among the synergic bridging satisfiers discussed in Lleida, a new working time regulation stayed central. This is now campaigned for by the civil society organisation 'Iniciativa per a la reforma horària'[13] (initiative for timetable reform) launched in January 2014 after a decade of lobbying against the current timetables in the Catalan society. This grassroots organisation is advocating for two interlinked changes in the way time is organised in the Catalan society. The first relates to the time zone, since due to their geographical location Catalonia and Spain should have Western European time as do Portugal and the UK. The second concerns changing the structures that articulate daily routines around long working days and late-night dinners, which resonates with the suggestions of workshop participants.

To date, the initiative has got the support of different local and provincial public institutions in Catalonia. They have succeeded in establishing a working commission in the Catalan parliament that from June 2014 has been discussing shorter working days and opening hours in retail, synchronising school and parents' timetables, putting forward prime television times and committing

Table 5.2 Consolidated positive matrix in Lleida

	BEING	HAVING	DOING	INTERACTING
SUBSISTENCE	Modesty, solidarity	Participatory democracy, communal property, basic needs coverage	Protection of local agriculture, sharing, working, providing basic income for the needy	Proper housing, integrated hospital care, dividing the city into smaller units
PROTECTION	Self-confidence and trusting others	Time and space for ourselves, guaranteed subsistence, understanding of relationship with nature, real information	Civic education	Civic-mindedness and civic education, time and space for quietness
AFFECTION	Understanding, openness, simplicity, proximity, solidarity	Work with one's inner self/spirituality, time, non-materialist values	Time to devote to others, promote the community, being exposed to contact with others	Time and space for relatedness
UNDERSTANDING	Perspective, transparency, objectivity, communication	Real information, plural education, possibility of seeing one's community from the outside, empathy	Promoting intuition, ourselves and others, simplifying life, valuing people for what they are	Subsistence society, transparency

PARTICIPATION	Gratification, willing, generosity	Direct participation, open ballots, simplicity, proximity of institutions, education focussed on promoting participation	Education promoting participation, supporting initiative	Citizens-administration interaction, proper leisure centres
IDLENESS	Simplicity, curiosity, understanding	Rational working times, less distractions such as TV	Maintain and respect facilities, promoting leisure activities in the districts	Treating public spaces as private, free activities for young people
CREATION	Acceptance, inclusion of different generations, cooperation, no expectations	Education policy that promotes creativity, work flexibility, basic needs guaranteed, time for chilling out, non-materialist goals	Inform and promote creative activities	Flexible timetables of courses and centres
IDENTITY	Respect, acceptance, tolerance, self-esteem, conscious of and knowledgeable about one's identity	Culture, knowledge, education that explains diversity, tolerance, participatory society	Promoting the community, getting involved, respecting	Public spaces of tolerance
FREEDOM	Tolerance, acceptance, honesty with oneself and others, fearlessness	Few needs, safety, education promoting tolerance and respect	Knowing, trusting, understanding, respecting	Spaces of respect, Public security

Source. Adapted from Guillén-Royo (2010)

employers to flexi-time and telework. The initiative has stressed the synergic role that more rational timetables would have in terms of health, leisure, the general pace in society, civic engagement, productivity at work and family relationships, among other socio-economic and wellbeing enhancing factors. The positive environmental effects of a timetable rationalisation have also been touched upon, although mainly focussed on the reduction in the emissions of greenhouse gases from the promotion of telework.

It is not common to consider addressing daily schedules as a sustainable policy as the latter is mainly concerned with abating pollution, promoting sustainable transport and sustainable production processes and encouraging renewable energy options[14]. However, there have been experiences of 'municipal time offices' in Germany and Italy during the 1990s trying to coordinate opening hours of key municipal institutions such as libraries and schools with public transport schedules and people's working hours (Reisch 2001) that despite their relevance for sustainability have not spread to Catalonia or Spain. As in the example of labelling locally produced food, acting on time sovereignty alone, it is unlikely to enhance both human needs and the natural environment because it does not account for its interdependent satisfiers. Participants in HSD workshops indicated that the fact of having more time away from work would not automatically make people relate, participate, use their free time to relax, to create, to get rid of consumerist pressures or to engage in nature conservation activities. Deeper changes in people's values were required and these demanded a greater focus on creativity instead of productivity at school, the availability of spaces and structures for civic engagement and the reduction of the amount of advertising, among other measures.

Understanding the set of interdependent singular and synergic satisfiers that constitute a scenario where needs are optimally actualised seems to be central in order to advance towards sustainable societies. More rational working times and time sovereignty might not initially qualify for the label of sustainable satisfiers (they could hypothetically give rise to more energy consuming activities for example). However, when they are implemented together with the set of synergic satisfiers that have emerged from HSD workshops they might contribute to a sustainable articulation capable of generating sharp reductions in carbon emissions and supporting the regeneration of local ecosystems. This suggests that drawing on the original HSD methodology can, by unveiling a system of interdependent synergic satisfiers contributing to human needs actualisation, be a helpful tool in exploring avenues for sustainable development.

Conclusion

This chapter has discussed how needs-based workshops can contribute to the identification of measures that support sustainable development processes. It started by comparing the original HSD methodology with The Natural Step framework and the stages of the deep learning process described by Theory U. The analysis indicated that the sequence and characteristics of HSD workshops, together with the quality of the satisfiers that emerge after each of the three phases, justifies using the HSD approach as a tool to support communities in the co-generation of sustainable development measures. However, whether the HSD methodology initially designed to identify needs-enhancing measures had to be adapted to specifically target environmental sustainability, or whether it could be used as originally proposed to arrive at satisfiers that were both synergic and sustainable, had yet to be investigated.

The first example from a study by Jolibert and colleagues in the Belgian province of Brabant-Wallon adapted the original HSD methodology to design, with the participation of local stakeholders, a sustainable scenario for the region. After a deliberative process that included time and space for an individual reflection on satisfiers, participants arrived at *sustainable convergent synergic* or *singular satisfiers*. These were defined as not hampering the fulfilment of any human need now and in the future following the definition of sustainable development in the Brundtland report (WCED 1987). Satisfiers addressed from issues of population and lifestyle such as 'social and environmental consciousness' and maintaining 'social protection' to issues of agriculture and forestry concerning 'sustainable timber production' and 'shorter production and sales chains', for example. The fact that the satisfiers obtained contained implicit recommendations for policy at different levels of governance (local, regional and national) suggested that the authors' adaptation of the HSD methodology could be easily adopted by policy planners to improve sustainable regional development.

The second example included in the chapter analysed the processes and outcomes of HSD workshops carried out in Lleida (Catalonia) with local residents with the aim of identifying endogenous and exogenous synergic bridging satisfiers. The *singular* and *synergic satisfiers* that integrated the utopian matrix unveiled the interdependent social, economic and environmental factors that would enable optimal satisfaction of needs in Lleida. The *synergic bridging satisfiers* that participants considered to be taking their society closer to needs fulfilment, pointed to measures and interventions that, although not always directly linked to environmental sustainability, if jointly implemented would enhance both human needs and the natural environment. This was illustrated through the example of the synergic bridging satisfier 'time sovereignty' that involved the rationalisation of timetables in their society and the flexibilisation of working times. This was meant to reduce emissions from the midday commute and from the slower pace that, as a consequence of timetable reforms, the whole society would experience. However, as participants in HSD workshops pointed out, achieving 'time sovereignty' will not by itself imply a transformation of unsustainable consumption patterns unless the interdependent satisfiers that constitute the utopian matrix are also present in their society.

Both adapting the HSD methodology to specifically target the goal of achieving sustainable development and using the original HSD methodology to map the local constellation of needs-enhancing satisfiers appear as useful strategies to inform sustainable development policies and processes. The former will result in policy recommendations that have been appraised as convergent, agreed by different stakeholders, sustainable, meeting the needs of present and future generations, and needs enhancing. The latter will enable a deeper insight into the interlinked personal, social, technological and economic transformations that are needed if their society is to advance towards sustainable development.

Arguably, a combination of the two approaches could appeal to policy-makers interested in addressing the root causes of unsustainable practices. The needs-based approach to scenario building developed by Jolibert and colleagues could be used to analyse sustainable development policies with stakeholders while the traditional HSD workshops with residents would capture the interdependent singular and synergic satisfiers that constitute optimal needs actualisation. Participants in community workshops could join stakeholder workshops representing 'residents' and contribute to the discussion on convergent sustainable satisfiers with institutional representatives and policy-makers. This would bring the debate on sustainable satisfiers closer to the discussion at the grassroots and would enhance its achievement through a discussion on the synergic bridging satisfiers or policy measures arrived at by the community.

Finally, an alternative approach to sustainable development policy, more in line with the grassroots-oriented goal of HSD would be to identify, after HSD workshops with local people or stakeholders, those grassroots initiatives that are already campaigning for the realisation of *synergic* or *bridging synergic satisfiers*. In Catalonia, this would imply, for example, supporting the activities of the 'Initiative for timetable reform', which national institutions have done by endorsing the creation of a parliamentary commission to discuss the rationalisation of timetables and a new working time regulation. Other grassroots organisations campaigning for the *synergic* or *synergic bridging satisfiers* identified by participants in Lleida are also operating. An example is the 'Process Constituent'[15] (Constitutional Process) advocating for direct democracy institutions that allow Catalan citizens to give their opinion on important political, social and environmental issues such as the ones concerning food sovereignty, the use of fossil-fuels in public transport and the dominance of unsustainable production processes in the economy. Drawing on the HSD methodology to understand the interdependent satisfiers that support optimal needs fulfilment and environmental sustainability and then support grassroots movements engaged in the implementation of synergic satisfiers resonate with the bottom-up approach implicit in the HSD proposal. However, as I discuss in Chapters 2 and 8, it might not accord with the way sustainable policies and policy-making are currently articulated at the national and international levels.

Notes

1 More information about The Natural Step framework is available at www.naturalstep.org/the-system-conditions, accessed 5 February 2015.
2 Backcasting methods have been commonly used to address sustainability regarding transportation systems, regional planning and corporate strategies but it is increasingly applied to investigate pathways to low-carbon lifestyles (Neuvonen *et al.* 2014).
3 www.naturalstep.org/en/abcd-process, accessed 7 April 2015.
4 www.naturalstep.org/en/abcd-process, accessed 7 April 2015.

5 Scenarios have been used for learning and communication to orient decisions for military-strategic planning, private organisations and public policy, e.g. during the 1970s, the Royal Dutch Shell company performed pioneering work in scenario building (Jolibert *et al.* 2014: 35).
6 www.thenaturalstep.org/sustainability/backcasting/
7 The quote defining the Eco-Change project is taken from the following webpage: http://ecochange.vitamib.com/news/ecochange-final-conference/genereal-information (accessed 14 April 2015).
8 More information about the Eco-Change project can be found in their website, www.ecochange-project.eu/, accessed 29 January 2015.
9 The report 'Our common future' by The World Commission on Environment and Development (WCED) presented to the UN General Assembly in 1987 defines sustainable development as 'development that meets the needs of the present without compromising the ability of future generations to meet their own needs' (WCED 1987: 43).
10 Lleida is a medium sized city in the west of Catalonia with a population of around 140,000 people. Lleida has a relatively high GDP per capita (126, EU-27=100) compared to the average in Catalonia (122) and Spain (104). The relative wealth of the city and its geographical and economic characteristics as the service centre of a relatively prosperous farming region are related to consumption and production practices typical of western societies with high levels of waste, intense use of private transportation and a high level of energy use (Guillén-Royo 2010).
11 Workshops were carried out in May 2009, a year after the economic crisis was first felt in the country. In May 2011 many local youngsters joined the protests of the 'indignados' ('the outraged') in Spain, setting up a campsite in one of the main squares in Lleida. The 'indignados' or 'indignats' movement was very diverse, among their demands were: bringing to a halt the austerity measures that were negatively affecting education and health services; increasing participation of civil society in political decisions; and in Lleida, supporting the right to self-determination of the Catalan people.
12 The government of Catalonia has a webpage informing about the 'venda de proximitat' scheme (in Catalan), http://agricultura.gencat.cat/ca/ambits/alimentacio/venda-proximitat/, accessed 3 March 2015.
13 The website of the grassroots organisation for a timetable reform is the following (in Catalan) www.reformahoraria.cat/, accessed 11 April 2015.
14 Information about the areas of intervention of the sustainability department of the Catalan government is available (in Catalan) at http://mediambient.gencat.cat/ca, accessed 15 April 2015.
15 Information about the Constituent process in Catalonia is available here, www.proces constituent.cat/ca/english, accessed 14 April 2015.

References

Carlsson-Kanyama, A., Dreborg, K. H., Moll, D. H. and Padovan, D. (2008). Participative backcasting: A tool for involving stakeholders in local sustainability planning. *Futures*, 40(1): 34–46.
Cruz, I., Stahel, A. and Max-Neef, M. (2009). Towards a systemic development approach: Building on the Human Scale Development paradigm. *Ecological Economics*, 68: 2021–30.
Cuthill, M. (2003). From here to utopia: Running a Human-scale Development workshop on the Gold Coast, Australia. *Local Environment*, 8(4): 471–85.
Freeman, R. E. (1984). *Strategic Management: A Stakeholder Approach*. Boston: Pitman.

Guillén-Royo, M. (2010). Realising the 'wellbeing dividend': An exploratory study using the Human Scale Development approach. *Ecological Economics*, 70: 384–93.

Guillén-Royo, M. (2012). The challenge of transforming consumption patterns: A proposal using the Human Scale Development approach. In Bjørkdahl, K. and Nielsen, K. B. (eds), *Development and the Environment. Practices, Theories, Policies*. Oslo: Akademika Publishing, pp. 99–118.

Guillén-Royo, M. (2014). Economic growth and human needs satisfaction across socio economic groups in Peru: An illustration using the Human Scale Development approach. Fourth International Degrowth Conference for Ecological Sustainability and Social Equity, Leipzig (Germany), 2–6 September.

Guillén-Royo, M. (2015). Human needs and the environment reconciled: Participatory action-research for sustainable development in Peru. In Syse, K. and Mueller, M. (eds), *Sustainability and the Good Life*. Oxford: Routledge.

Hodgson, J. and Hopkins, R. (2010). *Transition in Action: Totnes and District 2030: An Energy Descent Action Plan*. Scripted and edited by J. Hodgson and R. Hopkins. Totnes, UK: Green Books.

Holmberg, J. (1998). Backcasting: A natural step in operationalising sustainable development. *Greener Management International*, 23: 30–51.

Hopkins, R. (2011). *The Transition Companion*. Cambridge: Green Books.

Hopkins, R. (2013). *The Power of Just Doing Stuff*. Cambridge: Green Books.

Jolibert, C., Paavola, J. and Rauschmayer, F. (2014). Addressing needs in the search for sustainable development: A proposal for needs-based scenario building. *Environmental Values* 23: 29–50.

Max-Neef, M. (1991). *Human Scale Development: Conception, Application and Further Reflection*. London: Apex Press.

Mitchell, J. A. (2001). Propuesta metodológica en el diseño de un asentamiento humano en una zona rural del centro oeste de la República Argentina. *La casa de América*, pp. 209–39 (ISBN-970-694-063-4).

Neuvonen, A., Kaskinen, T., Leppänen, J., Lähteenoja, S., Mokka, R. and Ritola, M. (2014). Low-carbon futures and sustainable lifestyles: A backcasting scenario approach. *Futures*, 58(0): 66–76.

Phdungsilp, A. (2011). Futures studies' backcasting method used for strategic sustainable city planning. *Futures*, 43(7): 707–14.

Reisch, L. A. (2001). Time and wealth: The role of time and temporalities for sustainable patterns of consumption. *Time and Society*, 10(2/3): 367–85.

Scharmer, C. O. (2009). *Theory U: Leading from the Future as it Emerges. The Social Technology of Presencing*. San Francisco, CA: Berrett-Koehler.

Scharmer, C. O. (2010). The blind spot of institutional leadership: how to create deep innovation through moving from egosystem to ecosystem awareness. Paper prepared for the World Economic Forum. Annual meeting of the new champions, Tiajin, People's Republic of China, 13–15 September.

Smith, B. P. and Max-Neef, M. (2011). *Economics Unmasked. From Power and Greed to Compassion and the Common Good*. Cambridge: Green Books.

van Notten, P. W. F., Rotmans, J., van Asselt, M. B. A. and Rothman, D. S. (2003). An updated scenario typology. *Futures*, 35: 423–43.

WCED (World Commission on Environment and Development) (1987). *Our Common Future*. Oxford: Oxford University Press.

6 Engaging with communities
Human scale development-based participatory action research

Introduction

Human Scale Development (HSD) relies on people's participation in every stage of the development process. This implies that researchers and practitioners interested in using the HSD framework would be expected to engage with communities or groups in a horizontal manner and not focus on prescribing solutions as in traditional expert-user relationships. Personal involvement is particularly important when addressing strategies for sustainable development as they usually imply a set of interdependent individual and societal transformations that can neither be identified nor implemented from a detached position. Reproducing Garmendia and Stagl's argument when discussing public participation for sustainability in Europe: 'when facts are uncertain, values in dispute, stakes are high and decisions urgent, scientists can provide useful input only by interacting with the rest of society' (Garmendia and Stagl 2010: 172). Horizontal researcher–participant relationships characterise Participatory Action Research (PAR) designs in the social sciences. These are approaches to research and practice based on collaboration at the many stages of a study or policy-making process including the diagnosis of problems, design of solutions, implementation and evaluation of strategies or programmes (Reason and Bradbury 2008).

This chapter argues that PAR is the most suitable research design for researchers willing to study HSD processes. It links with discussions in Chapters 3, 4 and 8 on participation and presents the characteristics, strengths and weaknesses of participatory methodologies addressing one of its most common critiques: the reproduction, exacerbation and generation of power imbalances (Cooke and Kothari 2004a; Cornwall 2011). It also touches on the use of PAR perspectives in adult education programmes aiming at empowering marginalised groups and communities. Adult education is a central topic in the sustainable development debate. It is included in one of the UN Sustainable Development Goals (SDGs) as life-long learning but it is often understood by more radical educators as a participatory process with a problem-solving orientation and an empowering potential (Morgan 2009). The latter perspective resonates with the example included in this chapter of a PAR study in Acostambo, a rural municipality in the Peruvian Andes. The adults' education initiative in Acostambo was started together with an organic vegetable gardens project (Guillén-Royo 2015) that had been identified by participants as having synergic effects on human needs. A participatory and desk analysis of the PAR project suggests a positive contribution to human needs through increased knowledge and social cohesion, and to environmental sustainability through new organic agricultural practices and a greater respect for the environment in the community (Guillén-Royo 2015).

Participatory Action Research: opportunities and limitations

Participatory Action Research (PAR) can be described as an 'inquiry that is done by or with insiders to an organisation or community, but never to or on them' (Herr and Anderson 2005: 3). This is a general definition that agrees with most approaches to PAR in the social sciences as it stresses collaboration and horizontal relationships. In development studies, PAR is often associated with research on inequality, marginalisation, oppression and poverty. This stresses the empowering potential of the methodology, describing it as a combination of academic research, adult education and political action through a participatory methodology that enables the poor and marginalised to become the main actors in their own development process (Fals Borda 1987).

Participatory approaches in development emerged when it became evident that decades of development work had not managed to change the power structures that maintained the poor and marginalised in their positions. Until the nineteen seventies, development practice had drawn on the conceptualisation of issues such as poverty, nutrition, health and education done by outside experts that were in charge of proposing solutions and ways of action often dissociated from the realities of the people concerned (Rahnema 1990). Regardless of whether this approach to development was based on the substitution of industrial inputs or on exporting primary goods, the progressive implantation of industrial activities was seen by donors and international organisations as the only way to improve the material conditions of the poor (Sachs 1992). Such an understanding of development stressed what people were lacking, and did not take into account their capacity, knowledge or potential to design their own strategies for personal and social progress.

This approach to development based on a linear connection between economic growth and poverty reduction was discussed in Chapter 3 under the 'trickle down' effect. It follows the tenets of the positivist paradigm in economics based on objective truths, causal relationships and the belief in value-free inquiry (Wicks *et al.* 2008; Tashakkori and Teddlie 1998). Contrary to positivist approaches to science that believe in the existence of a single reality that is best studied through detachment and independent analysis, proponents of participatory development adopted a research paradigm close to constructivism; where it is no longer possible for researchers to detach themselves from the reality and the people they are investigating. As Fals Borda put it: 'to participate means to break up voluntarily and through experience the asymmetrical relationship of submission and dependence implicit in the subject/object binomial' (Fals Borda 1987: 332). This subject/object or expert/user binomial can be broken by the researcher/practitioner

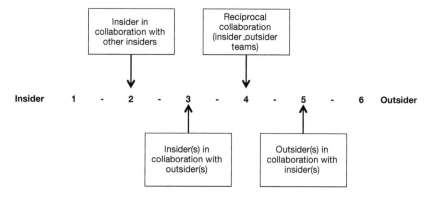

Figure 6.1 Continuum of positionality in research
Source: Adapted from Herr and Anderson (2005)

taking a position closer to participants. Following Herr and Anderson's *continuum of positionality* represented in Figure 6.1, participatory development would entail moving from a situation in which researchers are complete outsiders in their relationship with participants (position 6) to a situation where they get closer to a reciprocal collaboration (position 4) or even to a collaboration led by insiders (position 3).

Participation, action research or action science and participatory action research are terms that have often been used interchangeably.[1] However, there are differences between them (Herr and Anderson 2005). While traditional action research is more concerned with increasing the efficiency and sustainability of organisational practices; participatory research stresses the role of equity, self-reliance and power struggles. Hence, the former concentrates on specific problems that affect an organisation or community, while the latter undertakes a wider scrutiny of the structures in a society. These differences relate with the disciplinary interests of the scholars behind the development of PAR who specialised in topics such as organisational learning, adult literacy, health prevention and rural development. Thus, one could argue that PAR builds on both traditions. On the one hand it is concerned with the socio-economic and political imbalances affecting some groups or organisations. On the other hand it is committed to support, through the direct involvement of the practitioner or researcher and the use of participatory methodologies and the design and implementation of measures to reverse unjust situations.

Action research in organisations

The development of PAR as an alternative approach to social research in the seventies and eighties relates to earlier work on organisational learning and education by Kurt Lewin in the US and Paulo Freire in Latin America.

Behavioural psychologist Kurt Lewin (1946) proposed that knowledge should be created by engaging in problem-solving and studying the process itself. His perspectives were widely applied in the US as a strategy to involve workers in the design of organisational solutions but they were soon criticised as consultants used them as a mere efficiency exercise. Drawing on Lewin's work but expanding on the underlying causes of organisational problems, Argyris argued that organisational learning required an increased collaboration and connectedness across the organisation (Argyris *et al.* 1985). Through workers' and managers' participation in problem-solving processes, organisational learning would be produced and unwanted situations could be confronted. Key in Argyris' work is the belief that change cannot happen without challenging the values and assumptions that maintain the status quo. It is not problem-solving that is the core of Argyris' action science, but the understanding that internalised practices have led to the current situation and that there will not be a lasting solution without a deconstruction of these practices (Herr and Anderson 2005). When underlying values and assumptions are changed, learning becomes double-loop, compared to traditional single-loop learning based on the individual ownership and management of knowledge (Argyris and Schön 1974).

Drawing on Lewin's and Argyris' work but expanding it to account for a wide array of theories from evolutionary economics to socio-technical approaches together with critical approaches to power, action researchers have engaged in the study of sustainability transitions in business. A good example is Reason and colleagues' project *Lowcarbonworks* aiming at understanding the actions of people involved in firms that adopt low carbon technologies (Reason *et al.* 2009: 9). By working closely with people involved in six different organisations through periodical visits to engage in everyday activities and meetings, formal interviews and the creation of special events such as workshops and conferences, the researchers reflected together with participants on their experiences with low carbon transitions. The goal was identifying in a collaborative way the lessons that could be learnt from their projects and supporting them by making participants aware of their internal processes, providing them with tools to enhance conversation and collaboration, and uncovering distortions between intention and action. After the five-year study, researchers concluded that to facilitate the development of low carbon solutions in corporations, 'enabling environments' or spaces within organisations where dialogue and coalition building are encouraged were more important than specific carbon saving technologies or other technical solutions.

PAR in development studies

Participatory development became popular in the nineteen seventies through two interrelated strands of inquiry; the first focussing on learning and marginalised populations and the second linking academic research with participatory rural development. An overview of the strands and characteristics of the participatory development and PAR movements is far beyond the scope of this section. An extensive introduction to participatory and action research covering its influence in Africa, Asia and Latin America can be found in Reason and Bradbury's (2008) edited book; particularly in chapter 2 by Marja Liisa Swantz, Chapter 3 by Anisur Rahman and Chapter 20 by Robert Chambers. As the HSD proposal was developed as a reaction to the frustration generated by top-down, mechanistic, power-relations reproducing development strategies in Latin America, I focus this section on the Latin American strands of PAR represented by Freire's influential work on the *conscientisation* (or the process of developing consciousness in order to change reality) of the marginalised and Fals Borda's inquiry on grassroots generated research and action.

Educator and philosopher Paulo Freire (1970) and his Brazilian and later Chilean collaborators developed a series of literacy projects based on people's engagement in the learning process. This included co-defining the topics of courses and training sessions and reaching joint decisions on the articulation of knowledge exchange. The goal was twofold; in addition to helping participants become literate, they would be encouraged to engage in social critique and thus supported in breaking with the oppressive structures that bounded them to a marginal position in society (Herr and Anderson 2005). This process would be undertaken through dialogue; the main methodological instrument proposed by Freire. Thus, he distanced himself from traditional pedagogical strategies based on the reproduction of power structures with the educator as expert and the student as recipient or user of the knowledge. Freire's approach to literacy has been widely influential both in developing and developed countries and in addition to his work in Brazil and Chile it has inspired, among other international and national initiatives, the International Network in Participatory Research, launched in September 1977 and literacy campaigns in Guinea Bissau, Nicaragua and Tanzania (Herr and Anderson 2005; Nyirenda 1996; Rahman 2008).

An interesting and contemporary example of the adaptation and extension of Freire's approach is Susan Pick's educational work in Mexico. Inspired by Freire, psychological behavioural theory and Sen's capability approach, Susan Pick and her collaborators have designed a framework to empower the poor and marginalised through educational programmes (Pick and Sirkin 2010). Pick and her colleagues agreed with Freire that education is a key tool to support autonomy, self-control and internally motivated action. However, they go beyond the collective to place the stress on the psychosocial roots of people's agency that manifest in feelings of shame, fear or guilt and impair their access to development opportunities drawing on, among other theories, Fishbein and Ajzen's (1975) Theory of Reasoned Action and Sen's capability approach (Sen 1999). They consider that increasing people's agency cannot rely only on the transmission of knowledge but demands the transfer of adequate skills and the opportunity for people to practise new behaviours so they feel entitled and capable to take control over their lives. The framework for Enabling Empowerment (FrEE) implemented by Pick and colleagues in Mexico and other Latin American countries through a strategy named 'programming for choice' consists of participatory seminars where people (for example women interested in starting a micro-enterprise) would learn relevant skills and would be encouraged to practise and reflect on them in a safe and supporting environment before using them in real life. It has reportedly had a remarkable success in expanding the life choices of participants (Pick and Sirkin 2010).

Focussing less on education and more on the horizontal collaboration and engagement of people in their own development processes, Colombian sociologist Orlando Fals Borda argued for a 'science of the proletariat' or 'people's science' derived by people under their current conditions (Rahman 2008). Drawing on the works of Spanish philosopher Ortega y Gasset and inspired by Marxism, Borda integrated perspectives from action researchers and emancipatory educational programmes in what he named as PAR; a combination of research, theory making and political activism (Fals Borda 1987).

> Fals Borda called for such action research to give the people a true sense of ownership of the inquiries so as to autonomously develop their own independent analysis of the reality lived by them, in a truly 'subject-subject' relation with the outside researchers.
>
> (Rahman 2008:50)

An example put forward by Fals Borda was the process followed by a community in Nicaragua to obtain a census using PAR. This demanded that local participants challenged their internalised patterns of dependency and paternalism and got involved in the design and implementation of the survey. He concluded that the data obtained was more reliable than it would have been, if old patterns of submission had not been challenged, as people would have given false answers. He also claimed that the local community felt ownership of the data and that they learned about themselves and became prepared to take the lead in their own development processes (Fals Borda 1987).

Fals Borda (1987) proposed four techniques that give PAR its transformative dimension. The first concerns collective research, an inquiry that should be made by the group based on dialogue and consensus about potential actions and their consequences. The second highlights the importance of collectively going through the history of the group and its members to capture those elements that prevailed at one point and had succeeded in providing dignity and pride to the marginalised. The third uses folk culture to engage with participants and carry out transformative actions. It implies considering music, art, dance, storytelling, public representations, ancestral beliefs, sports and other types of expressions as potential resources for transformative action. The fourth implies adapting the communication style to the audience to which it is directed (illiterate or literate people, institutional representatives, and academics).

> There is an obligation to return this knowledge systematically to the communities and workers' organisation because they continue to be its owners. They might determine the priorities concerning its use and authorise and establish the conditions for its publication and dissemination.
>
> (Fals Borda 1987: 344)

As Rahman (2008) explains, the understandings of PAR maintained by Freire and Fals Borda influenced, and were influenced by, other contemporary movements such as the 'emancipatory research' in Germany, the Participatory Research Network of the International Council for adult education and the South Asian alternative development paradigms based on the promotion of popular self-determination in the nineteen seventies and eighties. The work of Robert Chambers (1994, 1997) also fits in this international movement as the principles and methods of PAR resonate with those in Participatory Rural Appraisal (PRA) and Participatory Learning and Action (PLA), two 'sets of approaches, methods, behaviours and relationships for finding out about local context and life' (Chambers 2008: 297) that were presented as alternatives to large questionnaire surveys in the 1980s and 1990s (Brockington and Sullivan 2003).

International organisations such as the World Bank, ILO, UN agencies and NGOs contributed to the spread of participation in development practice from the late nineteen seventies onwards (Rahnema 1990). As Rahnema (1990) explains, there were at least six reasons that justified this generalised interest in participation: 1) the increase in project efficiency and productivity that local participation entailed; 2) the reduction in local resistance to government interventions as participation brought organisations closer to people; 3) the higher effectiveness of directly targeting the poor or marginalised; 4) the fact that the knowledge acquired through immersion in local realities and the networks created increased the effectiveness of future interventions; 5) the fact that governments were more likely to attract international funds if they supported participatory approaches; 6) the use of the concept of participation to support the privatisation of development through including more and more private actors in the design and execution of development policies. Many of the reasons are led by the requirements of efficiency and rapidity characterising many development interventions. Chambers argues (2008) that the generalisation of participatory practices often led to routine implementation of PRA and a focus on particular methodologies that worked against the pluralism and diversity that characterise PRA and PAR; thus reducing its empowering effect and its potential to unleash people's creativity.

Critiques and limitations of PAR

Since the generalisation of PAR designs and methodologies in the nineteen eighties, criticisms have arisen concerning its legitimacy to represent people's realities and the power relations it undermines, promotes or conceals (Cooke and Kothari 2004a; Rahnema 1990). Participatory methodologies, particularly those in PRA, such as seasonal calendars and wealth rankings[2], have been criticised for their focus on efficiency and on obtaining information rapidly. This focus on efficiency has often led to simplified, biased or misleading knowledge that has disempowered people instead of empowering them (Chambers 2008). In addition, the fact that participatory methodologies often encourage a specific representation of the world not necessarily shared by participants has also contributed to disempowerment. Henkel and Stirrat claim that in the case of many if not all participatory projects it seems evident that what people are 'empowered to do' is to take part in the modern sector of 'developing societies'. [. . .] In other words, the attempt to empower people through the projects envisaged and implemented by the practitioners of the new orthodoxy is always an attempt, however benevolent, to reshape the personhood of the participants. It is in this sense that we argue that 'empowerment' is tantamount to what Foucault calls subjection.

(Henkel and Stirrat 2004: 182).

Related to the above argument, Cooke and Kothari (2004b) claim that participatory approaches to development are particularly *tyrannical* as they exert unjust and illegitimate power over people and their communities. The methods, topics and goals of participatory development projects are generally decided by the organisations, research institutes or researchers that carry out the research. Thus, the engagement of local people in discussions, decisions, analysis, execution of projects and impact assessment is, although often negotiated along the way, heavily influenced by the construction of the particular reality of participation that legitimates the work and involvement of experts. The outcomes of such exercises are often a combination of the internalisation of the practitioners'/ researchers' goals by the locals and their strategic reaction to the participatory framework. This is a particularly stark critique that Mosse illustrates with the example of a participatory farming systems development project in rural India. He claims that participants' strong inclination for eucalyptus as preferred timber for housing was, 'like the desire for soil and water conservation, in effect a low-risk community strategy for securing known benefits in the short term (trees or wages) that might have been jeopardized by some more complex and differentiated statement of preferences' (Mosse 2004: 21).

An additional criticism of participatory development concerns its ability to reproduce, hide or intensify unfair power relations. Kothari (2004), drawing on Foucault's (1977) perspective on power based on the reproduction of unequal power relations through social practices and rituals, suggests three ways in which participation might reproduce power imbalances. The first concerns the choice of participants who might share some common traits (poverty, health condition, locality, etc.) but be affected by different types of power inequality at home, in the community, at the peasant association level, etc. that will not be unveiled when working with participants as a group. The second and third connect to the earlier discussion on empowerment as what comes out from participatory processes is often considered as the expression of the 'local culture' or of participants' reality. However, results of participatory exercises might be representing the norms and values that people have internalised as a consequence of a situation of oppression and might be covering up the power structures at play. This is especially the case when the goal is to reach consensus like in the HSD workshops, as consensus seeking risks hiding the complexities of people's everyday struggles.

These criticisms are important and necessary to reflect upon when engaging in participatory processes like the ones described in the HSD proposal. However, a long-term commitment with groups and communities and the combination of participatory and non-participatory methodologies can successfully diminish its negative effect. Local initiatives, communities and grassroots organisations that work with a long-term perspective will most likely find themselves navigating within an articulation of power relationships that sooner or later will become evident. Reason and Bradbury (2008), Max-Neef (1991) Smith and Max-Neef (2011) and many others (Cavill *et al.* 2015; Cornwall 2011; Pick and Sirkin 2010) give examples of long-term action research projects by NGOs, research institutes and governmental organisations that are succeeding in increasing the wellbeing of entire communities and regions. However, unveiling all forms of power imbalances is impossible. A long-term, needs-based PAR process will most likely unearth the forms of oppression most detrimental for needs satisfaction but might have a limited effect on those power imbalances that happen at the personal level or are too 'embarrassing' to discuss socially.

Human Scale Development and Participatory Action Research projects

Many students, researchers and practitioners basing their work on the HSD proposal have used the matrix of needs and satisfiers as a tool to enhance their own understanding (or the understanding of a particular organisation) of specific conditions or problems affecting a community. It has also been common to draw on the concept of needs and satisfiers to develop participatory workshops that engage groups of people in a critical reflection about the capacity of the socio-economic, cultural, political and technical characteristics of their society to support need satisfaction (refer to Chapters 4, 5 and 7 for specific examples). These uses of the HSD methodology contribute to a deep understanding of the problems and potentials for development present in a particular society. However, the matrix of needs and satisfiers was designed as a tool to support development practice and thus its 'ideal' use is in the context of real-life processes aiming at self-reliance, balanced relationship and human needs satisfaction (the three pillars of the HSD proposal). Participatory Action Research designs seem the most adequate frame for these sorts of projects as illustrated, among other experiences with grassroots groups, by the work of the Colombian Association for Peasant development that has succeeded in engaging local communities in HSD processes during the last 25 years (Max-Neef 1991, 1992; Smith and Max-Neef 2011).

Henkel and Stirrat (2004: 170–171) summarised the characteristics of participatory development as: a stress on bottom-up rather than top-down approaches; an emphasis on empowerment; a focus on the marginal; a distrust of the state and a 'celebration' of 'local' or indigenous knowledge. Some of these features resonate with the logic of the HSD proposal, which was intended to support grassroots organisations and communities in the design and implementation of their own development strategies. On the one hand, HSD encourages self-reliant development initiated from the bottom; which often includes a focus on marginal peasant communities and on their empowerment since traditional top-down policies are usually based on relationships of dependence. However, HSD is not only relevant for developing countries or in contexts of poverty and deprivation. As discussed in Chapter 5, the systemic approach to development stressing interdependence between human and ecological systems suggests that HSD is a suitable proposal for the analysis and support of human needs fulfilment in contexts of affluence; as global warming, biodiversity loss, consumerism, joblessness and many other associated poverties are not only affecting poor, marginalised people or developing countries.

Contrary to what Henkel and Stirrat suggest, a focus on the grassroots does not imply that participatory development proposals allocate a marginal role to local, regional and national institutions. Following Max-Neef and collaborators (Max-Neef 1991), the latter are important contributors to development both by encouraging embryonic local initiatives and by creating the institutions that will contribute to self-reliance. Hence, HSD would demand, for example, that state regulations and policies support the establishment of networks connecting local initiatives in different regions or countries; that financial institutions are structured around the local community and that educational opportunities to connect local and experts' knowledge are set into place. The importance of both local and external resources is reflected in the HSD methodology described in Chapter 4; as it stresses the importance of discussing both endogenous (mobilised by the community) and exogenous (supported by outside institutions) synergic satisfiers. This gives the grassroots the responsibility to define the scope of their own contribution to human needs satisfaction and to identify the external supports that will be required to achieve their objectives while, at the same time, it does not underplay the role of a supportive state.

Finally, it might be useful to highlight an important difference between the HSD and other participatory methodologies, such as the ones associated with PRA (Chambers 1997) and understandings of education as *conscientisation* (Freire 1970). Unlike the latter, the HSD process based on identifying synergic satisfiers through participatory workshops does not entail training or educating people in the particularities of a specific methodology or conceptual framework. As described in Chapter 3, when Max-Neef and his collaborators developed the list of human needs they intended to come up with a list that was 'easy to understand and for people to identify with' (Max-Neef 1991: 31). Decades of use of the matrix with people from rich and poor countries, with different levels of education and different socio-economic background suggest that they achieved their goal. As Max-Neef explained

> we used to arrive in Andean communities to be approached by local leaders with a photocopy of a photocopy of a photocopy, almost unreadable, ready to discuss whether their interpretation was correct and whether their projects satisfied the philosophy of Human Scale Development. It was moving to witness how such marginal communities adopted the principles and designed development projects that conventional experts would have been unable to conceive.
>
> (Max-Neef 2011: xxi)

Example 6.1: Human Scale Development and Participatory Action Research in Acostambo, Peru

In November 2011, I and two assistants from the *Universidad Nacional del Centro del Peru* in Huancayo, carried out an exploratory research project in Acostambo, a rural district in the Central Andean Highlands. The research was a part of my larger post-doctoral project aiming, among other things, at comparing the negative, utopian and bridging synergic satisfiers identified in HSD workshops by people living in different districts of the country (see Example 4.1 for a description of the larger study). The research team had previous knowledge of the socio-economic, political and cultural characteristic of most districts, including Acostambo, as two of us had previously been involved in the Wellbeing in Developing Countries (WeD) ESRC Research Group at the University of Bath, investigating the cultural constructions of wellbeing in Peru from 2003 to 2007 (Copestake 2008).

Acostambo is a district in Huancavelica, one of the poorest regions in Peru with 50 per cent of the population below the national poverty line.[3] Most of the 4,273 residents are farmers cultivating traditional crops (barley, potatoes, wheat, peas, beans and maize) although some people also work for the town hall, the local schools or the small shops located by the road connecting the cities of Huancayo and Huancavelica. Most people are poor despite the fact that throughout the years governmental and non-governmental organisations have been present in the district promoting innovation in farming practices, running disease prevention campaigns and supporting reforestation, among other issues. In addition, social assistance programmes targeting the elderly poor, child malnutrition, extreme poverty and illiteracy have also been implemented in the municipality, although the continuous outflow of population seems to indicate that they have been insufficient to provide a critical level of need satisfaction among the population (Copestake 2008).

The two phases of the PAR project

The research in Acostambo was articulated around two phases summarised in Table 6.1 below (see Guillén-Royo 2015 for a detailed description). The first phase carried out in November 2011 consisted of a survey and a set of workshops implemented in five Peruvian districts. The goal of the survey was to provide quantitative data to investigate the relationship between personal values and wellbeing across the five districts. The goal of the HSD workshops was to compare the satisfiers identified by people with different socio-economic backgrounds and experiences. Workshops followed the three-step structure described in Table 4.2 (Chapter 4) where participants discuss negative, utopian and synergic bridging satisfiers respectively. In Acostambo, the three workshops were held in a room in the town hall provided by the municipality. Each workshop was joined by an average of nine people, most of whom participated in more than one workshop. In total, 22 people got involved.

Table 6.1 Research strategy in the district of Acostambo

	ACTIVITY	DATES	DESCRIPTION
PHASE 1			
Survey	Survey to 100 people from the district	November 2011	Questionnaire on values, subjective wellbeing and environmental attitudes.
HSD workshops	3 HSD workshops with a total of 22 participants	November 2011	Three 3-hour workshops to identify problems and opportunities to satisfy human needs
PHASE 2			
PAR interventions	Implementation of the two top synergic bridging satisfiers	April 2012– January 2013	16 workshops linked to the organic vegetable gardens and adults' school
Interviews	Semi-structured interviews to residents in Acostambo	April 2012– January 2013	21 interviews on people's experiences with development projects
Post PAR survey	Survey to 21 PAR participants and 21 non-participants	January 2013	Questionnaire on values, subjective wellbeing and organic vegetable gardens to PAR participants and a matched sample of non-participants

Source: Adapted from Guillén-Royo (2015)

The dynamics of the workshops and the contents of the negative and utopian matrices have been discussed elsewhere (Guillén-Royo 2012, 2015). The categories that the research team used to summarise satisfiers in Acostambo are represented in Figure 6.1 below. Hereafter, I focus on the *synergic bridging satisfiers* resulting from the first phase of the study and the process followed to implement two of them. As Figure 6.2 shows the *synergic bridging satisfiers* suggested by participants were: monthly communal work, organic vegetable gardens, reforestation and a parents' school. They were considered to have synergic effects on human needs through their contribution to unity/social cohesion, quality local education and better material conditions (the three categories summarising *synergic satisfiers* in the utopian matrix). They were also appraised as endogenous since participants believed that the local community could initiate them. At the same time, the need to receive support from local organisations and institutions for the implementation of satisfiers to be successful was also emphasised.

Environmental concerns were taken into account when discussing *synergic bridging satisfiers*. Participants in the first workshops had expressed a concern with water pollution, the use of chemical fertilisers in agriculture and the unhealthy conditions of roads and dwellings due to undisposed waste and low quality materials. Thus, the introduction of organic vegetable gardens was intended to address, among other concerns, the negative effects on soils and people's health of industrial fertilisers; reforestation was linked to the progressive land erosion from the expansion of agricultural practices, and *faenas* or communal work was seen as an instrument for the maintenance of common spaces and the removal of litter from streets and local roads. The parents' school was not initially discussed as addressing any environmental impact but instead reflected people's concern about the low educational level of most adult residents, the lack of understanding among generations and the progressive abandonment of Quechua, their mother tongue, in favour of Spanish.

None of the initiatives suggested were completely alien to participants as they had either heard of them or participated in them as part of their traditions or of externally-led projects. Thus, it was not about creating new institutions or

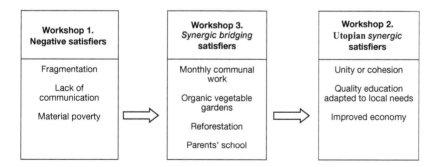

Figure 6.2 Summary of negative, utopian and synergic bridging satisfiers in Acostambo
Source: Adapted from Guillén-Royo (2012)

programmes but about bringing back those which seemed more promising in terms of needs satisfaction. For example, some participants had previous experience with organic gardens through their involvement in projects led by ADECAP (Association for the Defence and Development of Andean Communities in Peru) and Caritas (development association of the Catholic Church) in several neighbourhoods of the district. In addition, a local nurse had recently engaged women in the district on a project to increase the quality and variety of the vegetables grown in home gardens. This could suggest that needs-based PAR projects, despite their association with radical transformations, might be well suited to identify already successful interventions and strengthen their contribution to human needs. It also indicates, against what some critics maintain, that PAR projects do not necessarily ignore local institutions or organisations and create new ones that align better with the interests of the donor agency or the goals of the research project (Cooke and Kothari 2004b).

After the third HSD workshop, a preliminary analysis of the negative and utopian matrices and the bridging synergic satisfiers in Acostambo was submitted to the local council for their perusal. We did not receive a formal feedback from the council but after five months, when we returned to Acostambo to discuss the possibility of a follow-up through a PAR study, council members and former participants encouraged us to continue the research in the municipality. Having received the support of some local residents and authorities, we started the second phase of the project in April 2012 with the goal of extending it until January 2013. The aim of this phase was to study the process of implementation of the *synergic bridging satisfiers* or strategies identified in Phase 1, and analyse their contribution to human needs and environmental sustainability.

The second part of the study was articulated around periodical participatory workshops, action-based activities, in-depth interviews and a post-PAR survey with questions on personal values, wellbeing and the effect of the PAR-project on human needs fulfilment and environmental sustainability. In-depth interviews were used to acquire more knowledge about the processes and outcomes of recent development initiatives in the district. The goal was to triangulate previous knowledge from WeD (Copestake 2008) and the data from HSD workshops with the information obtained through interviews in order to better understand the factors that influenced development projects in Acostambo. Workshops and interviews were conducted by the two local assistants in close collaboration with me through Skype conferences, e-mail exchanges and sharing of video, audio recordings and written reports from PAR meetings and workshops. In January 2013, I travelled back to Acostambo to facilitate the two last workshops, carry out the post-PAR survey and present to participants an initial analysis of the findings including a new set of synergic satisfiers that had emerged in the last workshop.

A total of sixteen participatory workshops of around two-and-a-half hours were held from April 2012 to January 2013, attended by an average of 18 people, and a maximum of 33. The first three workshops took place in the municipality centre involving participants in the first phase. Workshops revolved around ranking the four *bridging synergic satisfiers* and discussing their feasibility. Participants appraised organic vegetable gardens as the most synergic satisfier, followed by the parents' school, the reforestation project and *faenas* or communal work. The *culture of asistencialismo* or dependence was called on to justify ranking communal work as least important. It was argued that nowadays people were used to getting handouts in exchange for participating in development projects and that they would not collaborate in communal works if there were not compensations or fines. This attitude is compatible with the history of paternalism, *clientelism* and material poverty experienced by many rural populations in Latin America that led HSD proponents to stress the importance of breaking relationships of dependence and promoting self-reliance at the personal and group levels (see Chapter 3 for a discussion).

Participants proposed to start with the two top strategies and during the second workshop they discussed how to implement them. The third workshop was not well attended and Roberto, one of the participants, suggested continuing the project in a *comunidad campesina*[4] (peasant community) consisting of people from the neighbourhoods of *Vistas* and *Condes*.[5] Roberto, a resident in Vistas, had participated in our workshops from the beginning and had kept the 36 members of the *comunidad* updated about the PAR project. The community was used to work with development agencies and NGOs and had been recently engaged in a nationwide reforestation programme by the Ministry of Agriculture. The latter was articulated around weekly meetings in the neighbourhood of Vistas, which created a habit of gathering on a regular basis. This and the fact that the community members had made explicit their interest in the organic vegetables initiative were used as arguments to persuade us to move the project to Vistas and involve the peasant community.

After two meetings introducing the research, the researchers[6] and the project, community members reaffirmed their interest in working with the two top *synergic bridging satisfiers* identified in previous workshops. The processes of organising and undertaking the organic vegetable gardens in Vistas have been discussed elsewhere (Guillén-Royo 2015). Hereafter, I concentrate on describing the processes and outcomes of the parents' school strategy and how these enhanced needs satisfaction among participants and supported positive environmental outcomes.

Parents' school in Vista Alegre

The fourth workshop in Vistas was devoted to analyse the parents' school's potential contribution to human needs fulfilment. Most community members knew about or had at one point participated in a parents' school. They highlighted their usefulness in achieving a greater understanding within the family and with close neighbours. As participants discussed the relationship between the parents' school and the nine fundamental needs, two topics generated a heated debate. The first was domestic violence, a *violator* or *destroyer*[7] in the language of the HSD proposal that affected some of the participating households. The second concerned being able to learn in Quechua, the mother tongue of most participants, as schools in the district were teaching exclusively in Spanish. Participants argued that being able to attend a Quechua speaking school would increase the satisfaction of their need for identity. This was easy to observe in the workshops as when participants switched to Quechua, they automatically became more relaxed and even otherwise quite serious people would joke and laugh.

After discussing the synergic characteristics of the parents' school, and in line with Freire's and Pick's approach to learning discussed earlier, participants were invited to identify the themes they would like to address during the PAR project. They suggested the following topics: personal values and ethics, domestic violence, citizens' rights and duties, family planning and conviviality norms. Following the participatory approach to education typical of PAR and HSD the research team suggested structuring the 2–3 hour parents' school sessions around short presentations and discussion groups, which the community endorsed. The community held sessions in the primary school of Vistas, after participants had arranged with the headmaster for its regular use. The research team was in charge of contacting local experts to give presentations and of arranging with the municipal council the lending of laptops or projectors. After the first sessions, upon request from participants, we also agreed on producing leaflets summarising the workshop discussions so people could share their new understandings with other family members. Response from 'local experts' was largely positive: the municipal health care centre facilitated the involvement of the general practitioner, the psychologist, the nurse and the obstetrician. The municipality governor and the leader of the office for the disabled also contributed with presentations. In general, the parents' school sessions were well attended and were also used to follow-up the organic vegetable gardens initiative and to discuss other project-related topics.

Several times along the way we emphasised that participants were the central part of the *escuela de padres* and that without their active participation and dialog we could not carry out the project. The group had a similar amount of men and women but it was clear that women were less comfortable than men speaking in public so in some sessions discussion groups were organised by gender. Not only the choice of themes reflected concerns over gender discrimination but also the contents of their discussions as for example, the most important negative value identified in the session on personal values and ethics concerned *machismo* or male chauvinism and the way it often degenerated into domestic violence. The importance of the topic was also reflected in the fact that the session on domestic violence was one of the best attended with 33 participants from the Vistas, Condes and Acostambo municipality centre. The session started with the local general practitioner and the psychologist giving a PowerPoint presentation with general information about the prevalence and characteristics of domestic violence in Peru and practical recommendations on how to prevent it. Physical violence was the topic chosen by participants for an in-depth discussion in small groups. The roots of physical and domestic violence were discussed in relation to socio-economic and individual factors such as *machismo*, parents' low education levels, the stress associated with teenage pregnancies, alcoholism and personal attributes such as revengefulness, jealousy and shyness.

We suggested that discussions about solutions or strategies to address domestic violence followed the HSD distinction between endogenous and exogenous satisfiers. Participants believed that endogenous solutions should rely on families spending more time together and sharing household chores, increasing communication and respect among its members and avoiding engaging in discussions when one of the partners (mostly the man) was drunk. Exogenous strategies were considered at the community and municipal levels. People proposed establishing a system by which couples experiencing problems could engage in a constructive dialogue with the support of a community mediator. They also discussed punishments that would shame aggressors in front of their neighbours. Other strategies included reporting the aggressor to the police or the municipal authorities and going to the psychologist to address the underlying problems of the aggressor. Consulting with the local psychologist was preferred over reporting the partner to the police. Participants agreed on the fact that non-repressive measures would have more synergic effects than repressive ones. As Anita, the leader of a local association summarised it:

> *Machismo* means that there is no support between partners [. . .] Women are mainly asked to cook and men to work outside the house [. . .] but men can also cook, they can also clean and wash and women can also do what men do, but this only happens when there is understanding, good communication. [. . .] women get used to this situation and this should not be the case, they become shy, they are afraid [. . .] taking the husband to the police should be done when there is no hope that the man can change but taking him to the psychologists is a solution for the whole family since very often children of abusive parents are also traumatised.[8]

After work in smaller groups, a representative from each group would present in plenary the main conclusions. Manuel, one of the participants who attended most of the workshops, a middle aged man with a position of authority in the community, gave a spontaneous speech after the session on domestic violence. Despite the fact that his opinion cannot be taken as representing the views of the community, it suggests that the participatory approach taken in the adults' school and the meetings around the PAR project were perceived as potentially empowering and synergic. Manuel said:

> In this workshop we have worked in depth on the subject, we have analysed it and then we have provided the solutions. I want to thank the researchers for this event they have organised. This small workshop is very useful and we should keep it in mind, we should not forget to work on improving our bad ways so we can finally create a good environment for our children, family and community [. . .] we leave this workshop with the head full of what we have shared and this should be put in practice by all of us.[8]

Due to the short duration of our PAR project it is difficult to assert that long-term personal and institutional changes came from people's participation in the parents' school.[9] However, what seems to be the case is that using a PAR design in combination with the tenets and methodology of the HSD proposal makes educational programmes more attractive for participants than traditional approaches to education. This was confirmed when the headmaster of the local school declared to be surprised that our workshops were better attended than the adult literacy course she was running in the same school; where she was not managing to attract more than four participants at a time. As Susan Pick describes for the case of Mexico 'the educational system in Mexico, as in many other developing countries is based on a paternalistic, hierarchical structure that emphasises rote memorization and the expectation that students unquestioningly comply with norms. Such a system does not encourage students to ask questions, to be analytical, and to address their needs, leaving little room for personal initiative, analytical thinking or creativity' (Pick and Sirkin 2010: xi). Participants also described that many teachers in the district were corrupt and that Quechua was neither taught at school nor was it included in literacy programmes. These factors might have contributed to their lack of interests in literacy initiatives from the formal education system.

Running the adults' school in parallel to the organic vegetable gardens had synergic effects on human needs. It gave participants the opportunity to meet, to get to know each other and provided them with another space in which to interact and cooperate. When people were asked in the post-PAR survey about the contributions of the organic vegetable gardens they stressed the fact that they had acquired new knowledge and that they had learned from each other, something that was also the objective of the adults' school. This increased interaction and cooperation among community members implicit in the implementation of the two *synergic bridging satisfiers* was found to be positively associated with a higher respect for the natural environment.[10] It also had a direct positive impact on the environment through the reduction of fertiliser use due to the success of the organic vegetable gardens initiative (Guillén-Royo 2015). These effects are not surprising, as strong community feelings have been identified by psychologists as being associated with pro-environmental behaviours and a greater care for the natural environment (Brown and Kasser 2005; Crompton and Kasser 2009).

A reflection on power

Among the critiques to PAR, the one concerning how participatory development processes address power is undoubtedly the most salient. As introduced earlier, Kothari (2004) argues that there are many ways in which PAR might reproduce or even intensify unjust power relations at the local or community levels. The first concerns the inherent power in exercises that invite or include some people in detriment of others. In our PAR project we started by inviting the 100 participants in the survey (all from the district of Acostambo) to join the HSD workshops. Other people we met and related to during the implementation of the survey were also invited. This loose recruiting strategy resulted in workshops being joined by a combination of people that included students from the local professional school, local public officials, shop owners and small farmers.

When the project moved to Vistas, around 2 km from the municipality centre, we provided transport for earlier participants who wished to continue with their engagement. People from other neighbourhoods and hamlets were not explicitly informed and thus were less likely to join the PAR project. In the end, only three to four people from neighbourhoods other than Vistas and Condes attended PAR workshops on a regular basis. However, we always stressed the fact that the project was open to anyone and people decided to attend or not attend as they saw fit. For example, several times participants did not show up even if they had previously agreed to do so. They usually explained their decision in terms of the requirements of the farming season, the weather conditions or their need to participate in other meetings or activities. In a way, they included or excluded themselves any time they felt they needed to. However, the fact that most participants belonged to the same peasant community in Vistas might have deterred other residents in the neighbourhood from joining, which would support Kothari's argument about PAR reproducing local structures of exclusion.

An additional criticism concerns the power dynamics hidden by decisions reached through consensus. This is especially relevant regarding the HSD methodology, as identifying the most synergic or negative satisfiers is often done through consensus. In the PAR project, we cannot rule out that some particular voices such as the ones of the governor, the justice of the peace and a handful of more educated peasants were more influential than others. However, the fact that the *synergic bridging satisfiers* chosen by early participants were later endorsed and implemented in Vistas, a much poorer and equal neighbourhood, suggests that these strategies had a much wider resonance than the one they would have had if they were only addressing the views of the better educated. One could argue, following critics of PAR, that people in Vistas had internalised their marginal position in society and were ready to accept any initiative that was likely to improve their situation. The concern about the internalisation of local power dynamics is a fair one, and it relates to the paralysing effects of the culture of *asistencialismo* or dependence reported by participants.

The *culture of asistencialismo* defined as 'the paternalistic social and development assistance traditionally given to the poor based on donations or gifts in exchange for political support (clientelism) or, more recently, in exchange for participation in health or education schemes (Guillén-Royo 2015: 134) was a threat to the potential empowering effects of the PAR project. Many in Acostambo had previously been involved in participatory projects led by NGOs and government agencies that had not delivered as expected. These experiences had made people sceptical towards participatory development projects that demanded personal involvement and did not offer food or handouts in exchange for participation. The paralysing effect of a history of *asistencialismo* can be found in the following comment endorsed by workshop participants: 'we are poor, but we have everything to overcome poverty. We have land, water and hands and if we are not able to succeed it is because some of us are used to receiving, to *asistencialimo*.'[8]

We were aware of the implicit power relationships inherent to the culture of *asistencialismo* and we avoided offering gifts or handouts in exchange for participation (although we still offered refreshments during workshops). This might have influenced the lack of interest of participants from the municipality centre at the beginning of Phase 2 and the later adoption of the project by the community in Vistas. The latter were poorer than the district average; which makes them more likely to have engaged in the project with the hope of improving their financial situation through increased sales of vegetables, for example. However, when people were asked in the post-PAR survey and in the last workshops about the effects of participating in the PAR project, they declared that they had become more knowledgeable and that their community and families were more united than before (Guillén-Royo 2015). Increased savings and sales of organic vegetables were considered less important outcomes of the project than the stronger bonds among community and household members and their improved general knowledge.

A final reflection concerns the discussion on the tyranny of participation initiated by Cooke and Kothari in the early 2000s. Participation, by appearing more democratic than traditional research or development strategies based on expert assessment, has a great appeal for those who believe that development has to be guided by the people concerned. However, by itself, it can be more authoritarian, or even tyrannical, than more conventional top-down or detached approaches because participation is always framed with a goal in mind, let it be research or project related, so in reality it is not a fully open process. This incentivises strategic reactions that might end up reinforcing feelings of *asistencialismo*, for example, reducing people's self-esteem and the possibilities of success of future development projects. However, attention to the processes participants and researchers engage in; the use of a wide array of research methods; the systemic understanding that HSD workshops enable; and the openness of researchers and practitioners to make mistakes and even give up pursuing specific projects, might avoid allegations of tyranny.

Conclusion

This chapter argues that when the goal of research is to engage with participants and achieve a deeper understanding of the synergies created through HSD processes, Participatory Action Research designs based on personal involvement with a group of people or community might be the most suitable approach. Participatory Action Research draws on two disciplinary traditions. The first relates with action research in organisations focussed on engaging experts, workers and managers in cooperative problem-solving by challenging entrenched values and practices. The second links to literacy and rural development projects concerned with reversing unjust situations through the empowerment of those suffering them. Both problem-solving and empowering participants through a deep analysis of reality resonate with the pillars of self-reliance, balanced articulations and human needs satisfaction that support HSD. They also align with the HSD methodology based on deliberative workshops aimed at identifying *synergic bridging satisfiers*; endogenous or exogenous strategies that contribute to human needs fulfilment at the local level.

In this Chapter I have used an example in the rural district of Acostambo (Peru) to illustrate how HSD workshops followed up through a PAR design, the use of quantitative and qualitative methods, and a direct involvement with participants all contribute both to a deeper understanding of the interdependences between the social, economic and environmental aspects of development and to a better fulfilment of participants' needs. I have also highlighted the fact that participator approaches to development can have pernicious effects if the challenges associated with power imbalances within communities and between participants and researchers/practitioners are not addressed. This became evident during the PAR project through the challenges of *machismo* and *asistencialismo* that could have threatened the success of the organic vegetable gardens and the adults' school initiative in Acostambo. Careful attention to processes during PAR projects and a long-term commitment with participants or communities can minimise the potentially tyrannical effects of engaging in participatory development.

Notes

1 For a comprehensive account of the history, methodology and debates on Participatory Action Research refer to Reason and Bradbury (2008), Herr and Anderson (2005), Cook and Kothari (2004a) and *The Journal of Action Research*.
2 Seasonal calendars are one of the techniques used in Participatory Rural Appraisal (PRA) to associate the activities carried out by participants with the time of the year they take place. Wealth rankings are also used in PRA and they aim to categorise the members of a group according to their level of wealth through participatory discussions on the meaning of wealth and poverty (Brockington and Sullivan 2003).
3 Regional poverty rates and population data are available at the National Statistics Office of Peru (Instituto Nacional de Estadística e Informática, www.inei.gob.pe/).
4 A *comunidad campesina* is a traditional local institution with a democratically elected board and voluntary membership informed by shared customs and ancestral links that coordinates, among other issues, the use of communal resources (Puntoedu 2013).
5 *Vistas* and *Condes* and all the names used in this chapter to refer to participants are anonymised.
6 I introduced the research and myself through a short video shown to participants from the peasant community during the second workshop in Vistas.
7 Violators or destroyers are satisfiers that, despite targeting the actualisation of a specific need, are detrimental for this need and reduce the possibility of satisfying other needs. Censorship and bureaucracy are examples of violators or destroyers suggested in the HSD book (Max-Neef 1991).
8 Translated from Spanish by the author.
9 However, the PAR project in general seems to have contributed to empower the community as Roberto, our contact person claims that after the PAR project participants became more engaged and showed a greater capacity and willingness to negotiate on equal terms with institutions (see Chapter 8 for a discussion).
10 The Post Par survey asked participants about the extent to which it was true that the organic vegetables project had contributed to instil into them a greater respect for the environment. Answers were on a five-point verbal scale from *completely false, not quite true, somewhat true, largely true* to *extremely true*. Most respondents agreed that the statement was 'somewhat true' (8 out of 21) or 'largely true' (10 out of 21).

References

Argyris, C. and Schon, D. A. (1974). *Theory in Practice: Increasing Professional Effectiveness.* San Francisco: Jossey-Bass.

Argyris, C., Putnam, R. and Smith, D. M. (1985). *Action Science: Concepts, Methods and Skills for Research and Intervention.* San Francisco: Jossey-Bass.

Brockington, D. and Sullivan, S. (2003). Qualitative research. In Scheyvens, R. and Storey, D. (eds), *Development Fieldwork.* London: Sage, pp. 57–74.

Brown, K. W. and Kasser, T. (2005). Are psychological and ecological well-being compatible? The role of values, mindfulness, and lifestyle. *Social Indicators Research*, 74(2): 349–68.

Cavill, S. with Chambers, R. and Vernon, N. (2015). Sustainability and CLTS: Taking Stock. Frontiers of CLTS: Innovations and Insights Issue 4, Brighton: IDS.

Chambers, R. (1994). The origins and practice of participatory rural appraisal. *World Development*, 22(7), 953–69.

Chambers, R. (1997). *Whose Reality Counts? Putting the First Last.* London: Intermediate Technology Publications (ITP).

Chambers, R. (2008). *Revolutions in Development Inquiry.* London: Earthscan.

Cooke, B. and Kothari, U. (eds), (2004a). *Participation. The New Tyranny?* 3rd edn. London: Zed books.

Cooke, B. and Kothari, U. (2004b). The case for participation as tyranny. In Cooke, B. and Kothari, U. (eds), *Participation. The New Tyranny?* 3rd edn. London: Zed Books, pp. 1–15.

Copestake, J. (2008). Multiple dimensions of social assistance: the case of Peru's 'glass of milk' programme. *The Journal of Development Studies*, 44(4): 545–61.

Cornwall, A. (ed.) (2011). *The Participation Reader.* London: Zed Books.

Crompton, T. and Kasser, T. (2009). *Meeting Environmental Challenges: The Role of Human Identity.* Godalming, UK: WWF-UK.

Fals Borda, O. (1987). The application of participatory action research in Latin America. *International Sociology*, 2: 329–47.

Fishbein, M. and Ajzen, I. (1975). *Belief, Attitude, Intention, and Behavior: An Introduction to Theory and Research.* Reading, MA: Addison-Wesley.

Foucault, M. (1977). *Discipline and Punish.* New York: Pantheon.

Freire, P. (1970). *Pedagogy of the Oppressed*, New York: Continuum.

Garmendia, E. and Stagl, S. (2010). Public participation for sustainability and social learning: Concepts and lessons from three case studies in Europe. *Ecological Economics*, 69(8): 1712–22.

Guillén-Royo, M. (2012). The challenge of transforming consumption patterns: A proposal using the Human Scale Development approach. In Bjørkdahl, K. and Nielsen, K. B. (eds), *Development and the Environment. Practices, Theories, Policies.* Oslo: Akademika, pp. 99–118.

Guillén-Royo, M. (2015). Human needs and the environment reconciled: Participatory action-research for sustainable development in Peru. In Syse, K. and Mueller, M. (eds), *Sustainability and the Good Life.* Oxford: Routledge.

Henkel, H. and Stirrat, R. (2004). Participation as spiritual duty: Empowerment as secular subjection. In Cooke, B. and Kothari, U. (eds), *Participation. The New Tyranny?* 3rd edn. London: Zed Books, pp. 168–84.

Herr, K. and Anderson, G. L. (eds) (2005). *The action research dissertation: A guide for students and faculty.* London: Sage.

Kothari, U. (2004). Power, knowledge and social control in participatory development. In Cooke, B. and Kothari, U. (eds), *Participation: The New Tyranny?* London: Zed Books, pp. 139–52.

Lewin, K. (1946). Action research and minority problems. *Journal of Social Issues*, 2(4): 34–46.

Max-Neef, M. (1991). *Human Scale Development: Conception, Application and Further Reflection*. London: Apex Press.

Max-Neef, M. (2011). Preface: The death and rebirth of economics. In Rauschmayer, F., Omann, I. and Frühmann, J. (eds), *Sustainable Development: Capabilities, Needs and Well-being*. London: Routledge.

Max-Neef, M. (1992). Development and human needs. In Ekins, P. and Max-Neef, M. (eds), *Real-life Economics*. London: Routledge.

Morgan, A. D. (2009). Learning communities, cities and regions for sustainable development and global citizenship. *Local Environment*, 14(5): 443–59.

Mosse, D. (2004). People's knowledge', participation and patronage: Operations and representations in rural development. In Cooke, B. and Kothari, U. (eds), *Participation: The New Tyranny?* London: Zed Books, pp. 16–35.

Nyirenda, J. E. (1996). The relevance of Paulo Freire's contributions to education and development in present day Africa. *African Media Review*, 10(1): 1–20.

Pick, S. and Sirkin, J. 2010. *Breaking the Poverty Cycle: The Human Basis for Sustainable Development*. Oxford: Oxford University Press.

Puntoedu (2013). Cinco claves para entender qué son las comunidades campesinas [http://puntoedu.pucp.edu.pe/noticias/cinco-claves-para-entender-que-son-las-comunidades-campesinas/], accessed 18 August 2014.

Rahman, A. (2008). Some trends in the praxis of participatory action research. In Reason, P. and Bradbury, H. (eds), *The SAGE Handbook of Action Research: Participative Inquiry and Practice*, 3: 49–62.

Rahnema, M. (1990). Participatory Action Research: The 'last temptation of saint' development. *Alternatives: Global, Local, Political*, 15(2): 199–226.

Reason, P. and Bradbury, H. (2008). *The Sage Handbook of Action Research: Participative Inquiry and Practice*. London: Sage.

Reason, P., Coleman, G., Ballard, D., Williams, M., Gearty, M. and Bond, C. (2009). *Insider Voices: Human Dimensions of Low Carbon Technology*. Bath: Centre for Action Research in Professional Practice, University of Bath.

Sachs, W. (1992). Bygone splendour. In Ekins, P. and Max-Neef, M. (eds), *Real-life Economics*. London: Routledge.

Sen, A. (1999). *Development as Freedom*. Oxford: Oxford University Press.

Smith, B. P. and Max-Neef, M. (2011). *Economics Unmasked. From Power and Greed to Compassion and the Common Good*. Cambridge: Green Books.

Tashakkori, A. and Teddlie, C. (1998). *Mixed Methodology. Combining Qualitative and Quantitative Approaches*. London: Sage.

Wicks, P. G., Reason, P. and Bradbury, H. (2008). Living inquiry: Personal, political and philosophical groundings for action research practice. In Reason, P. and Bradbury, H. (eds), *The SAGE Handbook of Action Research: Participative Inquiry and Practice*, 1: 15–30.

7 Supporting local sustainability initiatives

Introduction

This chapter discusses how the theoretical and methodological perspectives of the HSD proposal resonate with the principles and practices of local sustainability initiatives and might contribute to their long-term success. Sustainable communities and other local sustainability projects are often characterised by personal involvement, a local focus, and a systemic understanding of the relationship between people and nature. They are also generators of what Max-Neef called 'non-conventional resources' such as critical awareness, personal commitment, cooperation and experiential knowledge. Examples of the projects they commonly engage with include: promoting the local economy through food and clean energy production, using local currencies or alternative exchange mechanisms and reducing energy consumption and household waste. The holistic approach to environmental activism results in local sustainability initiatives often expanding their activities to tackle issues of marginalisation, inequality, poverty or joblessness and they often do this in dialogue with local and regional authorities and other voluntary or non-governmental associations.

This chapter is organised as follows. First, it explores how the three pillars of the HSD proposal are contemplated in the foundational principles and operations of sustainable communities; arguably the most holistic among local bottom-up sustainability initiatives. Then, it addresses how different community initiatives such as eco-municipalities, ecovillages and the transition movement have linked to the fundamental needs approach of the HSD proposal, either through their foundational principles or through the methodological suggestions of researchers and practitioners. Next, Inez Aponte[1] presents her experience using the HSD perspective on needs and satisfiers with members of the transition movement in the UK. She highlights the usefulness of the proposal to make people aware of the connections between transformative actions at the personal level and those at the community and national/global levels. Last, acknowledging diversity of goals and mechanisms across initiatives, I introduce the concept of 'necessary' *synergic satisfiers*, those that seem to be present in societies or communities where needs are optimally actualised and the negative environmental impacts of human activity minimised.

Human Scale Development and sustainable communities

During the last decades, local sustainability initiatives have been spreading around the world taking the form of community projects involving neighbourhoods, villages and municipalities or of issue-specific projects targeting environmental concerns such as energy and food production and consumption, food distribution, water regulation or private transportation. In principle, community-based initiatives have a greater potential to transform lifestyles than single-targeted policies or projects. They usually have a holistic and systemic approach to environmental challenges that acknowledges the interdependence between human and ecological systems and its complex interactions. They have also been influenced to varied degrees and through different actors (activists, planners, researchers, consultants) by the HSD proposal's approach to human needs and satisfiers.

Ecovillages, eco-municipalities, transition towns and other sustainable communities[2] have their roots in collaborative bottom-up initiatives to transform the ways people consume, produce and think about wellbeing and the natural environment. They share many principles and features between them: from the logic of participation in decision making, project development and execution, to the centrality given to low-carbon lifestyles and environmental conservation. Probably, their most distinctive feature is that they provide a living setting in which to experience low carbon lifestyles. This is a central aspect of sustainable communities, as in order to transform habits it is important to have the chance to experience and engage in alternative practices (Guillén-Royo and Wilhite 2015). Through experimentation of sustainable eating, travelling and heating for example, people and communities can develop new habits that place them at the forefront of lifestyle change. The environmental achievements of sustainable communities are increasingly acknowledged, from a 40 per cent smaller ecological footprint of the members of the Findhorn Foundation in Scotland (Sevier 2008) to the 1.2 tonnes average carbon savings per household participating in 'transition streets' in Totnes[3] (UK) or the limited 1 per cent growth in electricity consumption in Burlington (US) during the last 20 years (Phillips *et al.* 2013).

What are the characteristics of these movements and how do they relate to the HSD proposal? The question is pertinent if one wants to explore the potential of drawing on the HSD approach to needs and satisfiers to support communities already engaged in low carbon lifestyles. Table 7.1 below starts this exploration by outlining the main features of three types of sustainable communities from the perspective of the pillars of the HSD proposal: self-reliance, balanced articulations and human needs fulfilment. The goal is not to highlight the differences or similarities between these three approaches but to discuss some of their principles and practices with regards to their resonance with the foundations of HSD.

As discussed in Chapter 3, Max-Neef and colleagues did not understand self-reliance as self-sufficiency or autarchy but as the centrality of the community in decision making, policy design and the implementation of production and consumption strategies. Building strong, resilient communities is a core concern in most grassroots projects that place collective values and aspirations at the centre of sustainability planning. For example, the 'cyclic use of material resources'

Table 7.1 The three pillars of the HSD proposal and some key features of sustainable communities

	Self-reliance	Balanced articulations	Human needs fulfilment
Ecovillage			
'An ecovillage is an intentional or traditional community using local participatory processes to holistically integrate ecological, economic, social, and cultural dimensions of sustainability in order to regenerate social and natural environments.'[a]	The community as the core of production and consumption activities as 'all major functions of human living –residence, food provision, manufacture, leisure, social life and commerce –are plainly present and in balanced proportions' (Gilman 1991:11). Self-sufficiency or isolation are not a goal but stress is placed on the establishment of clusters and networks with other ecovillages to run common infrastructures and services.	Same level of importance given to self-discovery, spirituality and community building as to environmental practices (Kessler 2008).	Not explicit about human needs. Their stress on achieving a 'healthy human development' through the promotion of the physical, emotional, mental and spiritual aspects of a healthy life (Gilman 1991) suggests a central role of synergic satisfiers and non-conventional resources in the eco-village movement. 'Equality between humans and other forms of life.' Gilman (1991: 11). Linked to a systemic understanding of change as 'each area of change interacts with the other areas in unpredictable ways' (Gilman 1991:16)
Eco-municipality			
'An eco-municipality is one that has adopted a particular set of sustainability principles as guiding municipal policy and has committed to a bottom-up, participatory approach for implementing this.'[b]	Focus on decreasing environmental impact by reducing CO_2 emissions, increasing use of renewables, production and consumption of organic food and protecting natural areas, among other	Focus mainly on balanced ecosystems as the pillar on which sustainable economic and social structures are based as their concern is the increasing negative environmental impacts of industrialization processes	Human needs fulfilment as understood in the HSD proposal is one of the four sustainability principles included in the Natural Step Framework (see next section) on which the Swedish eco-municipality movement is based.

environmental goals. Some environmental targets concerning food and renewable energy imply the (re)localisation of production. Municipal involvement and community awareness are central in the movement.	and economic organization. Swedish eco-municipalities stress the importance of a strong network, formal membership and common environmental goals.		It is drawn on to argue for the compatibility of meeting needs and consuming less.[c]
Transition town			
'Communities taking an integrated and inclusive approach to reduce their carbon footprint and increase their ability to withstand the fundamental shift that will accompany Peak Oil' (Brangwyn and Hopkins 2008:3)	The focus is on the 'resilient' community, on (re)locating jobs and economic activity (food, energy generation and retrofitting of housing for example) and reducing resource use and environmental impact. People are the main asset of the transition town movement, as Hopkins claims 'you can think of it as a self-organizing system, driven by people's enthusiasm and ideas' (Hopkins 2013:49).	Attempting an integration of the personal, communal, local, regional and global. Initiating projects that are afterwards supported by local councils or higher levels of public administration. Networking and sharing experiences is also crucial for the transition movement. A website, newsletter and annual conferences facilitate sharing and dissemination.	Needs are understood as safety, competence, connectedness and autonomy (Hopkins 2011). Synergies are important since a resilient society, one prepared to confront the challenges of peak oil and recourse depletion is thought to improve need satisfaction. Some of the synergic satisfiers identified (cooperation, democratic participation, creativity, sharing and networking) correspond to Max-Neef non-conventional resources.

a Definition from http://gen.ecovillage.org/en/ecovillages. Accessed 18.12.2014.
b Definition from (http://www.instituteforecouncilities.org/Eco-municipalities.html, Accessed 02.12.2014)
c Terry Gips, economist and sustainability consultant from the US uses the Natural Step Framework to support institutions and communities towards sustainability transformations. Regarding the use of the HSD approach to needs he states that in his workshops 'you'll also explore the powerful work of Alternative Nobel Prize-winning economist Manfred Max-Neef that shows how we can meet the fundamental needs of every person, address our consumption addition and transform our lives and planet'. http://allianceforsustainability.com/terry-gips-on-tnsf/. Accessed 18.12.2014.

promoted by ecovillages takes the community as the place where most of the food and other bio-resources are produced, processed, recycled and disposed of (Gilman 1991; Litfin 2009). This central role of the local community sometimes spreads to education, energy production, the provision of financial services and even the organisation and delivery of social assistance. However, it is not always possible for local initiatives to be in charge of the provision and delivery of basic services as this depends, among other factors, on the technical and financial support that the State is prepared to provide and the level of decentralisation in the country. What seems clear is that most local bottom-up sustainable initiatives consider the community as the relevant dimension for the articulation of sustainable development practices.

In addition to the centrality of the community, strengthening self-reliance implies the emergence of networks that connect local initiatives. Max-Neef and his collaborators stressed the role of networks of grassroots initiatives in order to activate 'non-conventional resources' such as sharing, cooperating and participatory decision making, which would enhance the capacity of bottom-up projects to fulfil human needs. Gilman (2007) agrees with this perspective in his discussion of the ecovillage movement. He maintains that the future of the ecovillage lies in the

> growing 'ecosystem' of groups playing different roles in the movement – everything from the 'on-the-ground' centres of research, demonstration, and training; to specialized consulting groups, to urban neighbourhoods, to towns and villages, and to various networks and associations weaving these together.
> (Gilman 2007 in Arend *et al.* 2013: 7)

It is not uncommon to see several transition initiatives in the same city, coexisting with co-housing, renewable energy and urban farming projects. In Sweden, for example, some ecovillages are located within existing eco-municipalities, which suggests complementarities and overlaps that, although largely unexplored at this stage, might be worth investigating in terms of their synergic effects on human needs and the natural environment.

Balanced relationships at all levels (personal, institutional, between technologies, people and nature, and between micro and macro-levels) constitute the second pillar of the HSD proposal. This is also important for sustainable communities as the necessity of redressing traditional imbalances in the relation between economy, society and environment has traditionally been one of their foundational goals or principles. It is expressed by prioritising interventions to reduce the environmental impacts of transport, home heating/cooling, and food consumption but also in the fact that the strategies used to achieve low impact lifestyles are by and large participatory and take into account the consequences for employment, transportation, land use and market organisation of the environmentally-targeted measures.

The systemic understanding of development and social change advocated by Max-Neef resonates with sustainable communities' stress on direct involvement, participation and transdisciplinarity in their approach to the design of low-carbon solutions and the implementation of sustainability projects. Although expert knowledge is drawn on when required by the community, projects are not usually led by them but are designed and planned in collaboration. The stress on horizontal relationships also applies when dealing with policy-makers and politicians. As Hopkins (2011) reported, when in 2009, Ed Miliband, UK Secretary of State for Energy and Climate Change at the time, requested to attend the annual Transition Network conference, he was accepted on the condition that he attended as participant and not as speaker. In Hopkins own words 'this story symbolises the approach Transition takes to politics, of leading by example and of trying to get politicians to experience the buzz being created by Transition initiatives, rather than just protesting' (Hopkins 2011:23).

Finally, the fulfilment of human needs is a pillar that the HSD proposal shares with the different approaches to sustainable communities summarised in Table 7.1. Their overarching goal is to achieve needs fulfilment with a low environmental impact in terms of greenhouse emissions, resource use, biodiversity loss and waste generation. 'It is the idea that by taking back control over meeting our basic needs at the local level we can stimulate new enterprises – new economic activity – while also reducing our oil dependency and carbon emissions and returning power to the local level' (Hopkins 2013: 27). Thus the focus, even if not always made explicit, is on finding *synergic satisfiers*; those that satisfy more than one need with a positive, null or greatly reduced negative impact on the natural environment. As in the HSD proposal, most literature on sustainable communities considers human needs to encompass much more than the physiological requirements of the human body. Fundamental human needs such as affection, understanding, participation, creation, identity and freedom are considered central for the wellbeing of sustainable communities' members although they are not always worded using the HSD language but expressed in terms of basic or citizens' needs (Hallsmith 2003; Hopkins 2011). An exception is the eco-municipality movement where the HSD understanding of fundamental human needs is taken as a foundational principle. The sections that follow explore in more detail the different ways that HSD has influenced, or has the potential to influence, local sustainability initiatives.

Human needs satisfaction as a foundational principle in eco-municipalities

The Swedish eco-municipality movement is one of the examples of grassroots initiatives analysed by Max-Neef in his most recent book (Smith and Max-Neef 2011). The movement originated in the early eighties in Övertorneå; a small city of less than 5,000 inhabitants located in the north of Sweden on the border to Finland. In a context of economic recession, members of the community together with the municipal government initiated a process towards sustainable development that quickly spread in the country and beyond. Currently, 30 per cent of Swedish municipalities have adhered to the movement as well as local councils in countries as diverse as the US, Japan, Kenya, Ethiopia, Denmark, Finland and Chile.[4]

In order to define a sustainable society, the eco-municipalities movement draws on the Framework for Strategic Sustainable Development or Natural Step Framework. As already outlined in Chapter 5, the framework was developed by Swedish oncologist Dr Karl-Henrik Robért in collaboration with ecologists, physicists and medical doctors, among other scientists.[5] The framework is supported by four principles that are considered both sufficient and necessary for a sustainable society and can be applied by any type of organisation, from households, to local groups, communities, municipalities, business, religious institutions, government agencies or NGOs. The four principles characterising a sustainable society are the following (Holmberg 1998; Smith and Max-Neef 2011: 182–183):[6]

1) a minimal concentration of substances extracted from Earth such as fossil fuels, underground metals and minerals as their increased use has resulted in a build-up of hazardous substances and pollutants that weaken living systems and contribute to climate change;
2) a low concentration of substances produced by society such as greenhouse gases, synthetic chemicals, plastics and other substances that spread toxins in the environment and contribute to global warming;
3) a low or null level of degradation and destruction of the ecosystems and biodiversity; and,
4) the elimination of hurdles that society creates to satisfy fundamental human needs.

The fourth principle draws on the HSD list of nine fundamental needs and concentrates on the efficient use of resources to meet human needs, while respecting the first three principles. As Holmberg (1998: 35) puts it

> if we are more efficient, technically, organisationally and socially, more services with the possibility of meeting more human needs can be provided for a given level of impact in nature. Efficiency in that context, if the perspective is large enough, implies not only reduced resource flows per utility, but also improved means of dealing with social issues such as equity, fairness and population growth.

On the website of the Institute for Eco-municipality Education and Assistance,[18] directors Torbjörn Lahti and Sarah James explain how Eco-municipalities take a systemic approach in opposition to the traditional 'silos approach' commonly associated with top-down environmental policies. They explain that

> while many US communities in the United States are carrying out sustainable development projects such as green building programs, affordable housing, smart growth, or climate change initiatives, these largely are occurring on a project-by-project basis that might be called the 'silo approach' to sustainable

development. In contrast, the eco-municipality model uses a systems approach that involves widespread community awareness-raising and integrated municipal involvement, and using a common language to identify what sustainability means, such as the four APA sustainability objectives.[7] These approaches have been instrumental in creating an extensive track record of success.[8]

The success of eco-municipalities is exemplified by the fact that the early Swedish eco-municipality movement inspired Agenda 21, agreed to at the UN Rio Earth Summit in 1992. As outlined in Chapter 2, Agenda 21 was a non-binding, voluntary action plan with measures encompassing local, national and global action with the goal to reduce the impact of human activity on the environment (Agenda 21 1992). The experience of eco-municipalities was captured in some of its chapters; such as chapter 7 on the promotion of sustainable human settlements and chapter 4 on the transformation of consumption patterns. Unfortunately, these are two of the chapters where no significant progress can be reported at the global level. As Dodds and colleagues maintain 'while there are some good examples of progressive urban policy, the socio-economic inequalities and negative environmental issues within many urban areas remain widespread in both developing and developed countries; and slum populations are still rising' (Dodds *et al.* 2012: 7). Despite this bleak picture, Dobbs and colleagues claimed that in 2002, more than 6,000 municipal authorities around the world had started plans or developed policies to reduce the environmental impacts of everyday activities in their localities. In addition, eco-municipalities, and other sustainable community initiatives, continue spreading in Europe and the US, and are emerging in other parts of the world; suggesting a perhaps too slow but somehow steady progress towards environmental sustainability at the municipal level.

Drawing on the HSD approach, we could identify at least two factors that could strengthen the success of eco-municipalities in spreading low-carbon lifestyles at the local level. The first concerns the fact that, despite considering needs satisfaction as a foundational principle, human needs have not been included as one of the measurable targets to evaluate eco-municipalities' success. The 12 indicators used to monitor progress among Swedish eco-municipalities, for example, focus on environmental targets and do not include psychological, relational, social or needs-based measures.[9] To date, most indicators suggest that progress has been made in reducing some environmental impacts: for example, from 2007 to 2011 the number of journeys per inhabitant with public transportation in Swedish eco-municipalities increased from 54 per cent to 79 per cent; the percentage of renewable and reused energy in municipality buildings increased from 68 per cent to 75 per cent; and the percentage of environmentally certified schools and preschools from 11 per cent to 19 per cent. Nevertheless, it is quite likely that if human needs satisfaction had been included as a measurable target, the interventions designed to actualise needs would have increased the efficacy of environmental interventions due to the synergies between human and natural systems activated in the process of needs actualisation.

The second reflection stemming from approaching sustainable development drawing on the HSD framework, concerns the need to strengthen participatory processes in sustainability planning and being open to grassroots organisations taking the lead in designing and organising specific sustainability projects. The eco-municipality movement has always underlined the importance of popular participation and many decisions on environmental measures are done with the involvement of relevant stakeholders after awareness-raising campaigns are put into place and creative solutions have been developed through the generation of new spaces for participation (James and Lahti 2004; Phillips *et al.* 2013). In fact, one of the chapters of Agenda 21 where progress can be reported is the one stressing the role of civil society's involvement in decision-making processes regarding environmental issues (Hallsmith 2003; Phillips *et al.* 2013). However, a renewed focus on grassroots leadership and on needs-based participatory methodologies could enhance eco-municipalities' environmental achievements through interventions capturing human-nature synergies. The prototype tool described in the next section, and the adaptation of the HSD methodology by Inez Aponte discussed later, could support an increased stress on grassroots participation in the eco-municipality movement.

Contributing to ecovillages' success through a human needs-based tool

Unlike eco-municipalities, ecovillages are often intentional communities; communities purposefully created with the goal of experiencing sustainable living. They are relatively small (a recommended upper limit of 500 people); of 'a size in which people are able to know and be known by the others in the community, and where each member of the community feels he or she is able to influence the community's direction' (Gilman 1991: 10). Gilman (1991) coined the term ecovillage in the early nineties to identify communities that were created with the twin purpose of combining low impact living with community building. Their emergence and proliferation was encouraged by the increasing amount of evidence on ecological limits, the appearance of new communication technologies and renewable energies and the new levels of consciousness or awareness about the earth and the history of humans (Ergas 2010).

The Global Ecovillage Network, a network of sustainable communities that 'serves as an umbrella organization for ecovillages, transition town initiatives, intentional communities, and ecologically-minded individuals worldwide', reports having more than 13,000 eco-settlements registered around the world.[10] All these settlements have in common a commitment with low impact lifestyles, with placing the environment first and going beyond conservation to enhancing and regenerating natural ecosystems. Ecovillages are highly diverse and include from villages applying ecological design principles in Sri Lanka to educational centres such as Findhorn in Scotland.[11] Despite their diversity, they share an 'ontological commitment to holism and radical interdependence' which draws on system-thinking in Gaia theory – considering the Earth as a living organism

(Lovelock 1979; Litfin 2005), and permaculture – understanding human systems as reinforcing and intertwined with natural systems (Litfin 2009).

As discussed earlier in this chapter, ecovillages aspire to high levels of self-sufficiency through an understanding of human activities as part of a cyclical process, where production and consumption do not generate waste. 'Gray water and kitchen waste are recycled into community gardens; human manure is composted into landscape soil; rainwater is harvested for garden and home use; and woody waste from community forests warms the homes of the residents. To the extent that ecovillages are able to generate a local economy based upon community resources, money circulates internally and automobile use decreases. Central to each of these elements of ecovillage life is the creation of virtuous cycles, as opposed to vicious cycles, which regenerate the land, enliven the community, and sustain its members in a cohesive whole comprised of integrated human and natural systems' (Litfin 2009: 129). Thus, ecovillages could be considered examples of the practice of human scale development at the local level through their systemic understanding of the relationship between people, society, economy, technologies and nature and their commitment to participation and social cohesion.

However, ecovillages are not always successful in presenting a long-term alternative to consumerist, highly polluting western lifestyles. In 2003, Diana Leafe Christian reported that around 90 per cent of the aspiring ecovillages and community initiatives failed and that one of the most important reasons for this failure was the lack of a community vision, shared by all members of the settlement, that was flexible enough to be amended and transformed through participatory enquiry (Christian 2003). Drawing on this evidence, masters students Arend, Gallagher and Orell (2013)[12] suggested using the HSD approach to needs to design a participatory tool to support ecovillage members in the development of long-term strategies. Since the pillars of the HSD proposal and its systemic approach to sustainable development are very similar to the principles of the ecovillage movement, a more explicit consideration of human needs and satisfiers in community planning could be easily integrated in decision-making processes.

The prototype tool developed by the students was based on the 'sustainability wheel' used in ecovillage design education; permaculture principles,[13] and the nine fundamental needs of the HSD proposal. Through a series of iterations with ecovillage experts, the students arrived at a final prototype and a suggestion for a methodology for its application, based on The Natural Step framework discussed in Chapter 5. Graphically, the prototype presented three concentric rings with community vision and values at the core, surrounded by the HSD nine fundamental needs defining societal sustainability and the seven permaculture principles accounting for ecological sustainability. The outer ring represented the biosphere. In their iterative process of consultations, experts agreed on the fact that a main strength of the prototype tool was the inclusion of Max-Neef's theory of human needs. As the authors reported 'the experts liked that Max-Neef's human needs were the driving force in the centre of the wheel and that the prototype stimulates discussion on how to satisfy these needs within the boundaries of nature. It helped them to see the big picture, grounded in a shared understanding' (Arend et al. 2013: 26).

The prototype was intended to guide ecovillages' strategic planning. It could also be used as a tool to rethink and redefine the goals and vision of the community. The authors suggested organising participatory workshops following the ABCD planning method used by The Natural Step framework[14] for sustainability planning developed in the context of the eco-municipality movement. The ABCD planning method describes a participatory methodology in 4 steps based on Awareness raising, Baseline mapping, facilitating the emergence of Creative solutions and Deciding on priorities and strategies (refer to Chapter 5 for a more detailed explanation of The Natural Step framework). The ABCD planning method was drawn on by Arend and colleagues to structure a series of leading questions that communities could use when working with the prototype. Two questions framed the discussion on human needs and satisfiers. The first was included in the Awareness phase asking participants to reflect on the reasons they had to 'get together and find new, creative, innovative ways to satisfy their needs' (Arend *et al.* 2013: 31). The second was included under the co-creation or Creative solutions phase where ecovillagers would be encouraged to reflect on satisfiers that would allow the actualisation of human needs at the personal and collective level while being mindful to others and accounting for the seven domains of permaculture.

The planning process suggested by Arend and colleagues resonates with the discussion presented in Chapter 5 on the use and adaptation of the HSD methodology for sustainability planning. The prototype tool and the associated methodology could be considered yet another alternative way of using the HSD perspective on needs and satisfiers. However, the fact that the prototype is tailored to the logic and foundational principles of ongoing sustainable community initiatives such as ecovillages and eco-municipalities increases the likelihood of its adoption compared to the other adaptations of the methodology presented throughout the book. It will be interesting to follow the work of Johanne Gallagher and Peter Orell, two of the masters students co-authoring the thesis, who are currently introducing the prototype to several community projects in Western Australia.[15]

Supporting the transition movement through HSD workshops

The Transition Movement started in Totnes, Devon (United Kingdom) in 2006 with the goal of finding creative strategies to address climate change, reduced supplies of fossil fuels ('peak oil') and consumerist, high-carbon lifestyles. Currently there are transition groups and communities in 41 countries and the number is constantly increasing. As discussed earlier, the three pillars of the HSD are reflected in the processes and goals of the movement as their work to build resilient communities revolves around the (re)localisation of production and consumption, active networking, the promotion of horizontal relationships and a focus on creativity, motivation and strengthening community life. Hereafter, Inez Aponte reflects on her experience using the HSD approach with people engaged in Transition initiatives.

Box 7.1 Fundamental human needs and the transition movement, by Inez Aponte

As a practitioner working in the field of behaviour change, I focus on exploring the conditions which encourage public engagement with social and environmental issues. I have a particular interest in developing creative methods to translate academic research, such as the HSD approach to needs, into accessible, workable ideas to mobilise change on the ground. Working in 2009 as a trainer for the Transition Network, I delivered the two-day Launch training[16] on how to set up, run and grow a transition initiative. The programme covered both the practical aspects of Transition as well as what is referred to as 'Inner Transition', which deals with the inner or personal dimension of Transition. As part of the work with Inner Transition, a session called 'Inner Worlds' addressed models and notions of primal wounding, suggesting that our wounding on an individual and collective level leads us to engage in behaviours that are emotionally and mentally destructive. This in turn creates a world that passes on further wounding. While I agreed with the theory of wounding to a large extent, I felt the framework lacked the specific dimension of our relationship with and dependence upon the earth. Although the framework hinted at the necessity of a human-nature connection and there was an assumption that a healthy human would naturally feel respect and care for the planet we live on, there was no way of explicitly evaluating the impact of human psychology and subsequent behaviour on the natural world. Thus, I began my search for a framework that would enable groups to undertake this evaluation and I found in the HSD approach to needs and satisfiers a useful theoretical and practical reference.

Drawing on the HSD framework, I developed a core workshop which poses the question 'What do humans need to thrive?' and proposed a discussion on the issue with regards to the satisfaction of needs. To the standard HSD approach, I added a fundamental condition for needs satisfaction; a Living Earth (see Chapter 4 for an illustration). I began delivering this workshop and a number of associated practices to both *Transitioners* and *non-Transitioners*, people new to environmental issues as well as experienced activists. In total, over the last five years I have delivered these sessions to several hundred people from many different countries and as young as 12 years of age.

HSD bridging divides

Through delivering these workshops (entitled 'What really matters – understanding human needs and values') it became clear that the model of fundamental human needs, with my addition of the Living Earth, had the potential to bridge some of the divides I had observed within the Transition and other environmental movements, such as those between 'be-ers' and 'do-ers', experts and lay people and sustainable and unsustainable behaviours.

Regarding 'be-ers' and 'do-ers': although Transition stands out from many environmental movements with its emphasis on inner transition as an important counterpart to the doing aspect of the work, I have observed that the way in which inner transition is framed often alienates people who are not so comfortable with psychological models or reflective practices. Because each of the fundamental human needs can be seen as having both an inner and an outer dimension, we can safely start discussions about the impacts of the outer conditions on our lives and gradually move to questions of a more inward looking nature. This allows groups to engage with psychological questions in a non-threatening manner and to go as far as they are comfortable without forcing the issue.

Concerning experts and laypeople, I observed that some of the people I worked with had no interest or were actively put off by economics as a discipline. The HSD approach to needs and satisfiers allows participants to view the economy through a completely different lens and to see themselves as economic actors regardless of whether they are involved in activities that raise GDP or not. Parents who stay at home to look after their children, those caring for elderly relatives, community volunteers, unpaid creatives and the countless individuals who in conventional economic terms are counted as unemployed, and therefore unproductive, gain visibility in this process. Seeing themselves appear 'on the map' often leads to a sense of empowerment which, combined with practical opportunities for action, can inspire increased participation in society. Introducing the language of fundamental human needs and framing the purpose of an economy in a new way makes it easier to engage people hitherto disinterested in economics, social psychology or other expert fields.

Finally, understanding the difference between needs and satisfiers allows us to address barriers to sustainable behaviour on a systemic level rather than judging individual lifestyle choices. HSD can help us understand the underlying need that drives individual choices, the specific nature of the satisfiers used to meet the need and offer synergic alternatives. It also shows us that even when we are fully committed to living sustainable lives we may not have a choice to do so. The systemic nature of our environmental and social problems is revealed and we can place less emphasis on individual choice and more on collective action, thus reducing feelings of guilt and unleashing people's creativity to find solutions to their common challenges.

Transition as good HSD practice

Transition projects often intuitively meet many of the nine fundamental human needs in a synergic way.[17] The Transition movement's emphasis on awareness raising, valuing community, sharing and networking, drawing on the collective genius and appreciating diversity means that Transition projects readily provide synergic satisfiers for the needs for Participation, Understanding,

Creation and Affection. Depending on the project's area of focus other needs are also provided for. In Totnes alone there are several successful food initiatives, such as The Food Link Project[18] meeting the need for Subsistence in addition to all the above. In addition, projects such as Gardening for Health[19] add an emphasis on the physical and mental health benefits of food growing which provide an opportunity to meet the need for Protection. I would argue that this intuitive provision of synergic satisfiers is one of Transition's greatest strengths. Below I will elaborate on one of these examples, which exemplifies this intuitive process of satisfier 'emergence'.

The Transition Streets Project[20] was initiated in 2010 in Totnes with the initial aim of helping people make lifestyle changes that would enable them to save on their energy bills. To engage participants, leaflets were distributed inviting people to find another five or six households in their street to participate in a practical hands-on programme which promised to reduce energy bills and offered potential loans for solar panels for low income households upon completion. The sessions were self-directed with the help of a workbook after an initial introduction by a Transition facilitator. The group then met in each other's houses at an agreed time on a weekly or biweekly basis, going through the workbook which covered energy use in different areas: household energy, water, food, transport and waste.

The programme proved very successful in its initial goal: reducing energy consumption. The latest figures state that over 550 households have reduced their household bills by an average of £570 per year, which is the equivalent of 1.2 tonnes of carbon. What was not expected were the additional lasting gains in participants' wellbeing. The Transition Streets project had a considerable impact on social cohesion, providing many with satisfiers for Affection and Participation through new friendships, Protection due to an increased sense of community, and Creation and Identity through community projects initiated by group members. Projects started by Transition Streets groups include a community cinema, a community orchard and Food In Community, a scheme using waste from farms to provide meals for low income families[21] (Beetham 2011; Ward *et al.* 2011).

HSD contribution to Transition – becoming conscious of our needs

There are a number of ways the HSD model can support the work of the Transition movement. Despite my earlier observation that Transition provides so many synergic satisfiers, there is very little awareness among *transitioners* of the fundamental human needs model. So a lot of these synergic satisfiers come about coincidentally in as much as the projects do not consciously set out to meet these needs. This lack of awareness can lead to certain needs being overlooked or a project not maximising its potential by missing how, with a few adjustments, it might become more successful, lasting or inclusive.

Being explicit about what our needs are and understanding the impact of our choice of satisfiers offers opportunities for evaluation of practice that is often lacking when needs or values are assumed rather than articulated. It is often not until things go wrong that we realise that perhaps we weren't working towards the same objective after all. The strength of using HSD in Transition lies in the way the model can articulate both the inner dimensions of needs satisfaction and external societal influences.

Being explicit about needs also means we don't overlook some in favour of others, creating unnecessary and destructive imbalances. An often neglected need in Western culture is the need for Idleness. Activists have to deal with both the awareness of the ecological and social pressures we are facing and a culture that emphasises productivity as a measure of human worth. It is no surprise that many *Transitioners* become overworked and burn out. Understanding that the needs for Idleness, Affection and Creation are universal human needs that if not satisfied to a certain extent create 'poverties' and distress may be one way of preventing this.

By becoming conscious of our fundamental needs we can start to analyse how our satisfiers are provided, who provides them and where there are and aren't choices for adequate satisfiers that do not negatively impact the Earth. A Transition approach that worked consciously with the nine fundamental needs would quickly make it clear that action must take place on the personal, community and global/state levels. At the personal level, we must examine our personal story around these nine needs and the way we choose to satisfy them. 'How did I come to my values and are they serving me?' At the community level we must address the impact my community's choice of satisfiers is having on my own life, my community and the earth. 'How did we come to our collective values and are they serving us and the earth?' At the global/state level we should question the systems of legislation, ownership, education and communication that are in place to allow me to satisfy my needs and their impact on my community, other communities and the earth (Rauschmayer and Omann 2015).

Addressing these three levels, it becomes apparent that certain impacts on our needs satisfaction cannot be easily influenced by local action alone. National legislation often inhibits (positive) changes groups seek to implement in their local community. These types of changes require larger networked and often political solutions. Transition's position hitherto has been to stay out of the political arena as much as possible, which some say has contributed to its success. However when operating from a true HSD perspective it becomes untenable to avoid all political affiliation and can be frustrating when there is energy for political action which then has to be suppressed or ignored.

In summary, embedding HSD into Transition culture (as well as in the ecovillage and eco-municipality movements) may contribute to the project in at least five important ways. First, used at the initial stages of a group's formation it may become a useful tool for preventing unnecessary conflict, both within the group and in interaction with other groups or individuals (Spies 2006). Second, it provides a unified language for both Inner and Outer Transition which can help bridge the gap between be-ers and do-ers. Third, a deeper systemic understanding of people's motivations may provide ways for Transition to appeal to a wider public and find ways to engage those resistant to change or locked into unsustainable behaviour. Fourth, if energy becomes available for more outwardly political action it could be harnessed and redirected. Even if Transition wishes to maintain its apolitical stance it can then provide a sign posting function for different political activities. And fifth, it would allow the development of shared indicators across sustainable communities which could be used to measure how well an initiative is performing in terms of needs satisfaction.

Sustainable communities: exploring *necessary* synergic satisfiers

Drawing on the principles, methodologies and practices of sustainable communities, one could argue that generating *synergic satisfiers* is one of their main goals. Following the HSD definition of synergic satisfiers presented in Chapter 3, cultivating ways of Being, Having, Doing and Interacting that respect and enhance human needs is likely to improve the natural environment, since satisfiers that contribute to environmental disruption will negatively affect at least one of the nine fundamental human needs and hence will not present the characteristics of synergic satisfiers. Through the Transition Streets example, Inez Aponte has illustrated how sustainable communities organise projects with synergic characteristics. Throughout the book, I have discussed other HSD-based studies that have also resulted in the identification of synergic bridging or synergic satisfiers with positive impacts on the natural environment. At this point, it might not seem too farfetched to suggest that there might be some *necessary* synergic satisfiers, akin to the universal satisfier characteristics of Doyal and Gough's *Theory of Human Need* (1991) discussed in Chapter 3, that are present (or should be present) in societies where human needs are actualised in harmony with the natural environment.

Table 7.2 brings together synergic satisfiers that have been explicitly or implicitly highlighted in articles, websites, reports, theses or books discussing sustainable communities. Thus, satisfiers are drawn from the literature used in this chapter, among others: Arend *et al.* (2013); Blaitt Gonzales (2009); Dawson (2006); Hallsmith (2003); Hopkins (2011, 2013); James and Lahti (2004); Kessler (2008); Phillips and colleagues (2013); Seyfang (2009), the websites referred in the end notes and other informal sources. This is a rough first exploration, where for the sake of simplicity, satisfiers are mentioned only in relation to one of the needs they are meant to fulfil. Much more work is required to perhaps narrow down the constellation of satisfiers to those whose interdependence and leverage make them 'super-synergic' or *necessary* synergic satisfiers; satisfiers that could be defined as necessary components of societies that get close to both human needs fulfilment and environmental sustainability.

As an attempt to initiate this task, I discuss hereafter some of the synergic satisfiers present in sustainable communities that could fall under the category of *necessary*. Regarding the existential category of *Being*, sustainable communities underline the importance for people of being inwardly strong, authentic and true to oneself. These attributes enable people to open up, become more tolerant and willing to trust and cooperate with others. Self-knowledge was already identified by Max-Neef in his 1989 Schumacher Memorial Lecture (reproduced in the 1991 HSD book) as the first step towards larger-scale transformations. As Max-Neef put it:

> Now, the point is that if I change myself, something may happen as a consequence that may lead to a change in the world. But we are afraid of changing ourselves. It is always easier to try to change others. The dictum of Socrates was 'Know thyself', for he knew how afraid human beings are to know themselves. We know a lot about our neighbours, but we know little about ourselves. So, if we simply manage to change ourselves, something fascinating may happen to the world.
>
> (Max-Neef 1991: 113)

When it comes to *Having*, people working and/or researching on sustainable communities highlight the importance of having production, consumption and leisure structures that promote connectivity and cooperation, ranging from consumption and production cooperatives to associations organising leisure activities. Increased connectivity at the personal and community levels emphasises the importance of structures for conflict resolution. Leading sustainable lifestyles might create conflict or tension within the group or community and at the level of the whole society (between groups). As Inez Aponte described, some *transitioners* might be more eager than others in their advocacy and implementation of a low impact lifestyle and might judge negatively other less committed members.

Having a methodology to share and understand the underlying needs that lead 'non-activists', or less engaged people, to pursue an environmentally harmful activity is thus important. Rauschmayer and Omann suggest using a four-step process

> that first aims to acknowledge these tensions, second helps the participant to reflect upon the internal reasons for the tensions, third supports the communication of these reflections to others and fourth, introduces a process of creativity to find ways of dealing with or even overcoming the tension(s). This process aims for thriving, through awareness for non-conflicting strategies and is therefore called 'THANCS'.
>
> (Rauschmayer and Omann 2015: 117).

It can be operationalised using the matrix of fundamental human needs to identify the root-causes of personal tensions and could be considered an example of the necessary synergic satisfier 'having a conflict resolution mechanism' contributing to the needs for protection and affection among others.

Regarding actions and behaviours, sustainable community members are cooperating, volunteering, and being pro-active to identify, plan and execute measures to satisfy human needs and preserve the natural environment. An example of the synergic effects of cooperating and volunteering can be drawn from the Sarasota's Food gleaning project in the US where volunteers collect, pack and deliver to a local food bank the excess produce from a local farm. As Hopkins (2013: 93) writes, quoting Don Hall from Transition Sarasota:

> the project is 'a win for food banks and those in need'[21] because it provides quality, healthy food to those who need it most. This is a 'win for local farmers' because small farmers benefit from a tax deduction for the full market value of all of the produce they donate, and 'a win for volunteers' because as Don explains, 'all volunteers are invited to take home one grocery bag full of produce in appreciation for their time. This usually keeps people in leafy greens for a week'.

When it comes to the spaces and environments people interact in, we can identify at least two differentiated sets of satisfiers: one that is related to a reduced impact of human activities on the natural environment and another that links with an increased contact with nature, where natural and human spaces have no clear physical or mental divisions. Integrating nature in everyday activities through gardening, collaborating in forestry or farming tasks, volunteering for the regeneration of river banks and rundown parks or promoting farmers' markets is common to most sustainable community initiatives. Increased environmental conservation and protection is done through direct experience and it does not rely that much on sometimes counterproductive information or awareness-raising campaigns on environmental limits and ecological boundaries (Crompton and Kasser 2009). Hence, closeness and direct experience of nature and the natural cycle of life appear as potential candidates for the tentative category of *necessary synergic satisfier*.

Finally, one of the things that stands out when analysing the matrix in Table 7.2 is that the fact of living in a community with its high levels of participation and interaction, sharing and exchanging, self-reliance and connectedness to nature becomes a *necessary synergic satisfier* by itself (Blaitt Gonzalez 2009). Many projects that start with the goal of reducing environmental impacts highlight as the most important outcome the increased internal cohesion of the community or the strong relationships that have been forged in the process. This indicates that 'community living' is of key importance when it comes to the emergence of synergic satisfiers and might function as a necessary component of a sustainable articulation. As Seyfang illustrates when referring to Athena and Bill Steen's sustainable housing project in the US:

Table 7.2 Sustainable communities and synergic satisfiers

	Being	Having	Doing	Interacting
Subsistence	Engaged, honest, equitable	Own produce, self-managed work, exchange systems, local markets, organised groups, gift economy, cooperatives, partnerships, connectedness, local banks/currency	Living communally, health prevention, sharing, volunteering, cooperating, networking	Low environmental impact (less waste, fewer emissions, less pollution)
Protection	Hopeful, trustful	Sense of community, access to healthy food, access to alternative health-care, conflict resolution mechanisms, connectedness	Recognising, praising, supporting, visioning	Low ecological footprint, low levels of pollution, public or private spaces to grow food
Affection	Tolerant	Strong family and community ties, conflict resolution mechanisms, community celebrations, children's playgroup, time sovereignty	Bonding across generations, loving nature, volunteering, growing own food	Shared or collective spaces, activities to express emotions
Understanding	Open, inclusive	Awareness of one's place in the whole system, interaction with peers, permaculture, system to resolve conflicts, participatory decision-making, organised groups, unconventional classrooms, simplicity, local banks/currency	Growing personally, living sustainably	Experiencing nature, free (not enforced) spaces or opportunities to share ideas

Participation	Authentic, willing to cooperate, inclusive	Sense of community, community work, participatory decision-making, conflict resolution, community celebrations, local markets, organised groups, simplicity	Cooperating, searching for sustainable solutions, meditating, volunteering	Opportunities to get involved in decisions, multi-functional spaces
Idleness	Open, determined	Flexible times, community celebrations, permaculture, local markets, Organised groups (production and leisure related)	Prioritising time for idleness	Spaces and times adequate for leisure activities, balance of public and private spaces
Creation	Empowered	Permaculture, community celebrations, local markets, Organised groups (production and leisure related), room for experimentation	Searching for sustainable solutions, recycling, contributing to build the surroundings and one's own space	Common spaces, celebratory events, outreach events
Identity	Authentic, sustainable	Sense of community, participatory decision-making, community celebrations, local markets, Organised groups (production and leisure related)	Cooperating, feeling part of a group, working for a more sustainable work, building own spaces	Communion with life, spaces for participation and collaboration
Freedom	Satisfied, hopeful	Flexible timetable, successful projects to build confidence, culture of simplicity and frugality, local banks/currency	Choosing to live an alternative lifestyle, reflecting on successes	Spaces or opportunities to share ideas freely (non-binding)

straw-bale buildings can be sustainable, but they are not necessarily so, and it is the process of building, in relationship with nature, the materials, and with other people, that makes a building sustainable. In fact, as their work has progressed it has become the social and community aspects of straw-bale building which have become more prominent and valuable to the Steens.

(Seyfang 2009: 125)

Conclusion

This chapter has explored how the theoretical and methodological underpinnings of HSD can contribute to the success of sustainable community initiatives. It has analysed sustainable communities from their resonance with the tenets of the HSD proposal (self-reliance, balanced relationships and human need satisfaction), which are, to different extents, present among the goals and everyday activities of people living in ecovillages, transition initiatives and eco-municipalities. However, the connections between environmentally sustainable practices and human needs-enhancing strategies are not always made explicit in the goals and practices of sustainable communities. This is particularly the case in eco-municipalities that, despite having human need satisfaction as one of their guiding principles, still measure their success in terms of environmental targets. This and the low rate of survival of local environmental initiatives suggest that incorporating participatory strategic planning methodologies or reflection tools based on the HSD proposal would probably enhance the synergies of their environmentally-oriented projects and contribute to their long-term success.

As Inez Aponte points out, the HSD approach to needs and satisfiers, and its associated methodology, offer an opportunity to analyse and compare what is working and why. This analysis would allow communities to identify the specific conditions that are conducive to or encouraging of sustainable behaviour and could support a better articulation of the effectiveness of such projects in delivering a combined goal of sustainability and human wellbeing and provide evidence with which to influence policy-makers. In addition, a reflection on needs and satisfiers through the THANCS method, for example, suggests that the HSD approach to needs might also support the resolution of intra-individual and intra-societal tensions that arise when people choose a low impact lifestyle.

Finally, it is important to note that many of the characteristics of everyday living in sustainable communities are already synergic satisfiers. In the last section we suggest an analysis of these satisfiers in terms of their *necessary* presence as components of a constellation of *Beings*, *Havings*, *Doings* and ways of *Interacting* that support human needs actualisation and environmental sustainability. Self-knowledge, participatory conflict resolution schemes, volunteering, cooperating and direct experience of nature are put forward as examples of interdependent *necessary synergic satisfiers*.

Notes

1 Inez Aponte is an educator and community activist and founder of Growing Good Lives where she uses the HSD approach to design and deliver seminars, training

and consultancy to 'unleash human potential for the common good'. She has been developing participatory learning processes since 1998 and has designed and delivered programmes for, among others, WWF, The Soil Association, Danish Institute for Studies Abroad, Lille Institute of Political Studies and Schumacher College, as well as activists working in the New Economy movement. She is an accredited Trainer for the Transition Network and works for Totnes-based Futurebound on their Leadership for Resiliency programme (www.growinggoodlives.com).

2 Burlingtons (Vermont, US) is another example of a sustainable community, defined as a 'healthy place to live' with a balanced relationship between the economic, social and environmental aspects of everyday living (Phillips and colleagues 2013).

3 'Transition streets' are groups of five to ten households working together to reduce their environmental impact by addressing energy and water use, waste production and family diet and cutting emissions from private transportation (Hopkins 2011).

4 See www.sekom.se.

5 Refer to www.naturalstep.org/en/our-story for a short description of the development of The Natural Step framework.

6 http://allianceforsustainability.com/terry-gips-on-tnsf/, accessed 1 December 2014.

7 These correspond to the four principles of The Natural Step framework.

8 www.instituteforecomunicipalities.org/Eco-municipalities.html/

9 The 12 'green indicators' reported annually by the Swedish Eco-municipalities to the National Association of Swedish Eco-Municipalities are: CO_2 from fossil fuels sold in the municipality; number of journeys with public transportation (journeys/inhabitant); per cent renewable fuel in public transportation; per cent farmland with support for ecological farming; per cent forestry with environmental certification, land and water areas with nature protection as a percentage of municipality area, collected waste (Kg/inhabitant), including recycled; mg/kg of heavy metals in sludge (lead, cadmium and mercury); per cent of renewable and re-used energy in municipality buildings; transport energy for emissions with car (kWh/annual employee) and CO_2 for emissions with car (ton/annual employee); purchase of organic food (per cent); per cent of environmentally certified schools and preschools (www.sekom.se).

10 http://gen.ecovillage.org/, accessed 25 April 2015.

11 www.findhorn.org/, accessed 25 April 2015.

12 The masters degree thesis can be downloaded from www.bth.se/fou/cuppsats.nsf/all/750f 11b043e07a6cc1257b88004aad14/$file/BTH per cent202013 per cent20Gallagher.pdf, accessed 5 December 2014.

13 See www.gaiaeducation.net/index.php/en/programmes/ecovillage-design-education, for a graphical representation of the Sustainability Wheel. Permaculture is an approach to agriculture that accounts for natural processes to use land more efficiently. It was coined by Mollison and Holmgren (1978) to represent a holistic approach to human and natural systems that considers them as mutually enhancing (Litfin 2009). The seven domains of permaculture on which ethics and design principles are applied are building, tools and technology, education and culture, health and spiritual wellbeing, finances and economics, land tenure and community governance, and land and nature stewardship. Ecovillagers as well as members of most sustainable community projects are familiar with this framework and they use it as a reference for the creation of a sustainable culture (Arend *et al.* 2013).

14 www.naturalstep.ca/abcd, accessed 26 August 2015.

15 Contact Johanne Gallagher (irishdivan@gmail.com) and Peter Orrel (orrell65@gmail.com) for any query about their current practice as community facilitators.

16 See www.transitionnetwork.org/training/courses/launch, accessed 6 January 2015, for a description of the transition LAUNCH training.

17 See www.transitionnetwork.org/about/, accessed 6 January 2015, for a description of transition principles.

18 www.transitiontowntotnes.org/groups/food-group/food-link-project/, accessed 26 August 2015.
19 www.gardeningforhealth.org.uk/
20 www.transitionstreets.org.uk/
21 In inverted commas in the original.

References

Agenda 21 (1992). Agenda 21, report on United Nationals Conference on Environment and Development, Rio de Janeiro, Brazil, 3–4 June. https://sustainabledevelopment.un.org/content/documents/Agenda21.pdf, accessed 17 February 2015.

Arend, C. O., Galllagher, J. and Orell, P. (2013). Reinventing the wheel to guide ecovillages towards sustainability. Masters thesis, Blekinge Institut of Technology, Karlskrona, Sweden.

Beetham, H. (2011). *Social Impacts of Transition Together*, (www.transitiontogether.org.uk/wp-content/uploads/2012/07/SocialimpactsofTransitionStreets-finalreport.pdf, accessed 27 January 2015).

Blaitt González, R. (2009). La estructura social de comunidad y su aporte en la búsqueda de sostenibilidad: El caso de las ecoaldeas. Boletín CF+S 42/43. Marzo 2010, (http://habitat.aq.upm.es/boletin/n42/ac-rbla.html, accessed 16 December 2014).

Christian, D. L. (2003). *Creating a Life Together: Practical Tools to Grow Ecovillages and Intentional Communities*. Gabriola Island, BC, Canada: New Society Publishers.

Crompton, T. and Kasser, T. (2009). *Meeting Environmental Challenges: The Role of Human Identity*. Godalming, UK: WWF-UK.

Dodds, F., Schneeberger, K. and Ullah, F. (2012). Review of implementation of Agenda 21 and the Rio principles. Stakeholder Forum for Sustainable Future, (https://sustainabledevelopment.un.org/content/documents/641Synthesis_report_Web.pdf, accessed 17 February 2015).

Doyal, L. and Gough, I. (1991). *A Theory of Human Need*. New York: Palgrave Macmillan.

Ergas, C. (2010). A model of sustainable living: Collective identity in an urban ecovillage. *Organization & Environment*, 23(1): 32–54.

Gilman, R. (1991). The eco-village challenge. *In Context*, 29: 10–14, (www.context.org/iclib/ic29/gilman1/, accessed 16 December 2014).

Gilman, R. (2007). Broadening the ecovillage movement. In Joubert, K. A. and Alfred, R. (eds), *Beyond You and Me*. Hampshire: Gaia Education, pp. 216–20.

Guillén-Royo, M. and Wilhite, H. (2015). Wellbeing and sustainable consumption. In Glatzer, W. (ed.), *Global Handbook of Well-being and Quality of Life*. Frankfurt: Springer.

Hallsmith, G. (2003). *The Key to Sustainable Cities – Meeting Human Needs, Transforming Community Systems*. Gabriola: New Society Publishers.

Holmberg, J. (1998). Backcasting: A Natural Step when making sustainable development operational for companies. *Greener Manage International*, 23: 30–51.

Hopkins, R. (2011). *The Transition Companion*. Cambridge: Green Books.

Hopkins, R. (2013). *The Power of Just Doing Stuff*. Cambridge: Green Books.

James, S. and Lahti, T. (2004). *The Natural Step for Communities*. Gabriola Island, BC: New Society Publishers.

Kessler, S. (2008). Eco-villages. Studying in sustainable communities around the world. *Abroadviewmagazine*, 62–3.

Litfin, K. (2005). Gaia theory: Intimations for global politics. In Dauvergne (ed.), *Handbook of Global Environmental Politics*. Cheltenham: Edward Elgar, pp. 502–17.

Litfin, K. (2009). The global ecovillage movement as a holistic knowledge community. In Kütting, G. and Lipschutz, K. (eds), *Environmental Governance: Power and Knowledge in a Local-Global World*. Abingdon: Routledge, pp. 124–42.

Lovelock, J. (1979). Gaia: Una nueva visión de la tierra. Barcelona: Tusquets.

Max-Neef, M. (1991). *Human Scale Development: Conception, Application and Further Reflection*. London: Apex Press.

Mollison, B. and Holmgren, D. (1978). *Permaculture*. Lesmurdie Progress Association.

Phillips, R., Seifer, B. F. and Antczak, E. (2013). *Sustainable Communities. Creating a Durable Local Economy*. Abingdon: Routledge.

Rauschmayer, F. and Omann, I. (2015). Well-being in sustainability transitions: Making use of needs. In Syse, K. L. and Mueller, M. L. *Sustainable Consumption and the Good Life. Interdisciplinary Perspectives*. Abingdon: Routledge, pp. 111–25.

Sevier, L. (2008). Ecovillages: A model life? *Ecologist*, 36–41, (www.theecologist.org/investigations/society/268714/ecovillages_a_model_life.html, accessed 16 February 2015).

Seyfang, G. (2009). *The New Economics of Sustainable Consumption*. Basingstoke: Palgrave.

Smith, P. B. and Max-Neef, M. (2011). *Economics Unmasked*. Cambridge: Green Books.

Spies, C. (2006). *Resolutionary Change. The Art of Awakening Dormant Faculties in Others*, (www.berghof-foundation.org/fileadmin/redaktion/Publications/Handbook/Dialogue_Chapters/dialogue5_spies_comm.pdf, accessed 27 January 2015).

Ward, F., Porter, A. and Popham, M. (2011). *Transition Streets*. Final Report. September 2011, (www.transitiontogether.org.uk/wp-content/uploads/2012/07/TransitionStreets-finalreport-27Sep2011.pdf, accessed 27 January 2015).

Part III

8 Challenges and limitations to the practice of Human Scale Development

Introduction

This book has discussed alternative ways of applying the HSD framework to the study of sustainable development processes. Three challenges to the practice of Human Scale Development have emerged as particularly salient throughout the discussion. The first is linked to the 'inner' dimension discussed in Chapter 7, as a sustainable development proposal, that does not manage to reach the values, feelings, expectations and life goals of those involved, will fail at engaging people. The second is related to empowerment and the extent to which Human Scale Development processes can be said to broaden the boundaries that frame participants' everyday life, so they might be able to challenge relationships of dependence. The third links to the traditional approach to sustainable development policy that separates environmental from social policies and subordinates them to the requirements of economic growth.

This chapter analyses the three challenges with the goal of initiating a debate around important conceptual and methodological issues concerning the practice of HSD. Hence, the first section discusses how people's 'inner' dimension is reached through HSD workshops and addresses potential criticisms concerning personal conflicts associated with sustainable choices, the question of 'adaptive preferences', and the influence of personal values on HSD processes. It also includes the findings of a study carried out at the University of Oslo in 2013 suggesting that the capacity of the HSD methodology to reach the 'inner' dimension depends on whether participants in a given workshop have similar personal goals or not. The second section returns to the concept of empowerment discussed in Chapter 6 and presents evidence suggesting an increase in people's capacity to engage in changing the institutions that affect their lives after participating in HSD processes. The last section discusses the holistic and systemic approach to sustainable development policy that HSD-based interventions demand with regards to the 'green economy' perspective and the steady-state and de-growth proposals.

The 'inner' dimension

The HSD participatory methodology was designed to support grassroots groups and communities in their progress towards a type of social, economic and political development that catered for human needs and their interdependence with the natural environment. One of the risks of participatory approaches to development involving poor or marginalised groups is that they might only improve 'the outer, fragmented aspects of reality, disregarding their close relationship with the inner world of the people living that reality' (Rahnema 1990: 214). A reality that he describes as characterised by a constant exposure to fear, prejudices, induced needs and greed. If the inner dimension that encompasses feelings, beliefs, values, needs and world-views (Rauschmayer *et al.* 2011) is not reached, participatory processes will likely lose their empowering and transformational potential. In the following, I address the HSD methodology's capacity to reach people's inner dimension as initially designed and present some reflections on the ways it can be adapted to confront personal conflicts regarding sustainable behaviours, to address the challenge of 'adaptive preferences', and to reinforce personal values that are good both for people's wellbeing and the natural environment.

My understanding of the HSD methodology based on deliberative workshops is that it attends to the 'inner dimension' by linking the personal with the communal and the different governance levels through the concept of satisfiers. As discussed throughout the book, satisfiers represent people's attributes (such as generosity or greed), actions (such as cooperating or excluding), institutions (habits, cultural values, customs, organisations, laws) and environments (public parks, clean water, etc.). Thus, if people feel marginalised, lonely, socially excluded, sexually discriminated, etc. it is quite likely that the satisfiers associated with these feelings will come up in the workshops in the form of attributes such as being racist or chauvinist and/or institutional characteristics such as lack of job opportunities for the lowly qualified, for example. Moreover, when people discuss *synergic bridging satisfiers*, those that represent needs-enhancing inter-ventions, they are encouraged to identify whether they are endogenous (have to come from the community) or exogenous (need external support) which will establish an explicit connection between personal, communal and societal level measures. In addition to the awareness gained from these discussions, when *synergic bridging satisfiers* are implemented in a cooperative manner, as in the case of Acostambo in Chapter 6 and the Transition Streets project described by Aponte in Chapter 7, social cohesion is strengthened and participants feel less lonely and marginalised. This has reportedly increased the actualisation of participants' fundamental human needs for affection, creation, participation and identity.

Scholars studying sustainability policy underline the conflicting nature of sustainability measures as people's preferences over environmental protection, economic efficiency and social equality (the three criteria of sustainability) might differ (Kaivo-oja 1999). At the personal level, people often experience sustainability-related choices as a conflict between their commitment to the environment and the beliefs, habits, needs and/or values underpinning their everyday practices. Rauschmayer and Omann (2015) define 'sustainability-related intra-individual tensions as the inner conflict experienced 'between a strategy (or a set of strategies) that is prescribed or recommended by sustainable development and our usual (or alternative) behaviour' (Rauschmayer and Omann 2015: 116). Examples of these tensions arise when people have to decide between driving a car to work and cycling or using public transport; between taking a plane to a conference and taking the train; between turning vegetarian and eating meat; and between living in a city centre flat and commuting to a house in the outskirts, for example.

If sustainability is understood as a value, as Rauschmayer and Omann maintain, it might conflict with everyday practices anchored on habits, culturally accepted behaviours and understandings of comfort and the good life. To address this inner conflict the authors suggest following a four step process aiming for *t*hriving *t*hrough *a*wareness for *n*on-conflicting *s*trategies (THANCS) that incorporates elements of the HSD methodology. As outlined in Chapter 7, the four steps to deal with tensions concern: 1) acknowledging the tension; 2) reflecting on the reasons for the tension; 3) communicating with others that share the same type of tensions or are affected by them; and 4) creatively generating strategies to resolve the tension. All these phases can be undertaken drawing on the HSD approach to needs and satisfiers. First people would be encouraged to reflect individually on the needs involved in the tension (for example need for affection as motivating for taking a plane for a weekend visit to one's family vs need for identity as environmentally concerned citizen by abstaining from flying) and then they would proceed through phases 3 and 4 of THANCS finishing with a deliberative process akin to that in HSD workshops where *bridging synergic satisfiers* or strategies to address the tension at the personal and collective levels would be co-designed (Rauschmayer and Omann 2015; Omann and Rauschmayer 2011).

Another challenge regarding the 'inner' dimension concerns the possibility that when working with deprived communities or communities that present great deficiencies in terms of needs fulfilment, HSD workshops might not be sufficient to get to the 'inner' or personal dimension of participants. As Nobel laureate Amartya Sen explains, it is quite likely that deprived people experience downward adaptation 'for example, people who are used to living in a persistent state of undernourishment, illiteracy and lack of basic healthcare may come to think of nourishment or school education or medical attention as a luxury, rather than as a need, so that even if we go by their own self-perception of needs, we may take an unjustly limited view of their deprivation.' (Sen 2013: 11). Downward adaptation or the 'adaptive preferences' problem is particularly salient among women in developing countries as they get used to discriminatory wage structures, physical abuse and unhealthy or unsanitary conditions, among other needs-challenging conditions (Nussbaum 2000).

As discussed in Chapter 6, participatory approaches to development such as the HSD proposal were a reaction to the traditional prescriptive approach to development that reinforced the disempowerment of marginalised groups. Both Freire (1970) and Fals Borda (1987) understood education and development research as an endeavour that needed to be undertaken in people's own terms and in collaboration with them and not using traditional top down strategies. The goal of switching the locus of decision making was to empower populations that had traditionally been oppressed and to support them in acquiring new knowledge that they could use to engage in their own development processes and demand authorities to support them. This was one of the traditions that the HSD engaged with and the associated methodology based on participatory workshops discussing needs and satisfiers was meant to be synergic in itself by raising awareness about the articulation of harmful satisfiers present in their societies such as discriminatory and oppressive practices.

My own experience conducting workshops with relatively marginalised people, from urban slum dwellers and Andean villagers in Peru to unemployed people in the South of Spain, suggests that adaptive preferences might not block the possibility of affecting the inner dimension of marginalised participants. Through a careful design of HSD workshops and attention to the groups within the group (for example men and women, highly- and poorly-educated participants, etc.) that are experiencing higher levels of deprivation or exclusion, people can effectively work together to identify synergic satisfiers and strategies. In past workshops, people with no reliable access to safe-drinking water have managed to address its lack as a hurdle for needs satisfaction; unemployed citizens have brought up the problems associated with exploitative labour market practices, and marginalised slum dwellers have made explicit the synergic effects of having a job against receiving benefits from the state or aid from NGOs (Guillén-Royo 2012, 2014, 2015). This suggests that the HSD methodology has the potential to get past downward adaptation or that downward adaptation is less prevalent among the poor than supposed by Sen and Nussbaum (Clark 2002). It is otherwise true, that group dynamics have the potential to be manipulated by those with power and that, as discussed in Chapter 6 and in the next section, these are usually men and those with positions of authority (communal or municipal leaders, teachers, doctors and local politicians for example). In cases where gender has been the factor defining deprivation, combining workshops by gender and workshops in plenary has proven a fruitful option.

Long-term experiences of deprivation or deficient need fulfilment might have an influence on people's values[1] and in turn on their capacity to engage in environmentally friendly practices and experience wellbeing (Crompton and Kasser 2009; Kasser 2002; Kasser 2009). Psychology research distinguishing between 'extrinsic' or materialistic goals such as those for financial success, image and status and 'intrinsic' goals oriented towards personal growth, community involvement and close relationships, suggest that this might be the case (Brown and Kasser 2005). Extrinsic goals are enhanced through feelings of insecurity, so when children experience controlling or divorced parents or poverty they are more likely to be led by extrinsic goals in their adult life (Kasser, Ryan, Zax and Sameroff 1995). As Kasser explains 'some experiments even support a causal role of insecurity in creating materialistic concerns, as making people consider economic hardship, poor interpersonal relationships, and even their own death leads individuals to care more about materialistic ways and to act in more ecologically destructive ways' (Kasser 2009: 184). In addition to acting at the societal level to reduce exposure to poverty and insecurity, promoting an alternative set of values is also a viable strategy to countervail the negative effects of materialism on wellbeing and the environment.

One way of encouraging intrinsic values such as *community feeling* is providing people with opportunities to cooperate in the design and implementation of their own development projects through, for example, HSD workshops. The positive experience of participating in terms of empowerment and relatedness is likely to increase their fulfilment of intrinsic goals (for self-acceptance, affiliation and community feeling) and thus the importance they give to these types of goals relative to extrinsic or materialistic pursuits. This relative stress on intrinsic values is associated with greater concern for others and the environment and a greater willingness to engage in social and/or environmental activism (Brown and Kasser 2005; Chilton *et al.* 2012; Crompton and Kasser 2009). However, the capacity of HSD workshops to activate intrinsic goals has not been empirically confirmed yet. The example provided below constitutes a first attempt to investigate the potential of the HSD methodology to influence value or goal orientation.

Example 8.1. Goal orientation and Human Scale Development workshops

In spring 2013, I carried out, in collaboration with three research partners and two research assistants[2], a small project at the University of Oslo, exploring the potential of HSD workshops to influence values and pro-environmental behaviours. As presented in Chapter 4 (Example 4.3) the project had two phases: the first consisting of a self-completion questionnaire on personal goals (drawing on the Aspiration Index[3] by Kasser and Ryan (1996)), subjective wellbeing, environmental behaviours and willingness to engage social and environmental activism. The survey was distributed to a convenience sample of 260 students and members of staff across faculties of the University of Oslo.[4] Answers to the questions were confidential but not anonymous as participants gave their contact details so they could be invited to join HSD workshops at a later stage.

The second phase of the study consisted of HSD workshops following the methodology described in Table 4.2 (based on three phases to identify negative, synergic and synergic bridging satisfiers) and a follow-up questionnaire that was made available on-line two weeks after the last workshop (returned by 24 of the 26 participants). After a long process of selection,[5] we decided to study the effects of participating in HSD workshops for relative intrinsic people (people with a more intrinsic goal orientation than others in the sample) when they participated with like-minded people and when they participated with relatively extrinsic people (people with a less intrinsic goal orientation than others in the sample).[6] Each of the two groups would be engaged in the same three-phase process leading to the generation of a negative and a utopian matrix and a set of synergic bridging satisfiers describing needs-enhancing measures or interventions for each group. In total, we conducted six three-hour HSD workshops with 26 people who had participated in the initial survey (ten of whom joined two of the three work-shops). The worst attended workshop had only four participants and the best attended, nine people. Workshops were facilitated by me with the support of a research assistant in charge of voice-recording the session (with permission from participants) and of taking notes about his perceptions of the discussion.

The effects of HSD workshops on the 'inner world of participants' are difficult to determine due to three factors: the lack of a control group (a group of people who did not join the workshops but answered the survey twice); the impossibility to get a purely relatively extrinsic group; and the small sample size with only 24 workshop participants (11 from the intrinsic group and 13 from the mixed group) answering the survey before and after the workshops. Understanding these serious limitations to the study, I undertook a simple statistical analysis of participants' answers using a T-test with paired samples to explore the relationship between workshop participation, goal orientation and pro-environmental behaviours. Results suggested that participating in the workshops might affect people's goal orientation, depending on the group they joined.

Relatively intrinsic people (n=11) participating with people with similar goal orientation became more intrinsic after HSD workshops as goals linked to image and money turned out to be even less important for them. The opposite was observed with relatively intrinsic participants who joined the mixed group (n=6) as their appreciation of goals related to community was greatly reduced. However, no significant differences were found among their relatively extrinsic counterparts (n=7) in terms of goal orientation. Regarding pro-environmental behaviours significant differences were only found concerning the frequency of conserving energy at home ('How often do you conserve energy in your home e.g. switching lights off in unused rooms, switching off unused appliances at the wall, etc.'), which was significantly reduced after participation among extrinsically-oriented people.

Hence, participating in HSD workshops in and of itself did not seem to be enough to activate and/or encourage intrinsic values and discourage extrinsic values. The only effect we can possibly point to is the effect that the group had on participants. Those who gave relatively more importance to intrinsic goals were either supported or discouraged in their values, depending on the relative goal orientation of people they attended HSD workshops with. Relatively extrinsic people did not change their goal orientation through participation and they could even become more environmentally unfriendly than before participating. A possible interpretation of the findings from this exploratory study is that HSD workshops might be reaching the 'inner' dimension, in terms or personal values or goals, of relatively intrinsic people. However, this effect might not always be positive; it seems to depend on the relative values of those they are participating with.

One reason for this negative reaction can be the difficulties to reach consensus in non-homogeneous groups. This is illustrated by the answers of those joining the last workshops (the workshops where *synergic bridging satisfier*, satisfiers that would bridge the negative and utopian matrices, were discussed) to questions on their experience in participating. On a scale from 1 (extremely dissatisfied) to 7 (extremely satisfied), people in the intrinsic group declared to be significantly more satisfied with the topics discussed (6.2 vs 5.2), the outcome of the workshops (5.8 vs 4.9) and the overall experience of participating (6 vs 5) than participants in the mixed group.[8] The positive atmosphere experienced in workshops with relatively intrinsic participants is described in the notes by the research assistant reporting on the events right after the utopian matrix was completed:

> Twelve o' clock: The time's up, but the conversation (about referendums and polls) continues as before. There appears to be an intention to finish the discussion thoroughly. In fact, new ideas are being brought to the round even now. Jon and Laura[9] discuss 'including' at workplaces and in one's local community. Jon suggests a fund at a local level for NGOs. Svetlana says that a criterion for receiving some of that funding could be that you're not part of an organization. Jon goes on, saying, the application threshold must be low. Something simple, easy [. . .] Einar commented on how much more pleasant this group was as compared to last time. Last time he was in a mixed group.[10]

One way of adapting the HSD methodology to reach the 'inner dimension' when people do not have similar values or goals is to give them the opportunity to reflect on needs and satisfiers on a personal level before engaging in a collective discussion. This was the strategy followed by Jolibert and colleagues when dealing with stakeholders in a regional sustainability project aiming at generating a needs-based scenario to achieve sustainability in the province by 2050 (Jolibert *et al.* 2014). As discussed in Chapter 5, they included a phase where people reflected individually on the satisfiers required to achieve the sustainability goal. After that first reflection, they invited stakeholders to share with other group members two of their satisfiers so they realised the differences and similarities between the satisfiers of each of the participants. This higher level of awareness was then drawn on when participants were asked to reformulate their satisfiers in ways that did not diverge from those of others and could be presented as collective satisfiers; agreed by all stakeholders.

Thus, adapting the HSD methodology for participants to be able to engage in a personal reflection on needs and satisfiers might be a way to overcome conflicts that arise when different stakeholders, or people with different interests and values, are participating in HSD workshops. Sharing one's satisfiers and one's concerns over other people's satisfiers increases trust among participants and this enables them to work together to refine them and reach a final agreement. As Jolibert and colleagues put it

> the issue is not about collective interests overriding individual interests, but as Johnson (2003, 2011) argues, the need to communicate clearly one's concern to prevent conflict or ameliorate the conflict resolution process, and to share different types of knowledge – local, experiential, political, moral, institutional – between different stakeholders who often have limited contact, e.g. the policy-maker and the resident or the farmer and the forester.
>
> (Jolibert *et al.* 2014: 43)

Whether Jolibert and colleagues' adaptation of the HSD methodology succeeds in changing participants' relative values is a matter for further study. However, the fact that they address conflicts likely to be rooted in personal values and attitudes suggests that they might have devised a way of tapping into important aspects of people's 'inner' dimension.

Participation and empowerment

Following the tradition of literacy programs in Latin America discussed in Chapter 6, the HSD proposal intended to reverse the balance of power operating at the local level by supporting grassroots organisations and local communities to plan and carry out their own development projects. Grassroots groups had traditionally been dependent on decisions happening at the regional, national or even international levels, as was the case during the adjustment policies of the eighties in Latin America outlined in Chapter 3. They were not commonly involved in policy-making or evaluation as this was the responsibility of the regional or national level administration. When project implementation included local communities, it often treated them as a workforce for infrastructural projects or as customers or users of new consumer products, agrarian inputs, social services or training courses (Green 2010; Rahnema 1990). This often ended up strengthening the relationships of dependence that participatory development intended to break.

Dependence in its personal and social dimensions is likely to hamper the potential for people to feel empowered. The World Bank defines empowerment as 'the expansion of assets and capabilities of poor people to participate in, negotiate with, influence, control and hold accountable institutions that affect their lives' (Narayan 2005: 3). There are many approaches to measuring empowerment; some are more process oriented and others focus on either material or psychological outcomes; some aim at universal measures, others are participatory and revolve around meaningful expressions of empowerment at the local level (Kasmel and Andersen 2011; Narayan 2005; Uphoff 2005). In addition, measurement can be done at the individual or group levels, although as Narayan suggests, the two levels reinforce each other and are not always easy (or advisable) to disentangle. In general, people are more able to collaborate and advocate for institutional changes if they feel empowered but at the same time collective action can improve the access to public services and other entitlements of individuals who, as a consequence, might feel more empowered.

There is some evidence that the HSD proposal has contributed to empower individuals and groups in a community. Max-Neef in his book with Philip B. Smith describes the experience of a rural community initiative in Colombia that, based on the principles of HSD, has successfully increased people's capacity to participate, negotiate and hold authorities accountable at many levels.[11] The initiative, that soon turned into a regional association (Association for Peasant Development), started in the late eighties when a group of farmers drew on the principles of Human scale development to reorganise their economic activities away from the production of charcoal from local timber, which was causing deforestation, to alternative productive activities. Since then, family income in the community has surpassed regional and national average income, groups and civil society organisations have blossomed, 4,000 hectares of land have been protected, programmes for the empowerment of children have been created and an increasing number of youngsters are sent to university to complement their local skills with those from formal education. Formal is not replacing traditional knowledge though. As Max-Neef posits:

> a fundamental principle promoted by the community is what they call the 'dialogue of knowledge' as a recognition of the importance of traditional cultural, spiritual and organisation values of the peasant that have been discredited by modern techniques and attitudes. Through this they make a continuing effort to recover and honour ancestral wisdoms.
>
> (Smith and Max-Neef 2011: 179)

The empowerment of local peasants is even more visible in the international seminars they have organised throughout the years, where they set themselves to discuss on equal ground with experts, academics and policies on their dreams about the future (Smith and Max-Neef 2011).

Another example that might illustrate the empowering potential of the HSD proposal comes from the Participatory Action Research (PAR) carried out during 10 months with a peasant community in Acostambo (Peru) discussed in Chapter 6. The research project finished in January 2013 with two participatory workshops aiming at identifying *synergic* and *synergic bridging satisfiers* that would continue improving human needs in the community when the PAR project was over. One of the *synergic bridging satisfiers* concerning the existential category of *Doing* was defined as 'gestionar y tramitar con las autoridades' (dealing with authorities) and captured participants' willingness to be more pro-active in their demands to local authorities, NGOs and national development agencies operating in their community. They argued that this satisfier would help them fulfil many of their fundamental human needs from participation to identity. Before the project was over, the community wrote two letters to the mayor, one to ask for support to organise a course in Quechua, their mother tongue, not currently taught in the local schools, and another asking for the garbage collection truck to reach their neighbourhood. None of the two petitions were positively taken by the mayor but after a council reshuffle and a follow-up by the community in terms of new petition letters and enquiries, the garbage truck now collects the trash once a week.[12] Members of the peasant community have also been more pro-active in their dealings with NGOs and public development agencies working in the community asking for agrarian inputs, training sessions and seed donations. In November 2014, Roberto, the person who suggested that the research team work with the peasant community in the PAR project, told us that participating in the project had made the community more enthusiastic and eager to work with external projects and take an active role. This was in contrast to what Vincent has called the traditional passive role that many communities in the Andes display as they deal with the avalanche of NGOs and government agencies wanting to engage them in their pre-defined projects (Vincent 2004).

Despite the Colombian and Peruvian cases suggesting that HSD contributes to people's empowerment, most research drawing on the HSD proposal revolves around exploratory or one-off workshops which are unlikely to have long-term empowering effects on participants. The study at the University of Oslo (Norway) described earlier, used a self-completion questionnaire around two weeks before and two weeks after participating in HSD workshops to elucidate, among other things, the potential effect of participation on people's willingness to engage in social or environmental activism.[13] Results suggest that people were less willing to start a campaign to address environmental (scale 1–9, mean score 7.13 vs 6.38, p<0.1) or social (6.88 vs 6.21, p<0.1) problems after their participation than before. They were also less willing to join ongoing environmental campaigns (7.70 vs 6.96, p<0.1). Relatively intrinsic participants in workshops with fellow intrinsic people experienced a sharper reduction in their willingness to start an environmental campaign or participate in environmental activism.[14] Hence, it seems that one-off workshops are not inherently likely to empower participants. Relatively intrinsic people, who commonly give great importance to community, personal growth and close relationships are the ones that might be more disappointed at the lack of 'opportunity structures' (a group or institution supporting their engagement) to build on the decisions arrived at in the workshops. Disappointment might lead to feelings of helplessness and result in a lower willingness to collaborate in future environmentally and socially relevant campaigns, thus disempowering and not empowering participants.

Two other considerations regarding empowerment and the use of the HSD participatory methodology are worth discussing. The first relates to power imbalances among workshop participants and the second to the issue of co-option of endogenous development processes by organisations or government agencies. As discussed in Chapter 6, unequal power relations between members of communities and within grassroots organisations (and regarding researchers and participants) can influence outcomes of exercises in HSD, as is the case with any other participatory development processes. Gaventa and Cornwall in their discussion on power and knowledge in participatory research draw on Hayward (1998) and Foucault (1977) to define power as 'the capacity to act upon boundaries that affect one's life' (Gaventa and Cornwall 2008: 176). They argue that Participatory Action Research processes can create the spaces in which to challenge dominant discourses and broaden boundaries that limit one's actions. They might sometimes result in zero-sum games, as some groups get more power in detriment of others but they might also have a synergic effect as the actions of some can enable action by others. The possibility that the empowerment of some groups might result in the empowerment of people outside the group resonates with the systemic perspective of the HSD proposal in its operationalisation by the Association for Peasant Development in Colombia, where the initial empowerment of a small peasant community has led to long-term programmes targeting the empowerment of peasant women, children and the elders in the whole region.

As described in Chapter 3, HSD is not concerned with upscaling local development initiatives through general policies at the national or international levels. As Max-Neef and colleagues explain:

> It is not the purpose of this document to propose a state model that promotes Human Scale Development. Rather, our emphasis is on empowering civil society to nurture this form of development. This is not to minimize the importance of the state but to develop further the potential role of social actors, of social participation and of local communities [. . .] We believe that in order to avoid the atomization and the exclusion of people – be it in political, social or cultural terms – it is absolutely necessary to generate new ways of conceiving and practicing politics
>
> (Max-Neef 1991: 11).

These 'new ways' of practicing politics assign a supporting role to the state as well as to public and private development agencies. The question remains of how this supporting role is going to be implemented without formal institutions co-opting the process of development.

Max-Neef and colleagues together with other participatory development theorists such as Rahman consider that the creativity and synergies unleashed through participation and endogenous development processes could be annihilated by governmental and non-governmental agencies taking over the initiative to start them and putting conditions on their characteristics (Max-Neef 1991; Rahman 1995). They argue that the role of the state and of public policies is to identify these embryonic initiatives, reinforce them and support their reproduction, like for example following Rahman's suggestion, encouraging successful groups in the region to support other groups to increase self-reliance and engage in their own reflection on human needs and satisfiers. This has been done with success by the Colombian community referred to earlier, which started when members of the Minga Asoryacocha, a peasant association based on full participation and direct democracy declared its natural assets 'Private Natural Reserves of civil society' and expanded the initiative to other Mingas and associations in the region, leading to the establishment of a network of related initiatives around the country (Smith and Max-Neef 2011). The activities of the Minga,[15] co-founder of the Association for Peasant Development are now funded and supported by local, regional and national level organisations and international agencies.[11]

Thus, the state does not need to lead HSD processes for them to be successful. On the contrary, based on a direct and participatory form of democracy, the HSD proposal suggests that states should 'respect and encourage' the diversity of endogenous initiatives by strengthening and supporting economic and politically decentralised regions and consolidating democratic institutions at all levels of governance. Undeniably, this is asking economic and political elites to delegate part of their power, which is obviously not very popular. However, as Gaventa and Cornwall (2008) explain, spaces for democratic participation are being mobilised constantly. Popular demands and international agencies are now pushing developing countries towards increased decentralisation and the expansion of participation opportunities at the grassroots levels and increased popular mobilisation and frustration with traditional forms of political participation are currently contributing to the expansion of participatory spaces (Collier and Handlin 2009). These trends, although relatively recent, do not seem to relent in the face of the recent financial crisis and the subsequent adjustment policies. Although more participatory spaces do not automatically imply that new voices become influential, the constellation of grassroots and local proposals for sustainable development that are appearing around the world seem to suggest that the empowerment of previously marginalised groups through participatory processes, as the one suggested by the HSD proposal, is currently underway.

Sustainable development policy

An additional challenge to the practice of HSD is the difficulty of integrating its holistic approach in sustainable development policy. Sustainable development, understood as 'development that meets the needs of the present without compromising the ability of future generations to meet their own needs' (WCED 1987: 43), is articulated around three interdependent dimensions concerning economic efficiency, social equality and environmental sustainability. Despite its purported interdependence, the sustainable development policies associated with the WCED definition as presented in the diverse outcome documents from international conferences, such as the UN Conference on Sustainable Development in Rio in 1992, the World summit on Sustainable Development in Johannesburg in 2002 and the UN Conference on Sustainable Development (Rio+20) in 2012, suggest a precedence of the economic pillar over the social and environmental ones. This is particularly visible in the 'green economy' proposal by the UNEP (UNEP 2011) articulated around institutional, economic and information-based measures directed to reduce environmental externalities through regulation and/or taxation, supporting green sectors, and increasing awareness about sustainability challenges while promoting 'sustained and inclusive economic growth' (Cosbey 2011; UN 2012).

As discussed in Chapter 2, stimulating and preserving economic growth, understood as GDP growth, has become a cornerstone of sustainable development policies. This has happened despite the evident difficulties in reducing total greenhouse gas emissions, for example, as the scale of the global economy expands (Jackson 2009). It has also happened despite the existence of alternative socioeconomic arrangements that could allow meeting needs now and in the future in the contexts of de-growing economies and steady-states (Daly 1974; Kallis 2011; Martínez-Alier *et al.* 2010); and the practices of sustainable communities already experiencing low-carbon lifestyles and high quality of life (see Chapters 2 and 7 for a discussion). The resistance to reduce the role of economic growth in sustainable development is as van den Bergh puts it 'a major barrier against sustainability policies' and 'unnecessarily restricts our search for possible sustainable systems and developments' (van den Bergh 2010b: 2051). He suggests being indifferent about economic growth and focussing policy on meeting environmental goals. Among the measures he advocates for, we find the implementation of environmental regulation, such as 'hard' ceilings to pollution, together with a system of taxes, incentives and information, are deployed to address 'non-rational' behaviours (due to customs, habits, social comparison, reciprocity, etc.). He claims that these measures might result in a decline, stagnation or increase in GDP but this should be considered as a by-product and not as a goal of sustainable development policy (van den Bergh 2010a).

Herman Daly in his proposal for a steady-state economy suggests that sustainable policy should revolve around the reduction of the physical scale of the economy until its stabilisation around a steady-state, defined by him as 'a system that permits qualitative development but not aggregate quantitative growth' (Daly 2008: 1). Measures to support a purposeful shrinking and stabilisation of the volume of the economy (that has nothing to do with an economic recession as the one experienced after the 2008 financial crisis) accord with van den Bergh's suggestions regarding environmental policy. However, they go beyond environmental regulation and taxation to encompass specific socio-economic measures such as agreements on minimum and maximum incomes, 100 per cent reserves requirement for banks, or the promotion of cooperatives and jobs in maintenance and repair of consumer products (Daly 2008). Daly's proposal resonates with what Gough (2014) calls *radical decarbonisation* which, although it does not necessarily result in a physically smaller economy, implies that sustainable development policy accounts for the complementarity of social and environmental policies. Accounting for the latter should lead to a rethinking of policies concerning, for example, the domains of consumption and work. Gough maintains that 'eco-social consumption policy' should 'prioritise collective investment and consumption over private commodities, foster local, community-based consumption, identify high-carbon luxury consumption, and improve diets to benefit both health and the environment' (Gough 2014: 15). The corresponding eco-social work policy 'would gradually reduce paid work time, foster alternative employment contracts, develop "co-production" in service delivery and encourage low carbon leisure activities' (Gough 2014: 15).

The green economy approach to sustainable development and both the steady state or radical decarbonisation proposals are compatible with an understanding of policy-making based on national or regional regulations and interventions. However, proponents of *sustainable degrowth*[16] indicate that it is quite unlikely that sustainable development policies, such as the ones necessary to avert the most dramatic consequences of climate change or pollution, might come about without 'revolutionary social change' (Kallis 2011: 878). The latter entails the mobilisation and cooperation of scientists, activists and practitioners experimenting and working together to present alternative social configurations and although it might not appeal to powerful politicians in the beginning, it might become an important movement impossible to ignore. This is the perspective endorsed by the many local sustainability initiatives emerging around the world and the belief around which sustainable communities such as ecovillages and transition towns articulate their activities and deploy their virtual networks.

A holistic and participatory approach to designing and implementing sustainable development interventions is also the one favoured by HSD projects. Interventions addressing social exclusion, poverty, literacy, health prevention and treatment, consumerism or other social, economic and political concerns appear to be directly or indirectly linked to projects to limit and reduce the environmental impacts of production and consumption practices. The latter does not only concern local ecosystems, since by reducing CO_2 emissions and waste in their locality and regenerating local ecosystems sustainable communities and associations such as the Association for Peasant Development in Colombia are contributing to halt the pace of climate change and biodiversity loss, for example.

The methodology associated with the HSD proposal based on participatory workshops has proven to be a useful tool to identify a constellation of satisfiers that contribute both to meeting human needs and environmental sustainability. In Chapter 7, we discussed the concept of *necessary synergic satisfiers*, those that are common across sustainable communities articulating a set of personal characteristics, actions, institutions and spaces that contribute both to human actualisation and environmental sustainability. Examples of policies and interventions referred to in the chapter were those contributing to self-knowledge, engaging people in cooperative and volunteering activities, creating urban environments that enable a direct physical experience with nature and participatory institutions for conflict resolution, among others. These satisfiers would probably have a limited effect fulfilling human needs if they were implemented as part of single policies to foster social cohesion, reduce crime and insecurity or increase people's access to green spaces. However, as satisfiers that emerge from a systemic view of society and its relationship with the natural environment and are articulated around participatory decision making and project implementation, they reinforce one another in contributing to human wellbeing and reducing environmental impacts.

The question remains on how to articulate measures at the local level that often require policies at the regional or national levels. Max-Neef suggests using HSD workshops to clarify in a participatory manner the synergic satisfiers that can be implemented, drawing on the potentials of the community and those that will need external support by local-regional or national level institutions. Thus, the connection between local and national level sustainability policy would be suggested by the grassroots and the State would ideally take the role of supporting the emerging initiatives and encouraging their development. One way of supporting the emergence of local interventions is by promoting what Max-Neef calls 'idea banks' that gather information on grassroots initiatives aimed at local self-reliance. 'Idea banks' would collect information on the use of *non-conventional* resources such as knowledge, solidarity and popular creativity, and on technologies and public policies conducive to HSD. Other policies to foster self-reliance would target adult education and life-long training programmes that established stable connections between researchers, practitioners and the general public 'in order to create a system of permanent feedback' (Max-Neef 1991:71). The latter becomes crucial as Human Scale Development is more about creating enabling environments for the generation of sustainable development strategies than about designing sustainable solutions that are not dynamic and flexible enough to be adapted to changing conditions (climatic, organisational, political, etc.).

Articulating sustainable development policies around the pillars of HSD (self-reliance, human needs satisfaction and balanced relationships between, for example, nature, technology and society) is not likely to result in economic growth taking centre stage even if the environmental impacts of production and consumption practices become sharply reduced through legislation, technological innovation and the generalisation of renewable energy. The reasons for this are that the satisfiers that are often in place in societies that prioritise material production, such as competition, materialist values, consumerism and acquisition, are often considered by people participating in HSD workshops as *pseudo* or *inhibiting* satisfiers without synergic or needs fulfilling characteristics. In addition to articulating sustainable development around the three pillars of HSD, Max-Neef specifies a set of guidelines or postulates that should frame a 'humane economics' or what could be the same an economic system that supports human needs fulfilment and environmental sustainability. These postulates that resonate with the synergic satisfiers emerging in HSD workshops are based on: shifting common understandings of the relationship between human beings and the market (job, commodities, housing, etc.) and putting the economy at the service of people; respecting a foundational principle stating that 'no economic interest, under any circumstances, can be above the reverence for life'; and respecting planetary boundaries through an understanding of the economic system as subordinated to the limits of the biosphere (Smith and Max-Neef 2011).

A list of policies for sustainable development cannot be expected to derive from HSD processes. The latter are, by and large, focussed on the local level and its articulation with the regional and national levels through stakeholder workshops and direct democracy institutions. The radically different institutional architecture that HSD proposes might seem too utopian and unrealistic. However, increasing evidence from studies and experiences in HSD indicate that its holistic approach to sustainable development is feasible and that it requires time, persistence and a good deal of flexibility. It would be interesting to establish a dialogue with academics and welfare-state experts on the potential articulations of an 'eco-welfare' state that contemplates the leadership of the grassroots in designing sustainability policies. Gough (2014:9) suggests that these types of states are more likely to emerge in Europe than elsewhere but the successes of the Association for Peasant Development in Colombia imply that they might also emerge in developing countries. To conclude, it is important to stress that the dramatic reduction in biodiversity experienced in the last 50 years, the more and more visible effects of global warming and the increased human pressure on water resources require integrated and interconnected action beyond the limits of the nation-state and should also rely on binding international climate agreements and, quite likely, higher energy prices from non-renewable sources (van den Bergh 2010b).

Conclusions

The chapter has revolved around three interrelated challenges concerning the use of the HSD proposal as a framework to support sustainable development processes. The first addressed the 'inner dimension' that has often been diluted in group-based participatory development exercises. I have discussed how the methodology revolving around participatory workshops on needs and satisfiers has the potential to reach the values, goals, attitudes, fears and emotions of the people engaged and how it can be adapted to address differences in values and intra-individual conflicts. An exploratory study in Oslo suggested that accessing the 'inner' dimension is easier when workshops are organised with people sharing similar personal goals. When this is not the case, strategies that allow people to reflect individually on needs and satisfiers before sharing it with others in the group might be more effective in supporting deep personal changes than the traditional HSD methodology based on group discussions.

The second challenge to HSD processes is connected to the purported effects of participatory development processes on the empowerment of individuals and groups. Linking with the discussion on participatory action research presented in Chapter 6, this section argues that long-term HSD processes seem to be effective in expanding the boundaries within which people operate, enabling previously marginalised groups or individuals to participate, negotiate and defend their rights across institutional settings. However, empowerment cannot be expected to derive from one-off/exploratory HSD workshops; the latter, by not providing the opportunity structures to build on the decisions arrived at in the workshops, might result in people feeling disappointed with collaborative endeavours and less eager to cooperate. The way participatory processes become diluted when co-opted by higher level institutions has also been addressed. If supporting the grassroots in their development processes implies co-opting their methods and upscaling their initiatives, traditional relations of dependence might be reproduced hampering any potential benefit in terms of empowerment.

Finally, the third challenge relates to the articulation of sustainable development policy from a HSD perspective. The fact that there is not a specific recipe to articulate different levels of governance to organise a transition towards sustainable development around the principles of self-reliance, balanced relationships and human needs satisfaction might seem a serious limitation of the proposal. HSD processes identify synergic and synergic bridging satisfiers that demand the implementation of economic, social assistance, industrial and participation-related policies that are not possible to envisage without the participation of the grassroots but that also require external support. In addition, certain articulations of satisfiers might not require economic growth as redistribution; cooperation, exchange and reusing might be the pillars of many new economic configurations which might reduce the support to HSD initiatives from powerful groups. The examples of sustainable communities discussed in Chapter 7 suggest that despite these challenges, HSD processes can set in motion sustainable development processes at the local level. How these processes are going to be synchronised with the structures of national welfare states and architecture behind international climate agreements demands, among other things, a programme of transdisciplinary debates led and articulated by the grassroots.

Notes

1   The concepts of goals and values are used interchangeably in this chapter.
2   The short project 'From values to action: supporting Norwegians to act on their pro-environmental values through participatory workshops' was a collaboration with Hal Wilhite (University of Oslo), Tim Kasser (Knox College) and Tom Crompton (WWF) and two research assistants (Nina Zelenkova and Martin Lee Mueller from the University of Oslo). The project was funded by the *Klimaforsk* programme of the Research Council of Norway.
3   We used the version of the Aspiration Index in Grouzet *et al.* (2005) asking about the importance of 47 personal goals on a 1 to 9 scale from 'not at all important' (1) to 'extremely important' (9). The standard scoring procedure in Kasser and Ryan (1996) was applied to obtain measures of intrinsic and extrinsic goal orientation. The difference between the two scores was used to calculate the relative goal orientation of participants, which in our sample ranged from -4.25 (the most extrinsically-oriented respondent) to 18.13 (the most intrinsically oriented) (see www.selfdetermination theory.org/aspirations-index/ for more general information on the Aspiration Index).
4   The questionnaire was distributed to students and staff at the University of Oslo (Norway) in canteens, study rooms, the central library's café and some classrooms. Most participants were students belonging to the faculties of humanities and social and natural sciences.
5   Initially, we intended to follow the HSD process described in Table 4.2 with two groups of participants: one consisting of relatively intrinsic people and the other with relatively extrinsic people. Our research plan involved inviting 20 people among the 50 top relatively intrinsic and 20 people among the 50 bottom scorers of the 260 who answered the questionnaire. Most top extrinsic people, who are on average more concerned with physical appearance, money and material possessions declined the invitation to participate. We contacted up to 100 top extrinsic scorers and only five agreed to join the workshops. So we decided to adapt our research strategy and work with a group of relatively intrinsic people and a mixed-group integrated by both relatively intrinsic and relatively extrinsic participants.
6   Most respondents considered intrinsic goals more important than extrinsic goals. Only 5 per cent of the total sample (N=260 people) gave more importance to extrinsic than to intrinsic pursuits. I use 'relative goal orientation' to indicate that all comparisons are made within the sample.
7   Response was on a 5-point scale, from 'I never do these things' (score=0) to 'I always do these things' (score=4).
8   The questionnaire distributed to participants two weeks after the last workshop asked: 'Please indicate the extent to which you are satisfied or dissatisfied with the following aspects of the workshop'. The aspects were: 1) the topic(s) discussed in the workshop; 2) participants' interaction with other participants in the workshop; 3) the outcomes of the discussion as collected on the matrix/board at the end of the workshop, and; 4) the overall experience as a participant in the workshop. Answers followed a 7-point verbal scale from 'extremely dissatisfied' (1) to 'extremely satisfied' (7). A t-test

with independent samples yielded significant results for differences between groups regarding the first aspect (p<0.05) and marginally significant regarding the third and the fourth aspect (ps<0.1). The total number of participants in the last two workshops was 14.

9 Participants' names are anonymised.

10 This is a comment written by the research assistant. Participants did not know which group they had been allocated to in advance and relatively intrinsically-oriented people could change groups if the time was more convenient to them.

11 Information about the *Asociacion para el desarrollo campesino* and the *Minga Asoyarcocha* can be found at www.adc.org.co/.

12 The proposal to organise a course in Quechua has not been pursued by the community. They justify this by claiming that courses in Quechua are not important for them as all in the community can already speak it and that it is not a useful language when one travels outside of Acostambo.

13 The four questions were: 1. How willing would you be to join a campaign to reduce the impact of your everyday activities on the environment? (such as: initiatives to improve public transport, to build more cycle paths, to make waste-recycling more convenient, etc.); 2. How willing would you be to start an initiative to address an environmental problem you are concerned about?; 3. How willing would you be to join a campaign to address socially relevant issues? (such as: initiatives regarding better care for the elderly, marginalised groups, newcomers, the disabled etc.); 4. How willing would you be to start an initiative to address a social problem you are concerned about? Answers to these questions were on a 9-point scale from not at all willing (score -4) to very willing (score 4) that was later recoded to calculate means (from not at all willing =1 to very willing =9).

14 Differences between the mixed or intrinsically-oriented groups were only significant regarding environmental initiatives as people in the relatively intrinsically-oriented group experienced a sharper reduction in their willingness to start a campaign (7.64 vs 6.36, p<0.05) than people participating in the mixed group (6.69 vs 6.36, ns.). Regarding joining ongoing campaigns, significant differences were reported regarding environmentally-related actions (7.70 vs 6.96, p<0.1) and for people participating in the group with only relatively intrinsically-oriented counterparts (8.73 vs 7.36, p<0.05).

15 Minga or Minka in Quechua refers to the collective work done by and for the community. It can also benefit one group or family that needs support from the community to build a house, fell trees, planting or harvesting crops (Alvarez and Copestake 2008).

16 Sustainable degrowth is another alternative approach to sustainable development that revolves around achieving a smaller economy through an 'equitable and demographic transition' (Martínez-Alier *et al.* 2010: 1741).

References

Alvarez, J. L. and Copestake, J. (2008). Wellbeing and institutions. In Copestake, J. (ed.), *Wellbeing and Development in Peru: Local and Universal Views Confronted*. Basingstoke: Palgrave Macmillan, pp. 153–84.

Brown, K. W. and Kasser, T. (2005). Are psychological and ecological well-being compatible? The role of values, mindfulness, and lifestyle. *Social Indicators Research*, 74(2): 349–68.

Chilton, P., Crompton, T., Kasser, T., Maio, G. and Nolan, A. (2012). Communicating bigger-than-self problems to extrinsically-oriented audiences. Report available at www.valuesandframes.org, accessed 4 May 2015.

Clark, D. A. (2002). *Visions of Development*. Cheltenham: Edward Elgar.

Collier, R. B. and Handlin, S. (eds) (2009). *Reorganizing popular politics: Participation and the new interest regime in Latin America.* University Park: Pennsylvania State University Press.

Cosbey, A. (2011). Are there downsides to a green economy? The trade, investment and competitiveness implications of unilateral green economic pursuit (1 March 2011). United Nations Conference on Trade and Development. http://r0.unctad.org/trade_env/greeneconomy/road2rioGE2.asp, accessed 23 March 2015.

Crompton, T. and Kasser, T. (2009). *Meeting Environmental Challenges: The Role of Human Identity.* Godalming, UK: WWF-UK.

Daly, H. E. (1974). The economics of the Steady State. *The American Economic Review,* 64(2): 15–21.

Daly, H. E. (2008). A Steady-State economy. Sustainable Development Commission, UK, 24 April 2008. www.sd-commission.org.uk/data/files/publications/Herman_Daly_think piece.pdf, accessed 23 March 2015.

Fals Borda, O. (1987). The application of participatory action-research in Latin America. *International Sociology,* 2: 329–47.

Foucault, M. (1977). *Discipline and Punish.* New York: Pantheon.

Freire, P. (1970). *Pedagogy of the Oppressed.* New York: Continuum.

Gaventa, J. and Cornwall, A. (2008). Power and knowledge. In Reason, P. and Bradbury, H. (eds), *The SAGE Handbook of Action Research: Participative Inquiry and Practice.* London: Sage, pp. 172–89.

Gough, I. (2014). Welfare states and environmental states. Paper presented at the ECPR workshop 'Green Leviathan, Ecological Insurance Agency, or Capitalism's Agent? Revisiting the Ecological State in the Anthropocene', in Mainz, Germany, March 2013. Available at http://personal.lse.ac.uk/goughi/, accessed 4 May 2015.

Green, M. (2010). Making development agents: Participation as boundary object in international development. *Journal of Development Studies,* 46(7): 1240–63.

Grouzet, F. M. E., Kasser, T., Ahuvia, A., Fernandez-Dols, J. M., Kim, Y., Lau, S., Ryan, R. M., Saunders, S., Schmuck, P. and Sheldon, K. M. (2005). The structure of goal contents across 15 cultures. *Journal of Personality and Social Psychology,* 89(5): 800–16.

Guillén-Royo, M. (2012). The challenge of transforming consumption patterns: A proposal using the Human Scale Development approach. In Bjørkdahl, K. and Nielsen, K. B. (eds), *Development and the Environment. Practices, Theories, Policies.* Oslo: Akademika, pp. 99–118.

Guillén-Royo, M. (2014). Economic growth and human needs satisfaction across socio-economic groups in Peru. An illustration using the Human Scale Development Approach. Paper presented at the Fourth International Conference on Degrowth, Leipzig (Germany), 2–6 September 2014.

Guillén-Royo, M. (2015). Human needs and the environment reconciled: Participatory action-research for sustainable development in Peru. In Syse, K. and Mueller, M. (eds), *Sustainability and the Good Life.* Oxford: Routledge.

Hayward, C. R. (1998). De-facing power. *Polity,* 31(1): 1–22.

Jackson, T. (2009). *Prosperity Without Growth.* London: Sustainable Development Commission.

Johnson, B. L. (2003). Ethical obligations in a tragedy of the commons. *Environmental Values,* 12: 271–87.

Johnson, B. L. (2011). The possibility of a joint communiqué: My response to Hourdequin. *Environmental Values,* 20: 147–56.

Jolibert, C., Paavola, J. and Rauschmayer, F. (2014). Addressing needs in the search for sustainable development: A proposal for needs-based scenario building. *Environmental Values*, 23, 29–50.

Kaivo-oja, J. (1999). Alternative scenarios of social development: Is analytical sustainability policy analysis possible? How? *Sustainable Development*, 7(3): 140–50.

Kallis, G. (2011). In defence of degrowth. *Ecological Economics*, 70(5): 873–80.

Kasmel, A. and Andersen, P. T. (2011). Measurement of community empowerment in three community programs in Rapla (Estonia). *International Journal of Environmental Research and Public Health*, 8(3): 799–817.

Kasser, T. (2002). *The High Price of Materialism*. Cambridge, MA: MIT Press.

Kasser, T. (2009). Values and ecological sustainability: Recent research and policy possibilities. In Kellert, S. R. and Speth, J. G. (eds), *The Coming Transformation: Values to Sustain Human and Natural Communities*. New Haven, CT: Yale School of Forestry & Environmental Studies, pp. 180–204.

Kasser, T. and Ryan, R. M. (1996). Further examining the American dream: Differential correlates of intrinsic and extrinsic goals. *Personality and Social Psychology Bulletin*, 22: 280–7.

Kasser, T., Ryan, R. M., Zax, M. and Sameroff, A. J. (1995). The relations of maternal and social environments to late adolescents' materialistic and prosocial values. *Developmental Psychology*, 31: 907–14.

Martínez-Alier, J., Pascual, U., Vivien, F.-D. and Zaccai, E. (2010). Sustainable de-growth: Mapping the context, criticisms and future prospects of an emergent paradigm. *Ecological Economics*, 69: 1741–7.

Max-Neef, M. (1991). *Human Scale Development: Conception, Application and Further Reflection*. London: Apex Press.

Narayan, D. (ed.) (2005). *Measuring Empowerment. Cross-disciplinary Perspectives*. Washington: The World Bank.

Nussbaum, M. C. (2000). *Women and Human Development: The Capabilities Approach*. Cambridge: Cambridge University Press.

Omann, I. and Rauschmayer, F. (2011). Transition towards sustainable development: Which tensions emerge? How to deal with them. In Rauschmayer, F., Omann, I. and Frühmann, J. (eds), *Sustainable Development: Capabilities, Needs, and Well-Being*. London: Routledge, pp. 144–63.

Rahman, M. D. A. (1995). Participatory development: Towards liberation and co-optation? In: Craig, G. and Mayo, M. (eds), *Community Empowerment: A Reader in Participation and Development*. London: Zed Books, pp. 24–32.

Rahnema, M. (1990). Participatory Action Research: The 'last temptation of saint' development. *Alternatives: Global, Local, Political*, 15(2): 199–226.

Rauschmayer, F. and Omann, I. (2015). Well-being in sustainability transitions: Making use of needs. In Syse, K. L. and Mueller, M. L. *Sustainable Consumption and the Good Life. Interdisciplinary Perspectives*. Abingdon: Routledge, pp. 111–25.

Rauschmayer, F., Omann, I. and Frühmann, J. (eds) (2011). *Sustainable Development: Capabilities, Needs, and Well-being*. London: Routledge.

Sen, A. (2013). The ends and means of sustainability. *Journal of Human Development and Capabilities*, 14(1): 6–20.

Smith, P. B. and Max-Neef, M. (2011). *Economics Unmasked*. Cambridge: Green Books.

UN (2012). Report of the United Nations Conference on Sustainable Development.

UNEP (2011). Towards the green economy. Pathways to sustainable development and poverty eradication. www.unep.org/greeneconomy, accessed 4 January 2015.

Uphoff, N. (2005). Analytical issues in measuring empowerment at the community and local levels. In Narayan, D. (ed.), *Measuring Empowerment. Cross-disciplinary Perspectives.* Washington: The World Bank, pp. 219–46.

van den Bergh, J. C. J. M. (2010a). Relax about GDP growth: Implications for climate and crisis policies. *Journal of Cleaner Production*, 18: 540–3.

van den Bergh, J. C. J. M. (2010b). Externality or sustainability economics? *Ecological Economics*, 69(11): 2047–52.

Vincent, S. (2004). Participation, resistance and problems with the 'local' in Peru: Towards a new political contract? In Hickey, S. and Mohan, G. (eds), *Participation: From Tyranny to Transformation.* London: Zed Books.

WCED (1987). *Our Common Future.* Oxford: Oxford University Press.

9   Conclusion

From destroyers to a sustainable system of synergic satisfiers

I first started drawing on the HSD approach to study the relationship between consumption patterns and wellbeing among poor people in Peru. I used data from interviews and focus groups with residents in a shanty town of Lima to analyse the products and services they bought in terms of their singular, synergic, inhibiting, violator or pseudo-satisfier properties (Guillén-Royo 2007, 2008). It helped me understand how the purchase of electric appliances, for example, was acting as a *violator* since many poor households were becoming heavily indebted buying above their means, enticed by the marketing practices of retail chains. At the same time, it became clear to me that reversing this situation could only be done in collaboration with people themselves, as the constellation of negative satisfiers supporting rising levels of debt among shanty town dwellers could only be unveiled with the collaboration of those affected.

As I began facilitating workshops with people from different backgrounds, the first thing I realised was that – as HSD proponents maintain – the language of needs is easily understood by most people. Furthermore, discussing human needs and satisfiers usually feels interesting because it touches on everyday experiences and is engaging since it makes participants (and facilitators) feel that change is possible. However, when working with the negative matrix analysing the ways of Being, Having, Doing and Interacting that are hampering needs fulfilment it was easy to feel discouraged, as the system of negative satisfiers which participants unveiled often seemed unbreakable. It might be hard to believe that communities can come up with sensible solutions if development is blocked by corruption at most administrative levels (as participants from wealthy parts of Lima highlighted), if nepotism and elitism control politics and the economy (as the unemployed in Granada/Spain claimed), or if indifference and individualism reign supreme (as students from the University of Oslo/Norway maintained).

Feelings of helplessness do not last long during HSD-based projects. When people discuss *synergic satisfiers* – those that contribute to the satisfaction of more than one need – they start co-generating a constellation of values, laws, organisations, actions and environments which they experience as peaceful and healthy. The process of unveiling synergic satisfiers is commonly reported as being needs-fulfilling, and people often feel – even if only for the duration of the workshop – the possibility of change, the harmony of balanced articulations, and of a reduced level of harm to themselves, to others and to the natural environment. Reflecting on the positive link between *synergic satisfiers* and the protection of nature claimed throughout this book is important if we are to sustain the argument that human scale development implies environmental sustainability. Given the global dimension of the negative impacts of human activity on the natural environment in terms of pollution, climate change, resource exhaustion and biodiversity loss, it might seem naïve to assume that needs-based participatory processes at the local level might hold the key to identifying and implementing effective sustainability measures.

As stated in Chapter 3, since fundamental human needs change only with evolution, the satisfiers that people identify as synergic today are likely to remain synergic for a significant period. In addition, accounting for the systemic relationship between needs and satisfiers implies that synergic satisfiers are 1) not harmful to any other human need as they would then be qualified as *violators* or *inhibiting*; and 2) not harmful to the natural environment, as by destroying nature they would limit the possibilities to meet human needs now and in the future. This understanding of interdependence is not only grounded in conceptual considerations, it is also based on a review of the HSD literature and my own experience as facilitator. I have yet to encounter a group of people who would propose a configuration of synergic satisfiers that would, say, imply high levels of emissions of greenhouse gases, the pollution of water sources, or the degradation of global ecosystems.

As an additional illustration to the ones discussed in Chapters 5 and 6 of the set of synergic satisfiers that emerge from HSD workshops, I will outline some of the preliminary findings from my research in five Peruvian districts introduced in Example 4.1. Initially, in the context of Peru, a country with high levels of inequality and social fragmentation, it could be expected that residents in lower and lower-middle income districts envisaged a utopian matrix characterised by higher consumption levels both in the private and public spheres. A preliminary analysis of the HSD workshops in these districts indicated that *synergic satisfiers* included a better access to quality education and health services, proper housing (including safe drinking water, quality materials and space for all family members) and good communication and transport infrastructures. An increase in public and private infrastructures, at the current technological level in Peru and almost elsewhere, will increase the use of concrete, steel and other building materials, put stress on already overexploited water sources and increase the amount of cars travelling on – as of yet – remote roads. However, the additional satisfiers proposed together with those infrastructural changes, included more greenery and public parks, public spaces free of advertising, increased levels of popular participation in education, policy-making and economic institutions, the promotion of self-acceptance and of valuing diversity, and the institutionalisation of opportunities for cooperation and exchange (Guillén-Royo 2014). Both the cooperative values inherent in the synergic satisfiers discussed and the stress on self-acceptance and acknowledging diversity suggests that new infrastructures would be envisaged, drawing on what Kasser (2002) calls *intrinsic values*, which generally are associated with pro-environmental choices (Crompton and Kasser 2009).

When discussing *synergic bridging satisfiers*, the link between policies and interventions that enhance both human needs and the natural environment in Peru was made even more evident. This was also the case in most examples analysed in this book, from the study in Lleida (Catalonia) presented in Chapter 5 to the example by Inez Aponte on the Transition Movement in the UK described in Chapter 7. Cooperating, sharing, exchanging, accepting, appreciating, integrating, restructuring, finding personal spaces and connecting with nature were ways of Doing describing the processes behind most *synergic bridging satisfiers*. An example identified by participants from Breña (a lower-middle income district in Lima) illustrates some of these points. Residents agreed on the fact that a scheme to invite congressmen to experience the everyday life and routines of rural people would have synergic effects on many human needs, as their policies would be influenced by their experience. If, for example, congressmen spent a week working with peasants in Acostambo and discussing needs satisfaction with them, they would probably understand that a stable source of clean water does not only depend on functioning pipes but on local rivers and streams not being polluted by agricultural chemicals, cattle manure, and household waste. They would be more likely to support local organic agriculture, on-site training for peasants, and greater coverage of the municipal waste-collection truck, which were some of the *synergic bridging satisfiers* that emerged from the workshops in Acostambo described in Chapter 6.

It is difficult at the current stage of knowledge to affirm that all constellations of *synergic satisfiers* will always be sustainable and that *synergic bridging satisfiers* will always support their emergence. Some of the examples presented in this and other studies suggest that this could be the case, but we do not have hard evidence based on inferential statistics on the linkage between *synergic* and *synergic bridging satisfiers* and the reduction of CO_2 emissions, or kilograms of waste, or on the amount of species preserved due to HSD processes. The analysis of the characteristics of sustainable communities discussed in Chapter 7 indicates that these local initiatives are able to significantly reduce the emissions of greenhouse gases from transport, deficient insulation and energy producing activities, for example. In addition, the successes of the Peasant Development Association in Colombia increasing the average household's income, promoting food sufficiency and conserving the local ecosystems through reforestation and regeneration programmes also suggest that HSD processes strengthen environmental sustainability (Smith and Max-Neef 2011). Conversely, the studies in Lleida (Chapter 5) and in Acostambo (Chapter 6) stress the importance of the processes characterising the HSD methodology, as they allow a deeper understanding of the interconnections between socio-economic and environmentally targeted interventions, an understanding which is essential for the success of sustainable development policies. All this might seem like scattered evidence, but it is nothing that a systematisation of the processes and outcomes of HSD experiences cannot turn into scientifically and politically acceptable arguments. To this I turn later in the conclusions.

Sustainable development and Human Scale Development

In this book I have addressed HSD as an alternative to the sustainable development approach suggested by the 'green economy' proponents; it is an alternative which is closer to the perspectives of the degrowth and steady-state paradigms. In Chapter 2, I discussed the reasons why the 'green economy model' of sustainable development – articulated around technological innovations, energy and resource efficiency, and top-down regulations which address institutional, economic, and information-based measures – is not proving successful to simultaneously progress towards the three dimensions of sustainability: social equality, economic efficiency and environmental sustainability. One of the main reasons is that the 'green economy' approach to sustainable development has articulated all the above around the promotion of economic growth (understood as GDP growth). The latter has replaced in practice the more general term 'economic efficiency', and its prioritisation in rich and poor countries has deepened environmental degradation through the stronger pressure on natural resources and higher levels of greenhouse emissions that a progressive expansion of the global economy entails.

The negative environmental implications of economic growth have been discussed in Chapter 2 through the concept of *decoupling*, defined as the reduction of total environmental impacts from human activity expected from organisational and technological improvements in efficiency. Following Jackson (2009), absolute decoupling was considered impossible with the existing technological possibilities. This claim was supported by evidence of increasing total global carbon emissions, municipal solid waste and the rate of biodiversity decline. The reason why the negative impacts of human activity on the environment have not decreased despite improvements in technological and organisational efficiency is that higher volumes of goods and services are being produced annually around the globe. The latter defines economic growth, which is still regarded as the solution to poverty, inequality, and the high levels of unemployment derived from financial and economic crises.

HSD, as well as other alternative views on SD based on ecological concerns (Daly 2008, Martínez-Alier *et al.* 2010, van den Bergh 2010), and on social concerns (Doyal and Gough 1991; Gough 2014; Sen 2013; Lessmann and Rauschmayer 2013) suggest a lacking relationship between an increase in quality of life and the availability of more goods and services in a society. On the one hand, a great deal of the production in developing countries is exported, and the revenues of these exports end up in the hands of international investors or local elites, or they are safely guarded in fiscal havens (Max-Neef 1991; 2014). On the other hand, countries that have managed to sustain a reduction in poverty and inequality have been those that have succeeded in creating well-functioning welfare states, not necessarily those that have grown more (Gough 2014; Muraca

2012). Finally, quality of life, as experienced by people, does not seem to result from having more material possessions either at the individual or at the societal level (Easterlin 2013; Kasser 2002). As studies on subjective wellbeing point out, creating societies with low levels of corruption and unemployment and strong social networks that promote non-materialistic values and good physical and psychological health is more effective for wellbeing than having societies that revolve around the accumulation of material possessions (Helliwell *et al.* 2012). In addition, following Easterlin's studies in rich, middle-income, transition, and poor countries, there is no sound evidence supporting that people's happiness increases together with the annual gross rate of real gross domestic product (GDP) per capita; the most common indicator used to measure economic growth (Easterlin 2013).

The three interdependent pillars of HSD are self-reliance, balanced articulations, and human needs satisfaction. As discussed in Chapter 3, HSD suggests a type of economy that is led by the local level and connects horizontally and vertically with other local, regional, national, economic, political, cultural and religious organisations in a balanced manner; without producing or reproducing situations of dependence or subordination. As Max-Neef maintains when he outlines the postulates of a humane economics for the twenty-first century: 'the economy is to serve the people, not the people to serve the economy' (Smith and Max-Neef 2011: 139). Common strategies followed by transnational organisations such as outsourcing parts of the production process are not in line with this postulate, as they 'produce unemployment in its place or origin and under-employment in the place where the work is outsourced' (Max-Neef 2011), or they are carried out to escape the tougher environmental regulations applied in the countries where the headquarters are located (Kearsley and Riddel 2010). In theory, the 'green economy' discourse does not support the subordination of society and the environment to the requirements of economic growth since it stresses the equal importance for SD of investing in clean technologies, implementing environmental regulations and tackling exclusion and inequality through social policy interventions. However, this subordination is already implicit in the fact that economic growth is still considered to be a goal of sustainable development, achievable through a 'green economy'.

Chapter 8 reflected on the challenge of integrating the holistic approach of the HSD proposal in sustainable policy. It suggested that this could hardly be done in the context of the 'green economy', due to its stress on growth. But it also suggested that alternatives – such as the ones articulated by the Steady-State proposal – were not necessarily better suited to incorporate HSD's holistic and participatory perspective. The fact that HSD supports grassroots leadership might not be welcomed by those who expect to find environmental agreements, taxation and ecological tariffs, caps on emissions, and other strong sustainability measures at the core of sustainable development (SD) policies. The analysis of the system of synergic satisfiers operating in sustainable communities such as ecovillages and transition towns undertaken in Chapter 7, suggests that deeper personal, cultural, organisational and structural changes need to be identified and implemented for human activities to be less harmful for the environment. Hence, SD, as HSD, demands a greater awareness of the complex interrelated satisfiers that enable meeting needs now and in the future. I have argued that the holistic perspective embedded in both the theory and in the practice of HSD offers this. But the price is the acceptance of a shared leadership between the grassroots, experts and policy-makers, and a willingness to subordinate the economic dimension of SD to the requirements of human needs and the natural ecosystems.

Further research

There is a lot to be learnt by proceeding with the study of the characteristics and implications of HSD processes. However, the flexibility of the HSD approach and the encouragement of human creativity embedded in participatory develop-ment processes imply that it might not be necessary to codify all the possible uses and adaptations of the HSD methodology, or even to record most of its empirical applications. In a sense, Human Scale Development is development at a human pace, at the pace of communities and societies who engage in deeply democratic processes of self-reflection, and who are willing to make mistakes in their search and implementation of needs-enhancing measures. A successful experience in HSD in a specific setting at a specific historical moment might not be articulated around similar satisfiers in other settings or under different circumstances. Thus, for those searching for 'quick fixes' or 'well-rounded' solutions to the complex problems challenging humanity, this is probably not the best framework to draw on. HSD relies on the resourcefulness of the grassroots, not on the adoption of strategies designed by institutions or organisations with great visions and even better intentions. Centrally or externally designed development plans, even if inspired by the approach to needs and satisfiers of the HSD proposal, might only be able to scratch the surface of the deeper transformations that sustainable development demands.

Still, studies on the methods, processes and outcomes characterising experi-ences in HSD can be useful, as they can help to give visibility to sustainable development processes not centred on material accumulation. In addition, they might contribute to enhancing our understanding of the relationship between optimal satisfaction of human needs and environmental sustainability.

Visibility

Chapter 7 discussed the characteristics of sustainable communities, how their principles resonate with the three pillars of HSD, and how they seem to be articulated around a constellation of singular and synergic satisfiers that promote both human needs and the natural environment by protecting surrounding natural areas, increasing local production of food and energy, investing in organic agriculture, reducing total consumption and engaging in creative solutions to reduce their environmental impact. These communities may often be labelled as constituting 'anecdotal evidence', but they are increasingly important both in terms of the numbers of people involved and in the dimensions of their environmental and wellbeing-related achievements. There is also a growing amount of literature describing their successes and the processes they undergo to engage local residents, authorities and businesses in supporting sustainable transitions (Christian 2003; Hallsmith 2003; Hopkins 2013; Phillips *et al.* 2013; Seyfang 2009). However, there seems to be a need for meta-studies and macro-analyses that provide an overview of the volume and scope of these local movements, their organisational structures and their environmental and social accomplishments.

To increase the visibility of already successful local initiatives, it seems relevant to engage in collaborative projects that map the different NGOs, grassroots organisations, sustainable communities and individual strategies, such as the ones voluntary simplifiers are engaged in, that have succeeded in increasing human wellbeing and environmental sustainability. It is quite likely that an initial effort in this direction is appraised as academically unsound due to the lack of quantitative data supporting an analysis, or due to the partial or scarce information available. However, an initial mapping of the main features of local sustainability initiatives worldwide can support further, deeper inquiries and field visits that will add to a better understanding of the scope and achievements of grassroots initiatives. Such a research programme might contribute to remove the label of 'anecdotal' to grassroots-initiated transformations and also the label of 'alternative' to sustainable development processes based on values, behaviours and institutions removed from the principles of accumulation, competition and expansion inherent in the capitalist system.

Optimal need satisfaction and environmental sustainability

The belief that a 'wellbeing dividend', the possibility of reducing environmental impacts while increasing wellbeing, is an important outcome of HSD development processes, has underlain many of the examples included in this book. Although examples of communities that engage in low-carbon lifestyles while enjoying a high quality of life are increasingly available, more empirical research is needed to support the politically controversial argument of a positive association between relatively low levels of consumption and human wellbeing. One interesting effort towards this goal is the Happy Planet Index (HPI),[1] a measure of sustainable wellbeing that incorporates satisfaction with life, life-expectancy and the ecological footprint in the calculation. As a result, countries that rank high according to the HPI are not the richest, as the richest countries have very large ecological footprints due to their high levels of CO_2 emissions from unsustainable consumption patterns. However, countries ranking high on the HPI manage to enable their citizens to live long and satisfactory lives. The latest calculation places Costa Rica, Vietnam and Colombia as the top three countries and relegates Norway and Australia, the two countries topping the UN Human Development Index to the 29th and 76th positions respectively (Abdallah *et al.* 2012). It is of course true that Colombia and Costa Rica both have high levels of inequality and that Costa Rica, for example, has not managed to reduce poverty from a 20 per cent level during the last two decades (Hidalgo 2014). As outlined in Chapter 2, there is much to discuss about indicators and their capacity to reflect the three dimensions of sustainable development. However, relying on alternative indicators such as the HPI, the Index of Sustainable Economic Welfare (ISEW) or the Better Life Index by the OECD appears as a better option to capture the interdependence between human wellbeing and the natural environment than continuing to draw on GDP growth to measure the success of SD policies (Costanza *et al.* 2014; Daly and Cobb 1989).

At the micro-level, the suggestion put forward in this book – that the constellation or system of synergic and singular satisfiers represented in Utopian matrices is sustainable – demands further investigation. Chapter 5 suggested through the study in Lleida (Catalonia) that synergic or synergic bridging satisfiers such as a 'timetable reform' or 'direct-democracy institutions' – satisfiers that are not often associated with environmental policies or interventions – are indispensable components of a local sustainable society. Chapter 6 contributed to the exploration of the interdependence between satisfiers through a participatory action research project that involved implementing an 'organic vegetables' and an 'adults' school' project in Acostambo (Peru). A careful study of the processes in which participants engaged suggested that the trust and knowledge they acquired through their involvement in the participatory learning process characterising the adults' school was a key factor in the success of the 'organic vegetable gardens'. The latter had positive effects on the local ecosystems through a reduction of the total amount of chemical fertilisers used in the community and a reported increase in people's respect for the natural environment. Finally, Chapter 7 analysed the satisfiers that are commonly present in sustainable communities. Self-knowledge, participatory conflict resolution schemes, volunteering, cooperating and direct experience of nature seem to constitute what I came to categorise as *necessary synergic satisfiers*: those that are likely to represent societies that experience low-carbon lifestyles and high levels of quality of life. The examples presented in this book, together with the available literature on the practice of HSD, point to the possibility of realising the 'wellbeing dividend'. I believe that we might be closer to achieving this through the deeper understanding that comes from a collective reflection on needs and satisfiers.

Note

1 www.happyplanetindex.org/about.

References

Abdallah, S., Michaelson, J., Shah, S., Stoll, L. and Marks, N. (2012). *The Happy Planet Index*. 2012 Report. London: New Economics Foundation.

Christian, D. L. (2003). *Creating a Life Together: Practical Tools to Grow Ecovillages and Intentional Communities*. Gabriola Island, BC, Canada: New Society Publishers.

Costanza, R., Kubiszewski, I., Giovannini, E., Lovins, H., McGlade, J., Pickett, K. E., Ragnarsdottir, K. V., Roberts, D., de Vogli, R. and Wilkinson, R. (2014). Time to leave GDP behind. *Nature*, 505: 283–5.

Crompton, T. and Kasser, T. (2009). *Meeting Environmental Challenges: The Role of Human Identity*. Godalming, UK: WWF-UK.

Daly, H. E. (2008). A Steady-State economy. Sustainable Development Commission, UK, 24 April 2008, www.sd-commission.org.uk/data/files/publications/Herman_Daly_think piece.pdf, accessed 23 March 2015.

Daly, H. E. and Cobb, J. (1989). *For the Common Good*. Boston: Beacon Press.

Doyal, L. and Gough, I. (1991). *A Theory of Human Need*. Palgrave Macmillan.

Easterlin, R. A. (2013). *Happiness and Economic Growth: The Evidence*. IZA DP No. 7187. January.

Gough, I. (2014). Climate change and sustainable welfare: The centrality of human needs. New Economics Foundation Working Paper. http://b.3cdn.net/nefoundation/e256633 779f47ec4e6_o5m6bexrh.pdf, accessed 1 April 2015.

Guillén-Royo, M. (2007). Consumption and wellbeing. Motives for consumption and needs satisfiers in Peru. PhD Thesis. University of Bath, Bath, UK.

Guillén-Royo, M. (2008). Consumption and subjective wellbeing: Exploring basic needs, social comparison, social integration and hedonism in Peru. *Social Indicators Research*, 89(3): 535–55.

Guillén-Royo, M. (2014). Economic growth and human needs satisfaction across-socio economic groups in Peru. An illustration using the Human Scale Development Approach. Paper presented at the Fourth International Conference on Degrowth, Leipzig (Germany), 2–6 September 2014.

Hallsmith, G. (2003). *The Key to Sustainable Cities: Meeting Human Needs, Transforming Community Systems*. Gabriola: New Society Publishers.

Helliwell, J., Layard, R. and Sachs, J. (eds) (2012). *World Happiness Report*. New York: Earth Institute, Columbia University.

Hidalgo, J. C. (2014). Growth without Poverty Reduction: The case of Costa Rica. *Economic Development Bulletin*, 18: 1–18.

Hopkins, R. (2013). *The Power of Just Doing Stuff*. Cambridge: Green Books.

Jackson, T. (2009). *Prosperity Without Growth*. London: Sustainable Development Commission.

Kasser, T. (2002). *The High Price of Materialism*. Cambridge, MA: MIT Press.

Kearsley, A. and Riddel, M. (2010). A further inquiry into the Pollution Haven Hypothesis and the Environmental Kuznets Curve. *Ecological Economics*, 69(4): 905–19.

Lessmann, O. and Rauschmayer, F. (2013). Re-conceptualizing sustainable development on the basis of the capability approach: A model and and its difficulties. *Journal of Human Development and Capabilities*, 14(1): 95–114.

Martínez-Alier, J., Pascual, U., Vivien, F.-D. and Zaccai, E. (2010). Sustainable de-growth: Mapping the context, criticisms and future prospects of an emergent paradigm. *Ecological Economics*, 69: 1741–7.

Max-Neef, M. (1991). *Human Scale Development: Conception, Application and Further Reflection*. London: Apex Press.

Max-Neef, M. (2011). The death and rebirth of economics. In Rauschmayer, F., Omann, I. and Frühmann, J. (eds), *Sustainable Development: Capabilities, Needs and Well-being*. London: Routledge, pp. 104–20.

Max-Neef, M. (2014). The good is the bad that we don't do: Economic crimes against humanity: A proposal. *Ecological Economics*, 104: 152–4.

Muraca, B. (2012). Towards a fair degrowth-society: Justice and the right to a 'good life' beyond growth. *Futures*, 44(6): 535–45.

Phillips, R., Seifer, B. F. and Antczak, E. (2013). *Sustainable Communities. Creating a Durable Local Economy*. Abingdon: Routledge.

Sen, A. (2013). The ends and means of sustainability. *Journal of Human Development and Capabilities*, 14(1): 6–20.

Seyfang, G. (2009). *The New Economics of Sustainable Consumption*. Basingstoke: Palgrave.

Smith, B. P. and Max-Neef, M. (2011). *Economics Unmasked: From Power and Greed to Compassion and the Common Good*. Cambridge: Green Books.

van den Bergh, J. C. J. M. (2010). Relax about GDP growth: Implications for climate and crisis policies. *Journal of Cleaner Production*, 18: 540–3.

Index

For Product Safety Concerns and Information please contact our EU
representative GPSR@taylorandfrancis.com
Taylor & Francis Verlag GmbH, Kaufingerstraße 24, 80331 München, Germany